ANN RULE

DON'T LOOK BEHIND YOU

AND OTHER TRUE CASES

ANN RULE'S CRIME FILES: Vol. 15

POCKET BOOKS

New York   London   Toronto   Sydney   New Delhi

Pocket Books
A Division of Simon & Schuster, Inc.
1230 Avenue of the Americas
New York, NY 10020

The names of some individuals have been changed. Such names are indicated by an asterisk (*) the first time each appears in the narrative.

First Pocket Books paperback edition December 2011

POCKET and colophon are registered trademarks of Simon & Schuster, Inc.

For information about special discounts for bulk purchases, please contact Simon & Schuster Special Sales at 1-866-506-1949 or business@simonandschuster.com.

The Simon & Schuster Speakers Bureau can bring authors to your live event. For more information or to book an event contact the Simon & Schuster Speakers Bureau at 1-866-248-3049 or visit our website at www.simonspeakers.com.

Cover by Tom Hallman, hand-lettering by James Wang

Manufactured in the United States of America

10 9 8 7 6 5 4 3 2 1

ISBN 978-1-4516-4108-0
ISBN 978-1-4516-4109-7 (ebook)

For everyone who has lost someone they love, never to find them—or learn the reasons they vanished. With my sincere hope that those who are lost will find their way home, or to God.

Contents

NORTH TO ALASKA

When I am asked to choose which murder cases are the most interesting for me to research and write, I always say they would be selected from a relatively recent unit in the homicide divisions of large cities: the "Cold Case" department. There is something infinitely satisfying about finding killers long after they have become confident that they have walked away free. Some have gone on to commit even more violent crimes, while others have lived out their years in "average Joe" anonymity.

And then there are those who enjoy a luxuriant lifestyle after their victims' lives ended violently because of the killers' ultimately selfish motives.

Even so, surely they must always be listening for a footstep behind them and sirens in the night, waiting to see the flash of a badge.

North to Alaska unveils at least two murders and a tangled and convoluted history that often results from weird family trees. Any rational person would speculate that one of the homicides should never have been solved—not after three decades. The single detective who traveled from Washington to Alaska to New Mexico to Maryland investigating it had virtually nothing going for him at first. Quite literally, the second murder was a "bare-bones" case with a dark secret. That secret probably would never have been discovered if not for the jaws of a bulldozer that dug deep into the earth. But as its operator cleared land for yet another of the ubiquitous strip malls that spring up like mushrooms around America, the remains of a body emerged.

Maybe the bones were those of a person who never wanted to be found.

Sometimes people whose lives are in turmoil step out of their own identities and leave broken hearts, financial problems, and stunted dreams as they seek to escape that chaos. Occasionally, they start over with a different name. Sometimes they commit suicide. If they are peripatetic travelers, as one of the vanished characters in this true case was, the reasons for their disappearances don't necessarily have to be horrific.

But in this case, they were.

PART ONE

PUYALLUP, WASHINGTON

Chapter One

It was midafternoon on a very warm day—June 4, 2007—when bulldozer operator Travis Haney paused to wipe the sweat from his forehead. He'd been demolishing an old farmhouse and leveling the topsoil on Canyon Road East in Puyallup (pronounced Pew-AL-up), Washington.

It was a prime spot for a shopping mall in the Summit district of Pierce County.

The Washington State Fairgrounds were close by, and land surrounding Puyallup was known for its rich soil and never-ending acres of daffodils.

But just as the Kent Valley had been paved over to make room for the burgeoning Boeing Company and the parking lots, apartment houses, malls, and other businesses necessary to meet the needs of a startling influx of new residents, Puyallup's daffodils were beginning to disappear, along with the small truck farms and strawberry fields in the valley.

It was dismaying to see the rich loam of the area buried under cement. But progress was progress.

The tall yellow home that had once stood on this particular piece of property was probably built more than a hundred years ago. The house had been empty for a while, but even without care, many of the old-fashioned roses, lilacs, and other familiar perennials had managed to survive among encroaching weeds. The house was slowly dying. Its front porch sagged; some windows were broken and seemed like dead eyes staring out as the demo teams moved in.

There had, indeed, been a ghostly presence surrounding the house, which no one wanted any longer. Workers didn't notice it much in the bright sunshine of summer days, but they certainly did as the sun began to set. In June, in the Northwest, that doesn't happen until almost 10 p.m.

The house itself was gone by June 4; all the splintered boards and walls with a dozen layers of wallpaper had been hauled away to landfills.

The last thing Travis Haney was thinking about on this Monday afternoon was hauntings and bizarre secrets. He moved the 'dozer close to the fence on the west/northwest section of the lot, idly glancing at the dirt the blade turned up.

And then a black plastic trash bag rose up through the disturbed earth. Haney lowered the bucket again and the next scoop brought up the rest of the bag. He dumped it onto a pile of dirt. He could see that it was torn. Curious, he hopped down from his perch and opened the bag along one side.

There were bones and rotted clothing inside and some tattered twine that might have been used to tie it all up.

Ann Rule worked the late-night shift at a suicide hotline with a handsome, whip-smart psychology major who became her close friend. Soon the world would know him: Ted Bundy, one of the most savage serial killers of our time. . . .

THE STRANGER BESIDE ME
Now in an updated edition!

"Shattering . . . written with compassion but also with professional objectivity." —*Seattle Times*

"Overwhelming!" —*Houston Post*

"Ann Rule has an extraordinary angle [on] the most fascinating killer in modern American history. . . . As dramatic and chilling as a bedroom window shattering at midnight." —*The New York Times*

HEART FULL OF LIES

"A convincing portrait of a meticulous criminal mind." —*The Washington Post*

"Fascinating. . . . The sheer weight of [Rule's] investigative technique places her at the forefront of true-crime writers." —*Booklist*

EVERY BREATH YOU TAKE

"Affecting, tense, and smart true crime." —*Washington Post Book World*

"Absolutely riveting . . . psychologically perceptive." —*Booklist*

Finding bones wasn't particularly unusual for crews who were demolishing buildings and houses and rearranging dirt. Haney mused that these bones must have been in the bag for a long time. They could have been the bones of a dog or even a small farm animal. The presence of shreds of cloth, however, made him wonder if whatever had died here might have been a human being.

Travis Haney called his father, Matt Haney, who was the chief of police of Bainbridge Island just across Puget Sound. Matt told his son to call 911. There was probably an explanation that wasn't ominous, but Travis's discovery should be reported.

Just in case. Because you never know.

Pierce County deputy Jason Tate responded to the address on Canyon Road, arriving at twelve minutes to four in the afternoon. As he headed toward the man standing next to the excavating equipment, he saw that construction had begun on some commercial buildings in one section of the property. There were a few people standing by, apparently curious about what Travis Haney had found.

Deputy Tate peered into the bag of bones. He wasn't an expert, but he suspected they might very well be human bones. He contacted the Pierce County sheriff's dispatch and requested that the forensic unit respond.

Adam Anderson arrived first. After studying the bones, he tended to agree with Tate. The remains *did* appear to be human. Anderson's supervisor, Steve Wilkins, headed out to the scene as the afternoon slipped into evening. On the way, he contacted the Pierce County medical examiner's office. They needed all the experts they could summon to establish the bones' species.

As the investigators on the scene waited, one of the men standing nearby said his family owned the property. He said his name was Owen Carlson and that he owned the True Value hardware store that was located nearby. Carlson gave Deputy Tate a quick history of some of the myriad tenants who had rented the yellow house over many decades.

"My family's had the old place here for years," he explained. "My sister has been in charge of renting it out since back in the seventies. She leased it to so many people, but she'll probably remember most of them—at least those families who stayed for a year or so. Myself, I only recall one family offhand. They lived here sometime in the midseventies; as I remember, it was a married couple and their daughter—or, rather, *her* daughter. They lived here about a year, I guess.

"There was kind of a strange thing, though," Carlson continued. "More than a year after they moved out, some women came by my store and asked me if I knew where they might be able to locate the older woman's husband and the younger women's father. They was trying to find him because, I guess, he'd just plain disappeared."

The store owner didn't think the women who contacted him were related to the family who had lived there; the little girl whom he'd seen actually living there was much younger than the two sisters, and the grown daughter was years older.

"They told me that they were from someplace in New

Mexico, I believe, and that their dad suddenly quit keeping in touch. Evidently, that wasn't like him. They wanted to walk through the property because this was the last location they had for him—our old house."

"So you took them through it?" Tate asked.

"Yeah—as I recall, I did, but I couldn't answer their questions; I just told them that everyone from that family had been gone for a long time. I had no idea where."

Asked if he knew the allegedly missing man's name, the witness shook his head. "It was odd, though . . ."

"What was odd?" Deputy Tate asked.

"One of the daughters said that her father's new wife was the type of person who would *kill* him."

"Kill him?" Tate asked, surprised. "Was she serious?"

"I don't know. I didn't know her—never saw her again. Don't even know her name—but I recall that her first name sounded like a nickname. She could have been exaggerating. My sister would know more, but she's on a trip and won't be back until Thursday evening."

Forensics chief Steve Wilkins arrived and studied the bones in the black trash bag. He verified that in his opinion they were not animal bones after all. They were human.

As Wilkins delicately examined the bones, Jason Tate looked down at the ground beneath the excavator, which was about fifteen feet away from the first bone find. He saw that there were several more bones lying there. He pointed them out to Wilkins and they marked their location with evidence flags.

A Pierce County medical examiner's deputy—Bert Osborne—agreed with Wilkins's opinion. Osborne had no doubt that these scattered bones had come from a *human being*. How long they had been buried in the earth was anyone's guess; it surely had been a long time as they were all denuded of any soft tissue. It would take a meticulous laboratory examination by a forensic anthropologist to determine if they were male or female, the possible ethnic background of the deceased, along with height, weight, and other characteristics that had existed when they had been part of a living frame.

Osborne and criminalist Wilkins made the decision to leave the bones where they were. In the morning, they would come back and set up a grid, beginning where the first bones were found and extending throughout the property so they could be sure they had discovered any bones that remained, as well as other items that might give them some clue to who the dead man (or woman) had been. They didn't know yet if they were looking at what had been a natural death, an accident, a suicide, or a murder.

If this *was* a homicide case, the investigators hoped against hope that a killer might have left something behind that would identify him—or her—too.

It grew late. The sun had set and it was murky dark when the investigators cleared the scene close to eleven. The entire area was sealed off with crime scene tape, and deputies working the Third Watch were stationed around the large lot to protect it until the sun rose and they could work in daylight.

Until they did, the mysterious bones would remain where they had probably rested for decades. Every single person who had entered the lot—both law enforcement and citizens—had been required to sign the sheriff's log that began when the first responding deputy arrived.

Pierce County detectives had virtually nothing to go on at this point. Whatever had happened, it had occurred a long time before and they would need to explore the tangled misadventures of those who had once lived or visited here. They might be seeking the identity of a vagrant who had only bedded down for a time. The deserted house would have been tempting for someone low on cash. It offered protection from the rain and wind. Probably no one asked for rent or even noticed that a so-far nameless man or woman had hidden behind the dark windows.

Deputy Robert LaTour arrived at the Canyon Road property at a quarter to nine the next morning—Tuesday, June 5—and took over the security watch from Deputy Jim Junge, whose peers called him "Jungle Jim." An hour later, a man who lived right next door to the bone site walked up.

He said that he hadn't talked to any of the investigators the day before, although the land was legally owned by his cousins. Still, he thought he might have something to add that might help.

"My uncle passed away some years ago," he explained, "and this property kind of went downhill. I moved in next door—right over there—in 1995. That was after my mother passed. I moved into her house."

"Any idea who the person we found might be?" LaTour asked.

The neighbor shook his head. Unfortunately, he had little to add to the old property's history *or* knowledge about who the tenants might have been over the years. By 1995 when he moved in next door, there didn't seem to be any tenants—at least not any who stayed very long.

Next, a woman approached Deputy LaTour. She was concerned because someone in her family had called her after seeing a TV news report the night before about the discovery of the unidentified remains.

"She told me to get a 'good criminal attorney,'" the woman said to LaTour. "And then she laughed because it was a joke."

But it wasn't too funny, now that she thought about it. "We lived on the property for ten years—from 1985 to 1995," the former tenant explained. "And we had a dog that used to dig up bones in the yard. The dog pen was right over there."

LaTour glanced at the area and realized that that was where the black plastic garbage bag of bones and some of the other bones were located. He asked the former tenant what she had done with the bones.

"Oh," she said. "I took them away from my dog and threw them in the garbage. I figured they were animal bones—but now that I think about it—they were kind of big."

Crime scene investigators (CSIs) Steve Wilkins and Adam Anderson, Clarence "Skip" Mason, and Steve Mell arrived at the bone site five minutes before eight the next morning, prepared to resume digging. With rebar posts and string, they marked off squares measuring two feet by two feet. This would enable them to accurately identify and revisit the location of whatever they might find.

Ideally, they hoped to find a good portion of the body in a makeshift grave and learn what position it was in when it was buried. Sometimes that made the difference in determining if the person had died of suicide or homicide.

They worked with trowels as well as shovels. If they found an actual grave, they would use brushes to carefully sweep dirt from bones. Now they began to dig and sift the earth they brought up.

It was tedious work and the sun was baking hot. When each square had offered up whatever it held, they checked it off on the grid. Throughout the nine hours the investigators toiled, they found several more bones.

But no real grave.

They tallied up a grim list of what they discovered:

1. One black plastic bag: containing two pelvic bones, a femur (thigh bone) that appeared to have been cut with some kind of tool, a tailbone (the sacrococcyx), several rib bones, some almost unidentifiable fabric, and several lengths of string.
2. From the Grid Squares: #14, three ribs; #19, one vertebra; #20, three vertebrae; #21, two ribs and one vertebra; #22, one vertebra, #27, one vertebra, three rib bones, and cloth; #32, a bone fragment; #40, some charred bones; #42, one vertebra and a collarbone; #42, bone fragment; #44, piece of black plastic bag.

On the west side of the grid, they found more vertebrae and a scapula (shoulder blade). North of the grid on the east side of the backhoe, they located another cut femur and more shreds of the plastic bag. On the east side of the dirt pile they found a small piece of metal, its use undetermined.

On top of the dirt pile, the sheriff's searchers collected more rib bones, more vertebrae, clothing pieces, a leather belt, and some twine segments.

Had any of the body parts been buried in lower ground that often became waterlogged, the searchers might have found what is colloquially known as "grave wax," where the flesh literally turns to a kind of soap. This transmogrification can remain for decades after death. It is, however, more often found in corpses located in lakes and rivers. The proper term for grave wax is "adipocere," but these bones were absolutely dry.

All of the found body parts and debris were packed carefully and taken to the County-City Building evidence room in Tacoma for safekeeping.

Chapter Two

By June 6, 2007, Pierce County detective Lieutenant Brent Bomkamp assigned Detective Sergeant Ben Benson as the lead detective on the mysterious case of the unidentified bones. Benson would have to investigate the background of the nameless remains by himself; his usual partner—Denny Wood—was working on another puzzling homicide and had to stick with that.

In his twenty-plus years in the sheriff's office, Ben Benson had worked in almost every department there. I met him when he was working undercover, exposing narcotics rings. When Ben was a road deputy and I was a reporter, I once rode in the shotgun seat of his patrol car. We were going more miles an hour than I care to remember through a violent storm during Third Watch on a 911 call. This was long before he was assigned to homicide cases. Along with Ed Troyer—now the media liaison for the Pierce County Sheriff's Office—and some of the other young deputies, I was a frequent guest on a radio show that was designed to let the public know what their local law enforcement officers were doing to keep them safe.

Benson, Troyer, and Brian Halquist, the radio show's producer, even helped me move my furniture into the new house I bought back in 1989. If my neighbors had known that my movers were the narcotics squad helping me out in their off-duty hours, I'm not sure what they would have thought.

But I never told them.

Later, Ben Benson piloted fixed-wing planes for the sheriff's office, photographing the ground below in all kinds of criminal probes. Ed Troyer, along with Benson and many other Pierce County detectives and volunteers, has participated in a number of charitable projects that Troyer organizes. A few years ago, they drove a convoy to Mexico to deliver refurbished ambulances and fire trucks to poverty-stricken areas. After the Japanese earthquake and tidal waves, Troyer collected a warehouse full of donated items to ship to Japan for the disaster victims. What he couldn't ship to Japan, he personally delivered to Alabama tornado victims.

Volunteering to help those in need is not, of course, exclusive to the Pierce County officers. Law enforcement personnel all over America are always among those first in line to aid in disasters.

Ben Benson was the one who was assigned to investigate this case of the buried bones single-handedly.

In that first week of June 2007, Benson knew within a few days after the unearthed bones surfaced that they were human. Now he learned that Dr. Katherine M. Taylor of the King County Medical Examiner's Office—the only forensic anthropologist in Washington State—had determined that the dead person was a male. She was able to determine his sex by studying the pelvic morphology, noting that the narrow subpubic angle and the sciatic notch were those of a man and did not demonstrate the wider pelvis women have that enables them to deliver babies.

In addition, Dr. Taylor saw that the heads of the thigh bones and other bony processes were "robust," something seldom found in females.

The few pieces of skull told her that the cranial sutures were firmly closed, and the vertebrae bore signs of a man who was almost certainly over forty.

Dr. Taylor couldn't really determine how tall this man had been; there weren't enough complete long bones to estimate that. The same was true of the nameless man's ethnic ancestry. Forensic anthropologists use cranial, facial, and dental uniqueness to indicate racial and other ancestral signs. But these remains had no face or teeth, and only a partial skull.

Although there was no skull per se, she was able to examine the occipital rim on the back of the head, forehead, and upper jaw. She could not tell, however, if there was *any* solid evidence of foul play.

"There are some cracks in the pieces of skull," she pointed out. "It's possible they were caused by a gunshot to the head—but they could have been caused by other things, too."

Dr. Taylor laid out all of the bones on an examining table, forming a partial skeleton. She then drew a chart showing the bones that were missing in white and shading in deep black those that had been found. (You can see this chart in the photo section.)

There was no evidence remaining of possible trauma and no soft tissue that might have once held a bullet, but Katherine Taylor looked at the spots where some bones had been truncated. She could discern that someone had used a very sharp instrument—most likely a power saw—to dismember this body. The breaks were too clean—too smooth to be the result of after-death drying and weathering. Someone had used the saw to slice through the bones at the thighs, upper arms, tip of the chin, and the shoulder blades.

Benson felt that it was unlikely that the body was that of a transient who'd taken shelter in the empty house. Why would anyone have gone to so much trouble to dismember a stranger? No. Someone had surely killed this nameless man and made sure that all identifying characteristics were separated from the rest of the bones.

Benson had no identification yet; he knew only that whatever had happened had taken place more than ten years earlier—quite possibly *decades* before. He believed the victim had been a middle-aged male and deduced that someone had wanted to hide his death and any connection he might have had to the old house on Canyon Road East.

But why? Motive has so much impact on whether a homicide can be solved. The detectives had no idea what human emotions and interactions had fanned flames hot enough to motivate someone to commit murder. And they undoubtedly wouldn't have until they could identify the disassembled body.

The information gleaned from Katherine Taylor's report narrowed down the parameters of positive identification, although there were still more questions than answers. Many tenants had come and gone from this house and acreage. Which of them—if any—might have had reason to commit murder and hide all signs that it had occurred?

Certainly the killer or killers must believe by now that they had, indeed, gotten away with murder. The Pierce County detective wondered if those responsible lived nearby and if they might not be feeling more and more anxious as the news of the body find accelerated on television and in the local papers. Unearthed and unidentified bodies are almost always good fodder for the top of the nightly news.

Lieutenant Bomkamp sent Benson out to find everyone who had once occupied the tall yellow house.

Or had reason to visit there.

Fortunately, some of the extended family members who owned the property in the Summit district west of Puyallup had remarkable recall. Over the years, Owen Carlson's sister Marilyn Miller had been mostly responsible for renting the house. She and her husband were reported to be on their way back from a trip to Kansas City. Her brother was confident that she would be able to trace rental records back many years.

While Ben Benson waited to interview Mrs. Miller, he reread the statement from the woman who had lived in the rental house from 1985 to 1995.

"We moved into the house on Canyon Road in 1985," she'd written. "I was seven months pregnant. When we moved out in 1995, our niece and nephew moved in and lived there for a few years before they built their first home. Then my brother-in-law and his family moved in. After that the Carlson family decided to sell the property, and the house has now been empty for some time."

Ben Benson realized that no one had officially lived there for six or seven years. He shook his head as he read the last comment on the former tenant's statement: "There is something we were told and we're not sure if it is a fact! A family lived there at some time and they had a nephew who had sex with dead bodies—so you might want to check that out . . ."

Was this an urban myth that had begun long ago? Deserted old houses often are the subjects of totally specious "ghost stories."

Or could it possibly be true? Benson was inclined to think it was probably the former, but he would follow it back to its beginning, as good detectives always follow every clue—as unlikely as they might seem.

In the end, he found no confirmation that the family of former renters had harbored a necrophile.

But even in the bright warmth of June days, there was something about the property that gave many of those who investigated the mystery shivers up and down their spines.

A rabbit running over their graves? Or just the knowledge that someone's violent death had been hidden here for so long?

*   *   *

Owen Carlson talked with his sister Marilyn Miller shortly after she came back from Kansas, and he immediately typed up a report for Ben Benson that contained everything either or both of them remembered. Carlson's narrative was of great help in giving the Pierce County investigators someplace to begin.

When she learned of the bones' discovery, Marilyn had consulted some loose notes in the file she'd kept on tenants since the house had become a rental in 1973. She found some information there about the family who leased it in 1978. Those notes triggered her brother Owen's memory.

"I recall now," he wrote. "They [this family] moved in in June 1978. It was about nine months after that when the three women who said they were from some southwest state—maybe Arizona or New Mexico—came into my hardware store at Summit. Actually, there may have been two young women—sisters. And their mother was with them. They were inquiring about their father. He had formerly worked in Alaska.

"The last time they had heard from their dad was when he lived in our family's house at 10309 Canyon Road East," Carlson continued. "They felt that he had met with foul play from his girlfriend or wife. They didn't feel comfortable with that lady, and, as I told the first deputy, one daughter thought this woman was capable of murder. Those women actually walked the property to see if they could discover anything. Meeting and talking with them under such circumstances made an impression on me at the time. The daughters told me they would file a missing person report."

According to their conversation and Marilyn's notes, the worried young women had come looking for their father on April 9, 1979.

Marilyn Miller still had a copy of the rental agreement signed in June 1978. It was signed by "Mrs. A. M. Hesse," who had given her first name as Geraldine, although she said she went by Geri. The rent would be $350 a month. At that time Geri Hesse had probably been in her middle to late forties.

It was a stroke of luck in a very difficult case for the investigators to discover how meticulous Mrs. Miller had been about details. "Mrs. Hesse drove a 1977 Thunderbird—with an Alaskan license: AJH828," she said. "She gave me a phone number for a man who worked for Century 21 real estate in Bellevue. I think he might have been a reference for her."

But all of that had been current *twenty-nine years* earlier. In 2007, would Ben Benson be able to trace "Mrs. Hesse" that far back?

Marilyn Miller said that Geri Hesse's daughters lived with her; one was a very pretty young woman, probably somewhere in her midtwenties. The other was much younger, a child about eight years old. Geri Hesse had given the impression that she also planned to live with a man named Ray Isaak, and he'd given a former address in Puyallup. In 1978, there had also been a yellow Chevrolet S-10 truck, license #8497AR, parked on the property, but which state had issued that license was lost in time.

Still, very few law enforcement agencies are lucky enough to find witnesses with both great memories *and* documentation. The Carlsons offered both. Owen and his sister promised to bring the lease that Geraldine Hesse signed in 1978 to the Pierce County sheriff's headquarters.

Owen Carlson had even come up with the names of the young women who feared their father had met with some sort of homicidal violence. They were Gina and Jacqueline Tarricone. Jacqueline had told Carlson that she usually went by the name she'd chosen for herself: Gypsy. She had given Owen a phone number in New Mexico. Whether she still lived there was something Ben Benson would check as soon as possible.

Carlson said that when his son Douglas, who was now forty-three, heard about the discovery of body parts on the family land, he remembered visiting the Hesse family when he was a teenager.

"He, my wife, and my sister Marilyn went over to their house," Carlson said, "and Douglas remembers that he noticed Mrs. Hesse had a number of new 'scars' on her face. As kids will, he asked about it, and 'Mr. Isaak' told him that Geraldine had recently had a face-lift so she could look 'thirteen or fourteen years younger.' I think Mr. Isaak was about that much younger than Geraldine Hesse."

Ben Benson asked them if they had heard from Geraldine Hesse's family since they moved out. Christmas cards? Letters? Any phone calls?

They had not. "When Mrs. Hesse moved out, she left no forwarding address," Carlson said. "She also left with rent due, and an empty oil tank—which was supposed to be left half-full. It's right here in her lease."

Geri, her husband or lover, and her two daughters sounded like a strange family. Not quite fly-by-nights, but close to that. Geri Hesse *had* probably been near fifty in the latter part of the seventies, old enough to have one grown daughter and another around nine. She had apparently been living with a younger man; perhaps she had had a face-lift so he wouldn't notice their age difference so much. Her older daughter was said to be "a knockout"— or she had been at that time.

One thought kept nagging at Ben Benson. Where was "Mr. Isaak?" Had he moved away with Geraldine and her daughters—or had he remained on the Canyon Road property until the earth gave up what was left of him?

And who was Isaak? Benson figured that he might have been the man who told Owen Carlson's son Douglas about why Geri had so many scars on her face. That, in itself, was fairly mean and must have embarrassed Geri. The younger man could have simply told the kid that that was a personal question and none of his business. But then, kids do ask awkward questions and the answer had certainly shut him up.

There were so many blank spaces in the backstory of this case. At this point, Ben Benson didn't realize that he was going to have to trace two extremely complicated family trees.

Chapter Three

There is nothing more important to a murder investigation than knowing just who the victim is. Aside from serial killings, sexually motivated crimes, and those that take place during robberies, most homicides are committed by someone close to the victim(s), often someone they know and even trust. Benson had virtually no solid clues to who the long-dead man might be, nothing beyond the possibility that his surname could have been Tarricone.

He hoped that the media's coverage might bring someone forward who knew something—*anything*—about the person whose bare bones offered no secrets about his identity. Truckloads of soil from the property had been run through a screen at the company where Travis Haney worked, without any personal property popping up.

Sergeant Benson gave his permission to release that soil; they had gleaned all they could from the lot on Canyon Road.

But as Benson watched the news flashes about the case, someone else did, too.

Jan Rhodes, who worked as an administrative staff assistant in the Major Crimes Unit of the King County Sheriff's Office in Seattle, watched the report on the grisly find in the Summit area of Puyallup and her heart began to race. She handled missing persons reports in King County and saw instantly that there were similarities to one of her cases.

There was really no reason that Jan Rhodes should know about a missing report on a man who almost certainly had disappeared in Pierce County—and not King County. And yet it had ended up on her desk. In fact, she had found it so compelling that she had kept the missing man's photograph on her desk. She was determined to find him—alive or dead. When she saw the news flash about body parts discovered in June 2007, it struck a chord with Rhodes.

"Oh my God," she said to herself as she frantically tried to scrape her cat off its sleeping place on her telephone book. She immediately contacted Pierce County and was directed from one department to another until finally she was told that a Sergeant Benson was the lead detective.

"We have a missing persons case," she said in an email to Ben Benson. "The man went missing about August 1978."

"Missing from where?" Benson asked when he called Rhodes.

"10309 Canyon Road in Puyallup. There may be an 'East' on the end of that address. For some reason, your department didn't take the missing report—so we took it. He's apparently been missing since 1978, but we didn't take the report until 1993."

Jan Rhodes told Ben Benson that she had been in touch with the man's daughter, who had stubbornly refused to give up looking for him.

"What's her name?" Benson asked.

"Gypsy," Rhodes said. "Gypsy Tarricone. Her father's name is Joseph Tarricone."

"Bingo!" Benson thought.

So the elusive Gypsy had been found. Benson hoped that she might have enough information to help him prove that the bones *were* those of her father.

"We have dentals on our missing man," Jan Rhodes said, "but I don't know if you found a skull?"

Benson told her that, regrettably, they had found only a few parts of the skull: the lower occiput (back), a piece of chinbone, but no upper or lower jaw.

And no teeth.

Even if the King County Sheriff's Office had dental charts of the father of the woman called Gypsy, they would do no good in identifying him unless the Pierce County investigators searching the property should find more portions of skull and/or jawbones. And that search had been called off due to lack of success after the first bone discoveries.

Sergeant Ben Benson was about to follow a dizzying trail that would lead him from the baking heat of the Southwest to the frigid temperatures in Alaska and on to the East Coast. And he would realize once again what strangers neighbors can be. It was no longer the way it was earlier in the century, when neighbors often knew almost everything about families who lived on their block. The extended Carlson family was the exception. But even they knew only bits and pieces of the lives of the tenants in their old yellow house.

"Jan Rhodes deserves so much credit for the effort she put into a missing case that wasn't even in her department's jurisdiction," Benson recalls. "She went back to old records and found the original missing report that Gina Tarricone, Gypsy's younger sister, had filed in January 1979!"

The report had not been filed with Pierce County, and Benson wondered why. It had been filed in the small town of Des Moines, Washington, which is in the southwest part of King County.

Odd.

The complainant's name was Gina Tarricone.

Benson set out to locate the elusive Tarricone sisters. The Des Moines police department still had the missing report Gina filed, and it was full of information.

Apparently Gina had gone to the Des Moines police department as she tried desperately to locate her father. She had given all the facts she knew to Detective Jerry Burger.

Benson found that the entire Tarricone family had been distraught over Joe's disappearance, but Gina was the official complainant. She was living with her brother Aldo at the time and she didn't have a car—so she went to the closest police station, even though she believed that her dad had gone missing in Puyallup.

*   *   *

If it was Joe who was missing, who then was the man known as Isaak? Benson checked missing persons complaints in Pierce County and Tacoma for 1979. He found nothing that seemed to fit. Next, he asked law enforcement agencies in counties north and south of Pierce County.

With Jan Rhodes's help, Benson learned that Gypsy and Gina's missing father was Joseph Anthony Tarricone, who would have been fifty-three in 1978. There was only a blurred photo of him available in the old file, but his daughter had given his description: six feet one inch, two hundred–plus pounds, brown eyes and graying black hair, partially balding.

In 1979, Gypsy and Gina had said that their mother—Joseph's ex-wife Rose—lived in Albuquerque, New Mexico, as did most of their five siblings. On that day in January, twenty-eight years before, Joseph Tarricone had been missing for about four months. He had failed to contact his elderly parents, his ex-wife, or any of his children.

Benson's eyes widened as he read further; apparently the last time anyone saw Tarricone, he had been visiting a girlfriend who lived near Puyallup, Washington.

The girlfriend's name was Renee, and her phone number was on the report, although it was hardly likely she still had the same number after so long. Chances were that she had married in the years between 1978 and 2007 and probably had another last name now.

Fortunately, Des Moines detective Jerry Burger had added many details to the missing report. Gina Tarricone had told him that her father owned a business in Anchorage. She said she and Gypsy had called his girlfriend several times over the years, but Renee had always said she was as mystified as anyone about where Joe might have gone. She did say, however, that she and her mother—Geraldine Hesse—had moved to a town north of Anchorage in the seventies.

That answered one important question. Geri Hesse had been the renter of the Carlsons' house. Maybe it was her older daughter—Renee—who had dated Joe. By Benson's figuring, that young woman would probably be in her fifties now, if she was still alive. But three decades was a long time. The Pierce County detective checked death records and found that Geri Hesse, the mother, had died in 2000.

No one seemed to know where her daughters were in the summer of 2007.

PART TWO

JOE TARRICONE

Chapter Four

Joseph Anthony Tarricone had come a long distance from the place he was born to meet his killer. His parents lived in New York—in Brooklyn—and they always would. But not Joe; he had itchy feet and the personality of a natural-born entrepreneur.

Joe was the Tarricones' oldest child and only son, and his Italian parents were thrilled with their dark handsome baby son when he was born in 1925. Two sisters joined the Tarricone family in the following years, but Joey was always the star, the innovator, whose expansive personality drew people to him all his life.

Most Italian sons adore their mothers, and Joe was no exception. Wherever he might travel, he would always keep in touch with her. Her name was Clara, and Joe never failed to remember her with gifts on her birthday and on Mother's Day. He called home to New York frequently. Among the things that Joe and his wife, Rose, argued about were the huge phone bills that came in. He explained that he wasn't going to put a time limit on his conversations with his folks.

As Joe and his sisters were growing up, the Tarricone household was full of music, noise, hilarity, and the redolent smell of ravioli, spaghetti, pasta fagioli, sausages and peppers, and pizza; Joe learned to cook from Clara, and it was to become one of his favorite pastimes as an adult.

All the Tarricones were devout Catholics. Going to mass wasn't a choice; it was taken for granted that they would attend on Sundays and holy days. Faith in God was another thing Joe learned in his childhood home and it stayed with him.

Joe met Rose in the early forties when they were both in their teens. They were soon dating exclusively and they made an extremely attractive couple. He was unabashedly handsome, with thick wavy dark hair, and dark-eyed Rose was very pretty. Her hairdo then was a faithful copy of the upswept, side-parted pompadour with the back tucked under into a pageboy that actresses Betty Grable and Rita Hayworth wore during the Second World War years. Photos of Joe and Rose in their youth remain in family archives: some photos obviously taken in photo booths, which offered four pictures for a dollar; others from school proms. There were shots of them together at Coney Island. Even sixty-five years later, their engagement photo is especially endearing.

Rose and Joe seem frozen in time, grinning as he hugs her and they look forward to their future together.

But they were opposites. Rose wasn't Catholic, which could have been a huge obstacle for them, but they dealt with that. Rose was quiet and a little shy. When Joe took her home to meet his family for the first time, she was

shocked by the life force that ran through the elder Tarricones' house. There were five Tarricones and they held
nothing back. Rose was startled by the arguments that
ended in hugs, and the clatter of unchecked emotions,
shouting, and loud music.

"But, you know," their daughter Gypsy recalls, "my
mother told me later that she enjoyed going to her in-laws'
house because she found it 'exciting.' She said it was
probably because they were 'so *nuts*!' Even though Mom
was a little overwhelmed at first, she loved her sisters-in-
law a lot. If she had had her choice, she and my dad would
never have moved away from New York.

"My dad was outgoing and loud. They were so different, but they loved each other."

Joe had all kinds of jobs, spaced between three active-
duty assignments in the armed services. He served in
World War II in the army. Later, he was in the air force,
and he was called up from his reserve status after that. He
was a natural salesman, a studied pitchman, and it was
difficult to keep up with his various careers—sometimes
door-to-door, occasionally from the back of a truck, sometimes behind a desk.

Joe Tarricone also had a wanderlust that surfaced often.
Where Rose longed to live in one house in one place and
to have her garden and her precious furniture around her,
Joe often came home in an ebullient mood and called out,
"Rose, pack up! We're moving! We're going to Florida!"

Or New Mexico, or Texas, or the Pacific Northwest.

During many of the early years of their marriage, Rose
was pregnant or recovering from childbirth. Claire, the

oldest, was born in 1947. Then came Aldo in November 1950, Joey two years later, and Gypsy in 1957. Gina came along in 1960, Rosemary in 1963, and Dean, the baby, in 1966.

Coping with seven children and a peripatetic husband who always saw rainbows over the next horizon wasn't easy for Rose.

"She left so much furniture behind," Gypsy remembers. "Sometimes she would cry over it, but she went where my dad wanted to go for so many years."

Joe Tarricone was thrilled with the birth of all of his children, and he was a loving and caring father, however bombastic his personality. He cherished each baby and took the time to walk the floor with them, tussle with them, hug them, and let them know that each was special.

He became the Pied Piper for kids on the blocks where he lived. He liked nothing better than to gather up his children and a lot of the neighbor kids every Sunday. He'd take them all to a movie, a ball game, or the zoo. He often took a bunch of them to Disneyland, enjoying it as much as the children did.

Joe cooked huge spaghetti feeds on Sundays and invited all the neighbors. Joe, Rose, and their youngsters probably lived longer in Albuquerque, New Mexico, than any other place. They became friends with the Bob Silva family who lived across the street. The Silvas had children just about the same age as the Tarricone offspring and it was a happy time for all of them.

"My dad figured out a way to make enough pizza for most of our neighborhood," Gypsy recalls. "He got these boards and covered them with clean linoleum so that he and the men on our street could roll out pizza dough in four-foot-by-four-foot sheets.

"He also made something he called 'Coo-Coo Fritz'; it was dough filled with mozzarella, Parmesan, and all different kinds of cheese. And then he would deep-fry it."

Joe Tarricone could energize any group and a lot of people loved him. Rose remained quieter and more thoughtful. As her children grew older, she wanted to get a job. Joe pictured a marriage much like his parents' union: he wanted to be the breadwinner and have Rose stay home. But Rose had had a taste of forced independence during the months when her husband was away in the service and she was alone with their children.

"She got a job in Old Town in Albuquerque," Gypsy says. "It was in a specialty candy store and she was really good at rolling chocolates—so good that she was offered a management job there. But the woman who had that job was older, and an alcoholic. Mom said she just couldn't accept if it meant that woman lost her job."

Joe made good money most of the time. He worked mostly in sales, selling everything from the Famous Schools job training courses to gas to meat. While he and the family lived in Seattle, he owned the Shamrock gas station under the viaduct in south Seattle. He had a huge billboard with his picture on it, and it said, HI! MY NAME IS JOE! That became a familiar sight to drivers.

When he sold memberships to Famous Schools, he outsold most of his peers. One year, he was given a valuable painting as first prize in a sales competition. Joe could sell anything, and his customers were always glad when he came by.

"When we were in Washington State," Gypsy recalls, "we lived in Lower Preston, a very small town east of Seattle, and our house had a Coleman stove. Sundays were still special days for us. Mom got us all up and dressed, and Dad dragged us to church at Our Lady of Sorrows in Snoqualmie. Mom started the spaghetti sauce the night before, and she stayed home getting Sunday dinner ready. We all went out for hot chocolate after church, and then we went to K-Mart. My dad loved chasing the Blue Light Specials there.

"When we got home, we ate spaghetti and meatballs. I came to dread Sundays because I was the one who had to wash all those greasy dishes!"

There was no question that Joe Tarricone forged deep bonds with all seven of his children. He and Rose had been married three decades, and they were living back in New Mexico when Joe came home and once again shouted, "Pack up, Rose! We're moving to Texas!"

For the first time, Rose said, "No, Joe—I'm not leaving my house. I'm tired of moving for thirty years. No more."

He didn't believe her, and his response was flip: "Then I'll divorce you."

"Fine."

"My dad was blowing smoke," Gypsy says. "But my mother meant it. She didn't want to move again."

Joe hadn't really expected to be divorced, thinking at first that Rose would change her mind about moving to Texas. And, of course, she didn't.

Their affection for each other didn't diminish, but Joe was still the eagle, flying free, looking for a fortune in the next town or the next state.

And Rose loved her garden and especially enjoyed knowing that she would be there when the perennials she planted returned each spring. She gloried in the permanence of being in her own house with her treasured furniture, curtains, and knickknacks around her.

Gina was sixteen, Rosemary was thirteen, and Dean was ten when their parents broke up. Claire, Aldo, Joey, and Gypsy were out and on their own. Joe promised to support his youngest children and he kept that promise; he would never miss sending a check to Rose for their school clothes and monthly expenses.

Not until the fall of 1978.

School was starting in Albuquerque, and Rose looked for the extra check Joe always sent to buy Gina, Rosemary, and Dean new clothes for school and money for books and supplies. Day after day she checked her mailbox, but the check never came. Nor did the monthly child support that had arrived in the first week of every month. There was no check in October, or ever again.

Rose and Joe were divorced by then, but she counted on him. That just wasn't like Joe. He had always been a good provider. Rose had gone to a legal aid office when she and Joe split up, and they helped her get the divorce. She also got her GED certificate, a high school degree, after all that time. Rose was only fifty and she still had three children at home. Although Joe's contributions helped out, she knew she would have to get a job, something she was actually looking forward to. After he vanished, she had no choice but to provide financially for the children.

Rose applied for a job with See's Candies and soon became a manager. She had no animosity toward Joe; it was just that their goals in life had grown so far apart. He kept his promise to come home at least twice a year to see their children and they had talked comfortably when he did.

A few years after her divorce, Rose Tarricone began seeing an aeronautical engineer and they eventually married. He saw how hard she had worked over the years, and he also worried about her chronic migraine headaches. Her new husband wanted her to relax, and she finally agreed to retire from her candy factory job.

No longer a married man, Joe Tarricone had been ripe for a midlife crisis when he received his divorce papers. In his midfifties, he was still a good-looking man, although his dark, wavy hairline had crept backward several inches. He embraced the style of men's fashions in the late seventies. Up until then he'd mostly worn work clothes or armed service uniforms. Now he chose brightly colored leisure suits, polyester bell-bottom trousers, wide neckties, or muslin shirts with embroidery. Heavy gold chains were de rigueur for hairy-chested men like Joe, and he soon bought a few.

He had married so young, he was suddenly single after thirty years, and it somehow felt wrong for a man who had always been part of a Catholic family. There was an emptiness that Joe wasn't prepared for, even though he was regularly in touch with his seven children and ex-wife. He wasn't broken-hearted, but he was lonely, and he was ready to date.

He was attracted to women a generation—or more—younger than he was. That wasn't unusual; many men in the grip of a midlife crisis seek to recover their youth by dating women young enough to be their daughters. Joe Tarricone was certainly one of them.

He was living in Seattle at the time of his divorce, working for Gerard's Meats. After dating many young women once or twice, Joe ended his frenzied dating and settled down to seeing just two women. They were both pretty and easy to get along with, and he wasn't sure which of them was right for him. He was honest with them and made no promises.

One was named Kim. She was the one Joe chose to accompany him to Gypsy's wedding in July 1977. He had flown the younger kids in from New Mexico, and he picked them up in California and drove them to the wedding in Lake Tahoe. His children liked Kim, and they all had a good time during the festivities. Naturally, Joe cooked for the reception and put together huge antipasto platters with cheeses, meats, peppers, olives, and tomatoes.

The other woman was Renee Curtiss. Joe first met Renee when he worked at Gerard's, and he had been very attracted to her, even though she was in her early twenties, thirty years his junior. She was the secretary at Gerard's Meats, efficient, very pretty, and fun to be around. The one thing that bothered Joe about Renee was that she wasn't taking care of her own daughter, Diana,* and was even rumored to have another child who lived someplace else—a son, Brent.*

The Carlsons had been mistaken about the relationships in Geri Hesse's family.

Diana, an eight-year-old in 1977, wasn't Geri's daughter, after all; she was Renee's daughter. Geri was her grandmother, but she might have told people that Diana was hers—in order to protect Renee's reputation. Renee would have been very young when she gave birth to two babies, probably in her midteens.

Joe hadn't found her to be a very attentive mother to either of her children. He disapproved of that. He had no idea who had fathered Diana and Brent; Renee didn't talk about it.

Joe had always put his own children first—and he vacillated over which of his young girlfriends to choose.

"On the drive back from my wedding," Gypsy remembers, "my brother Dean said Dad asked the kids which of his girlfriends they liked best, Kim or Renee? They told him they couldn't make that decision for him, although I guess all of us secretly wished he would choose someone closer to his own age."

In the end, Joe chose Renee. Unfortunately, in choosing Renee, Joe also got her mother, Geri. They came as a matched pair.

---

* The names of some individuals have been changed. Such names are indicated by an asterisk (*) the first time each appears in the narrative.

In 1977, he decided to move to Alaska. The pipeline construction was under way, and he could see tremendous potential there if he started his own door-to-door meat business. He'd learned the ins and outs of selling meat in big lots while he worked at Gerard's in Seattle and was confident about striking out on his own.

He brought Renee Curtiss up to Alaska to work for him. Geri Hesse was in the process of getting a divorce from Renee's father, and she soon followed, bringing her granddaughter, Diana, with her. Renee's son, Brent, was in one of the many foster homes he would live in.

Joe called his new company Alaska Meat Provisions. It was located on International Airport Road in Anchorage. He picked up the steaks, roasts, and ground meat from a wholesaler and delivered them to customers from Anchorage to Fairbanks while Renee managed the office in Anchorage.

In essence, Joe was supporting Renee, Geri Hesse, and Diana, although he never lived with them: they rented a house on Jewel Lake. Joe put a bed for himself in an unfinished room over his office.

Geri was much closer in age to Joe than Renee was, but it was Renee who fascinated Joe. He bought her jewelry and almost anything she said she wanted, along with presents for Geri and Diana.

It wasn't long before Joe fell completely in love with Renee. He knew she didn't love him as much as he cared for her, and he suspected she was seeing other men.

It didn't matter. Joe Tarricone was obsessed with Renee Curtiss. His children disapproved, his parents in New York weren't at all happy that he was divorced and chasing after a woman thirty years younger than he was, and all his relatives and friends worried about him.

They wondered what such a young and beautiful woman might want from him. Renee could probably have just about any man she chose, and they were afraid she was after Joe for his money. He scoffed at the idea, convinced that he would win Renee over in time.

In the meantime, he had a warm friendship with her, Geri Hesse, and little Diana. In a sense, he had another family group.

Renee had an Irish pixie look about her, thanks to her bright blue eyes, deep dimples, and her cap of dark hair. Her figure was perfect. She didn't *look* like a femme fatale; she resembled a wholesome college girl.

Being with her made Joe feel as though he was in his twenties again. His business was doing very well. Although he missed his seven "kids," who were scattered from New Mexico to the Northwest to Hawaii, he was in touch with them often.

His life was good in 1977.

Believing that the victim on Canyon Road was, indeed, Joe Tarricone, Ben Benson realized that his prime suspects were likely to be Geri Hesse and two of her own children—Renee Curtiss and Nick Notaro, whom Geri had adopted when he was a baby.

Benson began background checks on all of them. He found that Renee had been arrested several times for DUI (driving under the influence). In one instance, police had found her car stopped in the middle of the 405 freeway between Renton and Mercer Island in the wee hours of the morning. She was inside, passed out from alcohol. Renee was lucky indeed that there was little traffic on the usually busy freeway at that time of the morning. She would very likely have been killed had another car run into her vehicle—and so might the driver and passengers of that car.

Geri seemed to have a clean record, but Nick had a child molestation case on his record.

"I almost fell out of my chair," Benson recalled, "when I read that one of the complaining witnesses had mentioned that Renee's brother, Nick, had told her about killing a man and burying him in his mother's yard. The Tacoma Police detective who did his child molestation investigation never followed up on the 'murder' story."

Chapter Five

Joe and Renee worked well together in his meat business in Anchorage, so well that he announced one day that he was giving her half interest in Alaska Meat Provisions. She didn't even have to put any money into the company; he was happy to give her what he felt was her share.

Joe bought prime meat wholesale from a ranch in Colorado. He was able to sell some of it in sides and quarters. He and Renee rewrapped and packaged smaller quantities in the office, which wasn't really legal with the permits they had—but wasn't a major infraction either.

Geri Hesse got a job as a saleswoman at a Lamonts department store, and both women lived quite comfortably. Whether Joe asked to move in with them in the Jewel Lake house is unknown—but he never did live there, staying instead in his barren, small office quarters.

Strangely, at one point the two women invited another man to move in with them. Renee always chafed at the idea of being totally bound to one man. She met a German national named Kurt Winkler in a Greek restaurant called

Andreas in Anchorage where she worked part-time as a hostess. Kurt was an accomplished chef and appeared to have money.

Kurt was about thirty in 1976. He was much shorter than Joe Tarricone, and not nearly as handsome, but Renee was attracted to him and they dated. According to Winkler, they eventually became lovers.

Joe probably suspected that there was more than friendship between the two, but Renee said a long time later that he never confronted her about it.

Perhaps he didn't know. Kurt soon got a job with Campo Pacific, a company that offered catering service to workers in remote locations across Alaska. The pipeline provided high-paying jobs to thousands of them, and seeing to their needs meant more jobs for those who had flocked to Alaska and the pipeline. It wasn't that different from the Alaska gold rush a hundred years earlier.

Kurt worked eight or nine weeks up on the North Slope at a stretch, and then had two weeks off. At least he was supposed to work that rotation, but if his replacement didn't get off the plane, Kurt had to stay until they could fill that job. Often, Kurt was gone from Anchorage for fourteen or fifteen weeks.

Joe, of course, traveled much of the time. He drove his yellow truck from Anchorage to Fairbanks and back, going up the eastern highway and returning along the western route. It wouldn't have been too difficult for Renee to keep the two men from confronting each other. Neither of them spent much time in Anchorage.

Renee reportedly became engaged to Kurt Winkler.

Years later, Renee said she broke up with Kurt when she found out he had slept with one of her female relatives.

That may or may not have been true. One thing is certain, however: Renee Curtiss's life was always full of drama, usually centered around her relationships with men.

Gypsy and her sister, Gina, remained convinced that Renee had something to do with their father's disappearance. They had no idea how difficult that would be to prove.

Gypsy tried to file a missing report with the Pierce County Sheriff's Office, and asked for a meeting with then-sheriff Mark French.

"He wouldn't see me," Gypsy recalls. "I actually had to get a county commissioner to intercede—and I finally got French to talk with me. All I asked was would they just reinterview Renee Curtiss. He wouldn't even agree to do that!"

In reality, Pierce County investigators *never* interviewed Renee, and no missing report was ever filed in their jurisdiction. Sheriff Mark French retired under a cloud that centered on his alleged interest in pornography and had nothing to do with Joe Tarricone; it was not French's detectives' fault that they hadn't acted on Gypsy Tarricone's report—they weren't aware of it.

Gypsy was extremely frustrated. Both she and her younger sisters, Gina and Rosemary, would slip into depression every year as summer drifted into fall and their father was still missing.

"We felt that was the time when our father died," Gypsy remembers. "And no one seemed to care enough to investigate what had happened to him. So our brother Dean came up with an idea. We all got together and made up a story that Dad had left an insurance policy where the proceeds would go to Renee Curtiss and to Dean. So Dean called her, and we taped the call. She was very interested at the thought that she might get money from an insurance policy, but she sounded baffled that my dad was still missing.

"She kept saying, 'Well, I'll be darned,' as if she was surprised that my dad hadn't shown up somewhere. But she didn't want the insurance money enough to admit that our dad was dead."

Eventually, of course, Gypsy and Gina had found detectives who would listen to them at the Des Moines Police Department and at the King County Sheriff's Office. And, finally, in 2007, in Pierce County.

By the time Sergeant Ben Benson became the lead investigator on the case of the unidentified bones, Pierce County had a new sheriff, Paul Pastor, and things were very different there.

Benson wanted to talk to Renee Curtiss, but he needed to find out as much about her as he could before he confronted her.

Gypsy Tarricone had never stopped looking for her father. She even bought a book on how to find a missing person and tried some of the techniques suggested there. If she had to do it all by herself, she was prepared to do that. Gypsy is an upbeat, attractive woman with thick black hair, and her career is an unusual choice for a female; she is a merchant mariner and is often out at sea for months at a time, stopping in exotic ports of call. Occasionally, she will be the only woman on board.

Wherever she was, Gypsy thought of her dad, determined not to give up her search for him as decades passed.

"Whenever I thought of him," Gypsy recalls, "I always pictured Canyon Road and 104th. I recalled walking that long driveway to the house that was at the back of the lot. That would have been in 1990, a dozen years after he disappeared. I knew my dad was there somewhere. It was like a chain reaction—it all fit together. But I couldn't prove it, and I couldn't find him."

And she was right. She had gone up that driveway and felt so very close to Joe. She felt his spirit, but she still didn't know where he was.

That year Gypsy tried, in vain, to request a presumptive death certificate for her father from the medical examiner of Pierce County. One of the medical investigators wrote back to her: "We are not insensitive to your situation. However, we cannot issue a presumptive death certificate at this time. Mr. Tarricone was last seen in this county," he wrote. "However, the only evidence that he is dead is the length of time since he has been seen. In the absence of any known event that would reasonably have taken his life or a known location for this event, we lack jurisdiction to act on your request."

The investigator suggested that Gypsy "appeal to a court in the area where he last lived."

Although Alaska authorities were kinder to Gypsy and her siblings, they could not offer closure either.

By 1993, Gypsy had moved from New Mexico to Hawaii. When she contacted the King County Sheriff's Office in Seattle, she was told that they could not officially take on the case, but this time Gypsy had had a glimmer of hope; Jan Rhodes of the missing persons unit took her report anyway. Rhodes had a feeling.

Gypsy was out at sea when Jan Rhodes called Gypsy's union representative and asked to have a message relayed to her—Rhodes needed to talk to her. When Gypsy called back from her ship, she told Jan that she wanted to keep her dad's missing report in the system—whatever it took.

Gypsy wasn't about to give up in her search for her beloved father. Although so many law enforcement agencies had refused to take a missing report because Tarricone wasn't linked to their jurisdiction and others had marked the case "closed" or "inactive," when Gypsy tried again in 1993 she'd finally found a kindred spirit in Jan Rhodes.

Another solid supporter was Bill Haglund—whom Gypsy dubs "a great man."

Haglund was a chief criminal deputy in the King County Medical Examiner's Office who was known for his refusal to give up on trying to identify John—and Jane—Does, and he, too, stepped in to argue Gypsy's cause.

For over a decade, Bill Haglund had become a familiar image on television news shows. In the eighties and early nineties, Haglund could be seen holding one end of the sad parade of stretchers holding one Green River victim after another.

In 1993, when Haglund listened to Jan Rhodes describe the Tarricone case, he'd encouraged her to write an incident report on the missing man. He also suggested that an incident report and Tarricone's previous dental charts would allow them to enter Tarricone's information into the vast database of the National Crime Information Center.

The missing report on Tarricone drew a number of hits through NCIC over the next few years. But all of them were eliminated because when the victims were found— dead or alive—there was always something that didn't match. Their eye color was wrong; their height, weight, or age was wrong; fingerprints didn't match; or there was some other specific detail that did not fit.

A man's body was discovered at the bottom of a factory's smokestack in Bellingham, Washington, which was close to the British Columbia border. Could it be Joe? Forensic pathologists said it had been there for only six to nine months and was so badly burned that identification proved impossible. They believed that the man was alive when he jumped or fell into the stack because he had removed his clothing and folded it beneath him in a hopeless attempt to fight the heat. A partially burned plane ticket was found beside him—but heat had obliterated the destination listed.

The dead man in the smokestack could not possibly be Joseph Tarricone; he had died years after Joe vanished.

Most laymen have no idea how many lost souls disappear each year, many of whom will never be found or identified. Bill Haglund tracked every hit from the computers at NCIC that he possibly could. There were many Joseph Tarricones in America, all with different social security numbers, but none of them proved to be Gypsy's father. In the end, none of the computer hits told Haglund where Joseph Tarricone was.

There was one hit, though, that had an interesting connection to the missing man. Dianna Darnell, of the Wasilla Police Department in Alaska, called to say that a gun Tarricone had reported as stolen on January 16, 1977, had been located! Darnell worked for the State of Alaska, but she was stationed in the Wasilla police office in the town where Republican vice-presidential candidate Sarah Palin had once served as mayor and where she still lived. Tarricone's gun had been stolen thirty years before, a year before he disappeared.

In 1993, when the missing report on Joe Tarricone was entered into NCIC computers, the system connected thousands of police agencies, and the computer monitors notified Dianna Darnell in 1993 that the stolen gun was linked to Joe Tarricone. When the gun was located, Dianna Darnell wanted to return it to Gypsy Tarricone.

Still, the discovery of his long-lost gun came with no new information on who had killed Joe.

Jan Rhodes learned a little more about Joe's background when she got a phone call from Gypsy. Gypsy called from her new home in Hawaii and was surprised to learn that it had been difficult to locate her. She wanted to stay in touch in case there were ever any human remains located where Renee Curtiss and her mother had once lived.

Although it was clear that Gypsy loved her father and worried about him, there were many things she didn't know about him, and their contact had been infrequent after he moved to Alaska with Renee.

Fifteen years after her father vanished, Gypsy no longer knew where Renee Curtiss and her mother lived; they had moved often after they vacated the old yellow house. Still, she was encouraged to hear how positive Jan Rhodes was when she said she believed that she could find Joe Tarricone.

Chapter Six

It was on a June day in 2007 when Gypsy landed in Hawaii after her ship had returned from China. She planned to catch the first flight she could get to Seattle.

Suddenly her phone rang and a male voice identified himself as Sergeant Ben Benson from the Pierce County Sheriff's Office.

"You know that place on Canyon Road in Puyallup?" he began.

"Yes," she said cautiously, although she felt her skin prickle.

"Well . . . we found remains—"

"I knew it," Gypsy said. "I knew it! All this time. She killed my father there. Renee killed him!"

Although she was initially elated to hear that Benson was working on her father's disappearance, she didn't allow herself to totally trust the Pierce County homicide sergeant.

"Now," Benson said in 2010, "I'm one of her favorite people, but when we first met I was just another detective who had failed to locate her father years ago. I had to prove to her that I would stick with the case."

Gypsy told Ben Benson that her father had visited her in Hawaii in July 1978. It hadn't been a very good visit as far as she was concerned; Joe Tarricone was so besotted with Renee Curtiss that she was all he talked about, and he wouldn't listen to her warnings to take things a little slower. But Gypsy told Benson that her father had changed in the last year or so before he disappeared. She realized now that he must have been in the last months of his life during his visit to Hawaii. He had played with her children and taken the youngest out in his stroller, but he seemed different somehow.

"He was a very secretive man," Gypsy explained. "Even with his seven children. I do know he always carried lots of cash with him; he had a briefcase full of big bills, but we never knew where the money came from."

Gypsy said she was sometimes afraid that her father could have been into something that was illegal.

"He almost wasn't in his right mind, you know, not at the end. He was too crazy over Renee."

Joe had cooked for Gypsy's family as he always did and had even gone to a local supermarket to buy prime meat to fill her freezer.

"But he wasn't like he had been—he wasn't like my real dad," she remembers sadly. "He was crazy to get back to visit Renee."

Joe had also traveled to New Mexico in July or August 1978. He visited with his younger children, Dean and Gina; his ex-wife, Rose; and his best friend, Robert Silva—whom he'd called "Bobby Boy" for years. In fact, he stayed with the Silvas—who still lived right across the street from where Rose lived.

Benson later spoke to Silva and learned that Joe had come down to Albuquerque, carrying his big briefcase full of bills—probably a few thousand dollars. Joe and Bob Silva even went to Disneyland together for what would prove to be their final outing. For them, two grown men going to Disneyland wasn't unusual; the men were buddies going way back and Joe Tarricone had always enjoyed Disneyland. He had a childlike enthusiasm for the wonderland there.

Joe's ex-wife, Rose, sighed as she told Ben Benson she could not imagine how the tragedy weeks after she'd last seen him could have happened to Joe. She recalled that she had often said to Gypsy, "I can't understand why someone like your father would *ever* get mixed up with people like that—that Renee and her mother. That wasn't like him—"

Benson was learning that, with Joe Tarricone, all roads led back to the mystifying Renee Curtiss.

Ben Benson continued to search for what he could learn about the two women who had once lived in the old yellow house on Canyon Road. Geraldine and Renee hadn't kept up correspondence with the people who knew them slightly in 1978, and no one in Pierce County appeared to know where they were in 2007.

He had begun with computer searches for Renee Curtiss. Her driver's license had been renewed in Washington State on August 1, 2003, despite her many DUIs. Her date of birth was August 1, 1953. That would make her fifty-four in 2007. Her driver's license photo showed a brown-haired woman with a pixie haircut and blue eyes. She had a pronounced dimple on the left side of her mouth, and she smiled brightly at the camera. Unlike most driver's license photos, this one was attractive. Benson figured if she looked this good in her midfifties, she had probably been a knockout in her midtwenties.

Over the years, Renee had used several names with the same social security number: Renee R. Curtiss, R. R. Curtiss, Renee Wallach,* and R. C. Wallach.*

After she and her mother had left Puyallup twenty-nine years ago, without paying rent or filling the oil tank, they had lived in a myriad of places. Benson traced the addresses listed. Apparently they had moved first to Tacoma—only ten miles away from Canyon Road—and then lived at five addresses in Seattle; two addresses in Sausalito, California; two addresses in Bellevue, Washington; and briefly in San Carlos, Woodside, and San Francisco, California.

And he found Renee's current address: a condominium in Seattle.

Apparently she was still alive. At least Benson didn't find any death certificate for her. That she might have died was one possibility he had considered.

He drove by Renee's condominium and took surreptitious photos of it, noting that it was in a good neighborhood and definitely upscale. But he didn't knock on the door. First, he wanted to get as much background as possible on the mother and daughter's travels and activities since 1978.

Florence Geraldine Bogner Hesse—Geri—had lived with Renee at every address listed. They appeared to have been very tightly bonded. But, of course, when Benson checked death records, they indicated that Geraldine had died in 2000. He sighed; there was no way to interview her now, seven years later.

He learned later that, in an eerie way, Geri Hesse was still with Renee. Her ashes rested in an urn on the fireplace mantel in Renee's condo. Geri still accompanied her youngest daughter whenever Renee moved on.

Benson suspected that Renee and Geri might have been mother-and-daughter con artists who had used men to build their fortunes. If that was true, they must have been good at it; he found no felony criminal record for either.

During the months of June and July 2007, Benson found that Renee and Geraldine had a number of close relatives. Their extended family members lived in either Washington State or Alaska. Tracing their family tree proved to be a convoluted and difficult process, but Benson was able to make some initial connections.

He learned that Geri Hesse had a sister named Lillian. When Lillian gave birth to a boy, Ron, in July 1947, Geri had been envious. They had always been somewhat competitive; the Bogner sisters were born only fourteen months apart.

Geri, the younger sister, had no children at the time, but she heard about a baby boy who was born on July 9, 194 to a mother who gave him up. Geri arranged to adopt him in the fall of that year. At that time she was married—for a very short time—to a man named Notaro, and she named her infant son Nick. Benson figured that in the summer of 2007, Nick Notaro would be closing in on sixty.

Census records showed that Geri had subsequently given birth to a girl she named Cassie* on June 3, 1952. Her second biological child was Renee, who was born fourteen months later.

At some point, Geri had married again at least once; that would be where the "Hesse" name came from. Both Cassie and Renee had used Notaro as their last name until they married.

As the Notaro/Hesse family tree kept sprouting new limbs in Benson's investigation, he drew up a chart so he could remember the entire cast of characters.

The mystery of the man named Isaak was quickly solved. He was neither Geri's nor Renee's boyfriend; he had been married to Renee's aunt Lillian when Joe Tarricone vanished. At the time, her aunt had lived only a few miles from Canyon Road East.

Florence Geraldine had had numerous last names, and so had her daughters Cassie and Renee. Renee's cousins—Ron and Dean Isaak, who were Lillian's sons—talked to Ben Benson about their memories of the late summer of 1978. Their mother was currently living in Tacoma, and their father had passed away a few months before. That would be Ray Isaak, the man the Carlson family had met at the yellow rental house.

Renee's cousins recalled that Renee had thrown a "big

barbecue" party in the late seventies at the Puyallup house she shared with her mother and her daughter. A number of their relatives had attended the party.

Dean confirmed that Renee had had at least *two* boyfriends at the time of the party. She had lived for a while in Alaska, working, they thought, for Joe Tarricone. The other man was also living near Anchorage, Alaska. That man's name was Curt or Kurt. Dean recalled that he was a cook and that he'd come from Germany.

With the pipeline going in, Alaska had been the place to go for high-paying jobs if one was willing to work hard for weeks without time off. Kurt had practically lived on the job. Renee's cousin Dean said that Renee was very helpful in recommending him to Kurt and that had helped him get a job on the North Slope.

"Renee was like that," Dean Isaak told Ben Benson. "I mean, she's one of these ladies that likes to help family and stuff. She knew I was down and out . . . so she told me to come up to Anchorage. Kurt was living at this house they rented and I talked to him. They had me fill out an application and he said he'd take me in until I got on the pipeline. I was there a couple of weeks. I went and got a job in a bar as a bouncer. I wasn't there very long when I got called to work up there on the Slope."

Dean described the bleak pipeline construction site far up in the northern part of Alaska. "Ketchikan and Barrow. I think Barrow's the tip of the world."

Ron Isaak agreed with his brother about his cousin Renee. She was a "good egg" who tried to help her family. In fact, it had been for Ron's birthday on September 23,

1978, when Renee threw the big barbecue that Dean had described.

She wasn't normally a party giver, but she went all out for Ron's special day. Benson's ears perked up when Ron Isaak said that Joe Tarricone had attended that party.

"My cousin [Renee] told me that he kept calling from Alaska and wanting to come down, so she finally says to bring a bunch of steaks and stuff 'cause we were having my birthday party. And he came down."

"Did he bring a lot of steaks?" Benson asked.

"Oh, yeah," Ron said, explaining that Tarricone's business was traveling around Alaska selling meat out of his truck. "He brought a whole case of them."

"Remember anything else at that party between you and Renee and Joe that day?"

"Being as it was my birthday and I had a bar I'd built a couple of years earlier, she wanted to help me stock it. She told Joe to go down to the liquor store and get a gallon jug of rum. He came back with just a small one, and she told him, 'No, I want a *gallon* jug'—so he comes back with a gallon of vodka. She was handing it to me, and he got upset," Ron said. "So she took it back and whispered to me that once he left, I could have it."

Asked if Renee had seemed happy or annoyed when Joe showed up at her house, Ron Isaak remembered that she had seemed irritated with him despite his generosity with all the free prime steaks. "She mostly ignored Joe that night," Ron said.

Ben Benson realized that the night of the barbecue could well have been the last night that Joe Tarricone was alive: September 23, 1978. Or had the barbecue taken place on some other night—some night that was only close to Ron Isaak's birthday?

According to both of her cousins, Joe had done everything he could to please Renee at the birthday barbecue. He'd cooked all the steaks. There were so many that people at the party had even tossed the expensive cuts to the dogs.

But nothing Joe did had any positive effect on Renee.

Renee had bragged to her cousins that Joe had already given her a black Mercedes convertible, and she kept it—although she stored it at her aunt Lillian's house until it was repossessed by an Alaskan finance company a few years after Joe disappeared.

Renee couldn't seem to say anything nice about Joe Tarricone. She had even hinted to several of her relatives that she believed Joe was involved in something crooked—possibly with the Mafia. She said it was likely that Joe's meat company was only a front for some illegal operation, and that could be dangerous.

Neither Ron nor Dean had seen Joe since the night of the birthday barbecue. They had asked Renee about him.

"She said that he disappeared and that maybe he even got thrown in the ocean or something by the mob," Dean Isaak said. "But she really didn't know."

Their aunt—Geri Hesse—had seemed to be very worried about Joe when she didn't hear from him after the night of the party. She told relatives that she took it upon herself to check out Tarricone's business office when she went up to Alaska to stay for a while with her oldest child—her son, Nick.

"She said she found the place a mess—as if someone had trashed it. She thought there had possibly been a fight there."

Ben Benson was learning more about Renee Curtiss. He knew now that she had a sister, Cassie, and a brother, Nick, as well as aunts, uncles, and more cousins. The two cousins Ben talked to had spoken of her as a generous woman who went out of her way to help them when they were down on their luck.

On the other hand, the Tarricone family believed that she was a devil woman who would stop at nothing to get what she wanted—even murder.

Benson looked for more of Renee's relatives. Although Dean and Ron Isaak had spoken positively about Renee, their sister, Victoria, was more judgmental.

When Benson spoke to Victoria McMillan, she was aware that some human remains had been found on the property where her aunt Geri and cousin Renee had once lived. Victoria didn't know who the bones might belong to.

Victoria said she had thought Renee Curtiss was "shady" during a time when she was younger. "In fact," she said, "I thought she worked as a prostitute. Geri may have been, too, or she might have just introduced Renee to 'dates.'

"They always spent more than they earned; Renee was

always flying here and flying there with men, and she got really neat presents from them," Victoria said. "One time, Renee told me, 'If you're gonna give it up, you might as well get paid for it.'"

Benson knew that of the many places Renee listed on her job résumé, one suggested that she *might* be selling sex. She had been employed by Elite Models in Seattle.

Her cousin confirmed that Renee Curtiss had not one but two children, neither of whom she had raised herself. "Aunt Geri raised Diana, and Renee's son, Brent—I don't know *who* raised him. He was mostly in foster homes. I don't know who his father was, but Renee's son, Brent, was always in trouble. And I don't think he ever actually lived with her."

So Renee had been helpful to her male cousins but apparently hadn't taken responsibility for her own children. Ben Benson found her life story more tangled with everyone he interviewed.

By this time, Benson had already done an initial check on Nick Notaro, Renee's adopted brother, and noted that Nick had a criminal record, one for a sexual crime involving a juvenile girl.

Victoria asked Benson if it was Nick's wife they had found on the property on Canyon Road.

"No," Benson said slowly, puzzled. He hadn't heard anything about Nick's wife.

"Nick went to prison for killing his wife," Victoria continued. "But they never found her body."

"Is that right?" Benson said, letting that information sink in.

"Oh, then it must have been Renee's boyfriend—the one who disappeared," Victoria said calmly. "I guess he never showed up either."

"I was beginning to think this was a very strange family," Benson said later.

Ben Benson contacted Dr. John Stewart at the FBI's DNA laboratory and asked if he could send the bones that almost certainly belonged to Joe Tarricone to the lab to be tested. They had been kept sacrosanct in the chain of evidence system since they were found.

"Yes," Stewart said. "Send them by Federal Express to the Evidence Control Unit at our laboratory here in Quantico."

Dr. Stewart also asked Benson to send DNA samples from Joe Tarricone's close relatives. Benson sent portions of the still officially unknown victim's left humerus and left ilium, and he included DNA exemplars from Joe's sister, Mimi Kraft, and from his son Dean.

Even without a complete skull, there was a good chance the FBI lab could tentatively identify the bones as belonging to Joe Tarricone.

It would take a long wait to receive an answer, however. The FBI is overwhelmed with requests for DNA matches. This was a homicide case thirty years old and didn't demand the immediate attention that recent cases did. Indeed, it would be March 2008 when the FBI lab reported that they were unsuccessful in identifying the exemplars Benson had sent in using nuclear tests. But they *did* have better results with mitochondrial DNA comparison between Joe's relatives and the unidentified bones. This wasn't as conclusive as nuclear DNA. Still, it meant that only one person in hundreds would have the same characteristics in the mitochondrial DNA matches.

Benson and Dr. Kathy Taylor sent in another bone to be tested shortly thereafter, and this time the odds were much higher that Joe Tarricone was the victim.

Ben Benson continued to search for evidence and/or witnesses, checking out the backgrounds of all "persons of interest" in Tarricone's homicide. He still worked alone from the summer of 2007 until the early months of 2008. Denny Wood had been called up as a reserve officer and was on a foreign assignment.

Ben actually talked to Renee Curtiss in late summer. He had found that she was working—or had been working—for Henry's Bail Bonds near Pioneer Square in Seattle. He went there and talked to a black man, who introduced himself as Henry Lewis. Ben asked if he knew of a Renee Curtiss.

"She's right here," the bail bonds company owner said, and Benson found himself looking at Renee Curtiss in person for the first time. She was an attractive, well-groomed woman in her fifties who now had some hard edges. She smiled as she invited him to sit down at her desk.

Benson chose not to let on that he was a detective from Pierce County who was investigating the disappearance of Joe Tarricone, and Renee quickly assumed he'd come to inquire about bailing someone out. He acquiesced—inventing his "mythical sister's son."

"I told her I wanted to know the cost of bailing someone out and how the process would work," Benson remembers. "She told me everything. She knew the justice system backward and forward and explained to me what would happen. She asked what he'd been arrested for, and I said, 'Burglary—but it's kind of a hokey deal.'"

Benson was impressed that Renee really knew her stuff. She was clearly an intelligent woman. Benson left, without ever revealing who he was.

As it turned out, he wouldn't talk to Renee again for months.

Working solo made him only more determined to find vital information that had scattered like a broken string of beads over the prior three decades.

Chapter Seven

Geri Hesse's three children were separated by distance and circumstance over the thirty years since Joe Tarricone disappeared. Her older daughter, Cassie, lived a relatively stable life in Anchorage in a very nice home there. After Cassie's brother—Nick—confessed to the murder of his wife, she visited him in prison in Colorado only once, and that was when she accompanied her mother, Geri, and sister, Renee.

Even armed with the many addresses where Renee Curtiss and Geri Hesse had lived since they left their Canyon Road rental in 1979, it was impossible for investigators to trace just what jobs they'd held. They were both intelligent and streetwise women. Renee had worked as a model and an escort a few times, and she made a good impression as she entered parties and dinners and, sometimes, grand hotels on the arms of her clients. She was also a competent office worker. Geri had a variety of jobs—as a salesclerk and in the medical field as a nursing assistant—although she probably slowed down as the years passed and she grew older.

Renee and Geri had expensive tastes; they preferred upscale clothes and jewelry, and cars that people of wealth drove. Renee, of course, hadn't been able to keep the new Mercedes that she said was a gift from Joe Tarricone way back in 1978; the loan company picked it up from where she had hidden it at her aunt's home. Still, she had usually managed to drive a luxury car. It's quite possible that she wasn't looking for love when she chose to date men. A lot of them were considerably older than she was, and on a scale of physical attractiveness, could not possibly equal hers.

When the two women returned to the Northwest from California, and after Geri died, Renee soon met a retired Exxon executive, reputed to be a billionaire, who lived in one of Seattle's posher suburbs—Mercer Island.

Luther Wallach* was certainly attracted to her, and she soon moved into his palatial waterfront estate, living with him for quite some time. She encouraged him to throw lavish parties and to travel. She hoped to marry him but, at his age, he didn't want to become legally entangled with her. He may even have sensed that her affection for him had dollar signs connected to it.

When the shocking news broke about Renee and her purported connections to Joe Tarricone, Gypsy Tarricone received a phone call from a KIRO reporter, Deborah Horne. The Seattle-based CBS reporter was passing on the name of a man who was trying to contact Gypsy.

"I called him," Gypsy remembers. "His name was Richard and he lived on the other side of Puget Sound from Seattle. He told me he just couldn't believe the things he was hearing about Renee."

Richard explained that he had been the driver for Luther Wallach during the time she lived with her billionaire paramour.

When Richard knew Renee, she was beautiful, a glamorous hostess at their parties, and everything was "perfect." She chose gourmet food, the finest wines. In Richard's eyes—then—Renee was the epitome of class, seemingly born to the upper stratosphere of society in Seattle.

Richard thought that the old man might have married her in time, but the chauffeur saw that she kept pushing too hard and his boss wasn't about to be forced to the altar. Perhaps thinking that he would change his mind if he thought he couldn't have her, Renee packed her things and left Wallach.

Her tactics didn't work. Shortly after she walked out of his life, Wallach married a young woman whom Richard categorized as "trailer trash." The new bride had a small child. Ironically, when the Exxon billionaire died a little more than a month after their marriage, he left everything to the woman who had quickly replaced Renee.

Renee Curtiss was smart and manipulative—but she had one flaw when it came to ending up with wealth: bad timing.

Renee wasn't alone for long. Next, she dated another very wealthy man—Charlie Gunderson.* He wasn't a billionaire, but he had an executive position in a huge chain of auto parts stores. He was, as was her pattern in the men she chose, quite a bit older than Renee. Once again, she lived a lush life. But once again, it became obvious that her goal was marriage. Charlie, who had ties to Anchorage, Alaska, wanted only a lovely companion—not a wife with expensive tastes.

Renee hadn't learned from her previous relationships. Charlie Gunderson, too, balked. And Renee walked out, just as broke as she was when she'd met him.

For Renee, the third time was almost the charm. She soon met Henry Lewis, who owned one of the top bail bonds businesses in Seattle and was a beloved local fixture. How she met him—or any of the men in her life—remains clouded. It's quite likely that she may have gone to Henry's place of business after one of her DUI arrests.

Renee was growing older; she was nearing fifty and the men she chose to seduce weren't that much older than she was anymore. Henry "Fireball" Lewis was eleven years older than Renee and beloved in the black community, and he was a great friend to many big names in the Seattle music world, especially Jimi Hendrix, one of the greatest guitar players of all time.

Henry had been a baseball star in his younger years, and he'd owned Henry's Bail Bonds for almost two decades. He had several children who adored him and scores of grateful clients. His bail bond business was one of five or six in Seattle that people who found themselves under arrest or in jail turned to.

When *Seattle Times* reporter Natalie Singer interviewed Henry in May 2006, she wrote, "It's too bad you have to get arrested to see the office of Henry 'Fireball' Lewis.

Tucked inside a historic Pioneer Square building, Henry's Bail Bonds doubles as a Jimi Hendrix shrine of sorts . . . [Henry Lewis] reigns over the collection of framed Hendrix posters and T-shirts, just a sampling of the memorabilia he hopes to turn into a museum one day."

Some people even called Henry "the Jimi Man."

Jimi Hendrix was, according to experts, one of two of Seattle's massively talented guitar players, singers, and songwriters, both of whom died prematurely at the age of twenty-seven, both under suspicious circumstances where drug use and the possibility of foul play were considered. Kurt Cobain, the front man for Nirvana—one of the first grunge rock groups to fascinate a new age in music—was the other. They both grew up in Washington State and lived, as adult superstars, close to Lake Washington in the Seattle area.

Kurt died on April 5, 1994, by his own hand, according to Seattle police detectives, as he held a rifle to his head. His fans still dispute the official decision to rule that suicide was his manner of death.

Jimi Hendrix, widely considered to be the greatest electric guitarist in musical history, died in London on September 18, 1970. It would take pages to list the honors bestowed upon him by the music world.

Henry Lewis was born in 1942, the same year as Jimi Hendrix, and he was a longtime friend of Leon Hendrix, Jimi's brother, and the entire Hendrix family. Henry was part owner of the small red house in Renton, Washington, where Jimi lived in his teenage years and where he played his "broom guitar" before he could afford a real one. It had long been Henry's mission to keep Jimi's legacy alive, to see that that modest house was preserved and that suitable memorials existed in Jimi's honor in Seattle. The inside of his office was papered with homages to Jimi Hendrix.

When the city was prepared to tear down Hendrix's former home, Henry Lewis told the media, "I won't let that happen. To save it, I'll carry it on my back if I have to."

Lewis's world seemed a million miles away from Renee's.

Renee's life was a series of vignettes as she moved from place to place, man to man, and through lifestyles that were diametrically opposed. Henry Lewis hired her—she was always a good study and quick to learn new businesses—and he fell in love with her, much to his children's dismay.

Henry suffered from a bad heart, but that didn't deter Renee; they were married in 2006.

When Detective Ben Benson first met Renee in Henry Lewis's office, he had yet to find out about all of her activities and liaisons over the years. If he had, he certainly would have seen the pattern emerge again and again. Renee and her mother had sought out those things and people who would keep them living in style. For Renee, that had always meant seducing wealthy men by using her beauty and her ability to be whoever she perceived men wanted her to be.

Henry Lewis wasn't a billionaire, but he owned a number of properties that had greatly increased in value over the years. He wore a small fortune in gold jewelry, and there were times—as Henry told reporter Natalie Singer—that he had had his name and his fortune riding on $8 million out in bail money. He was good to his clients, tried to make them feel at ease, and trusted that they would show up on the dates their court appearances were scheduled. He even felt sorry for many of them. However, he wasn't a patsy.

"But they have to go to court," he told Singer. "There are no bad hair days."

He was devoted to the memory of a musical giant, a dreamer who hoped to have his own museum for Jimi Hendrix someday—but Henry Lewis was also a no-nonsense man. A businessman. When he fell in love with Renee Curtiss, he placed his trust in her, although that might not have been as wise an idea as he believed it to be.

After Henry Lewis married Renee, she and her sister, Cassie, continued to work in his bail bonds company. No one ever said that Renee wasn't a hard worker. For a time, she seemed to be an asset, but she came between Henry and his children. She was not the kind of woman they would have chosen for their father.

PART THREE

"Jane Doe Down . . ."
HEALY, ALASKA

Chapter Eight

Renee's cousin Victoria had blurted out a question about *who* had been murdered, and that surprised Ben Benson. With the rumor that there had possibly been another homicide hanging from the Hesse/Notaro family tree, Benson contacted the Alaska State Patrol to see if they had any record of such an event.

They had indeed. Nick Notaro, Renee's older brother, had confessed to killing his wife, Vickie, in October 1978.

Benson requested a copy of that murder file from the Records and Identification Unit in Juneau, Alaska. They promised to send a copy down for him to review.

It was six in the evening on October 15, 1978, and almost full dark when the Fairbanks detachment of the Department of Public Safety—the Alaska state troopers on duty—received a report from Wayne Walters, chief of police in Nenana. A dead body had been discovered by kids sledding and picnicking at a gravel pit at approximately Mile 317 on the Parks Highway just outside Healy. As troopers Roderick Harvey, James McCann, and Steven Heckman headed to the location given for the corpse, they didn't know whether the victim was male or female. If it had been there for weeks or even months, it might be difficult to tell—at least at first.

"The scene is located where there is a dirt road leading uphill from the Parks Highway on the east side of the road," McCann wrote in his first report on the unknown deceased person. "Approximately halfway up the hill, the road tops out and levels into a gravel pit area. There is what appears to be a parking area. There is evidence of many people having come to this area for target practice as well as picnics. There are numerous fired cartridge casings of various calibers strewn around on the ground, and there is a campfire area. Approximately thirty feet south of this campfire, there is a trail [where someone] had carried or dragged a body to the open edge of the embankment. From the edge of that embankment to the victim's head was about thirteen feet."

There was little that could be done in the icy darkness, so the scene was protected until daylight. With winter approaching, dawn would come slowly, but the troopers could see that the dead person's head was below the feet, and the arms were outstretched and over the head.

What was obviously the most-used trail into the brush had no matted-down vegetation. A narrower path, however, had crushed willow brush. It appeared that someone had taken that route and then pushed or thrown the victim over. Dropping to their hands and knees, the investigators gathered hairs and minute fibers that clung to the willows. They also found a pair of panty hose, size small.

They determined that the victim was a woman, but it wasn't likely the panty hose belonged to her; she was a good-sized woman, close to six feet tall, and probably weighing at least 170 pounds. She had been shot in the head once, possibly more times.

But who she was, none of them knew.

There were several establishments of one sort or another along the highway, and trooper Steve Heckman stopped at every one that was open to see if anyone might know the woman's identity. He began at the Clear Sky Lodge, and proceeded to Roscoe's, the Corner Bar, Moochers Bar & Grill, Coghill's store, and Parker's Patch. The Dew Drop Inn and the Tamarac Inn were closed, but Heckman did get one possible ID at Moochers.

A female bartender recalled a woman who matched some of the details in the dead woman's description: "She was from Anchorage and she sometimes traveled between Anchorage and Fairbanks with a man who looked Spanish. He drove a new black car," the bartender said. "I thought she might be a hooker—because of the way she dressed, and because of what she said about the neighborhood she frequented in Anchorage. I think she is half white and half black, almost six feet tall, slender and well built. She's probably in her twenties, dark brown curly shoulder-length hair. Very fine facial features. Oh, and a sharp nose."

This woman was a most perceptive witness, with a great memory for details. "She usually wears expensive clothing and good jewelry—she has a large diamond dinner ring and chain necklaces with coins on them. Her nails are long, and they're painted orange."

"Anything else?" Heckman asked.

"She speaks Spanish. I think—I'm not sure—and she may have come from New Orleans originally."

The unknown victim was also tall, and she had shoulder-length curly brown hair. However, she'd worn blue jeans, a cheap polyester blouse, and J.C. Penney sneakers. Her nails weren't long and polished; they looked to be the blunt-cut nails of a woman who did physical work. Although the bartender at Moochers was a superb witness, she must have been describing another woman passing through.

There was one way they might be able to identify the nameless victim: she had had extremely good dental work done. Trooper Rod Harvey took photos of her teeth and gave copies to five dentists who practiced nearby.

None of them recognized the work. Troopers tried to find a match with a half-dozen more dentists, but gleaned nothing that would identify the victim.

On October 17, 1978, Dr. Michael Probst arrived from Anchorage to perform a postmortem examination of the dead woman. He felt she was twenty-five to thirty years old, but it would be impossible to accurately pinpoint her date and time of death. Her body was frozen when she was found, and still somewhat frozen as her autopsy began. Ordinarily, the stiffening of muscles after death—rigor mortis—can begin a few hours to even twelve to eighteen hours after death. A body's muscles may be immovable from any time from twenty-four to thirty-six or forty-eight hours after death before the stiffening relaxes.

The Jane Doe victim's rigor mortis had come and gone.

Livor mortis—or lividity—occurs when the heart stops pumping, leaving the lowest body parts stained a purplish red with pooled blood, and that can take up to a dozen hours. This victim's lividity was, as expected, in her head, neck, shoulders, arms, and hands, which had all been on the downhill side of the trail. It was complete.

The dead woman had to have been dead a day or so before her body was discovered, but she could also have been deceased for a lot longer than that, given the thirty-one-degree temperatures charted for the Healy area for that October.

No one had reported anyone resembling the victim missing.

The cause of death was horribly easy to detect. She had fought for her life gallantly and sustained numerous scratches, cuts, and what were clearly defense wounds. The injuries had been inflicted both before and after death. X-rays taken before this postmortem exam showed two projectiles (slugs) in the body—one in the brain and the other in the abdominal/pelvic cavity.

Dr. Probst looked at the entrance wound in the victim's left temple first and found gunpowder *inside* the wound, but the rounded wound had no charring and no ragged (stellate) edge. He determined that this wound had been in the "close category," but was not a "contact." The bullet had traveled in a straight line through her brain, ending up in the *right* occipital (back) of the brain. The copper jacket had separated from the slug. This slug had fractured her skull, not to mention causing shock and hemorrhage in her brain.

It would have been rapidly—if not instantly—fatal.

The second entrance wound was in her lower back in the left lumbar region. It had entered her back and ended at her right iliac crest (hip bone), traveling back to front, left to right. This would not necessarily have been a fatal wound, if the victim had had immediate medical attention. It had been fired from some distance. While the bullet had gone through the back hem of the woman's blouse, it hadn't caused any singeing or melting of the material. A close-up shot would have.

The pathologist and the Alaska troopers observing the autopsy agreed: the back wound would have been the first, possibly as the victim was running away from her killer. The head wound came second, almost as if the shooter was clamping her head close so that she could not avoid the fatal shot.

Three days later—after the Jane Doe's description was published in nearby newspapers—a woman came forward. She gave her name as Laverne Isaacson and said she owned the Healy Hotel.

"One of our maids is missing," she explained. "She's about twenty-five, more than five foot eight, and she's kind of chunky. I'd say she weighs about one hundred sixty pounds or so. I believe she has some Indian blood—she has brown hair and brown eyes. She wears glasses. She's a good person, and we're worried."

"Why is that?" Rod Harvey asked.

"Well, she went to pick up her husband from the hospital in Fairbanks on September 21. And she never came back to Healy—hasn't shown up for work . . . it's not like her."

"What's her name?"

"Vickie. Vickie Notaro. When I asked her husband, Nick, about where she was, he told me that they had a fight that night. They were staying in a hotel there—and he said she just up and left him."

The Jane Doe was no longer unidentified; she was the late Mrs. Nick Notaro, Renee Curtiss's sister-in-law. The Alaska detectives had been able to pinpoint the last day she was seen alive—they found a motel owner in Fairbanks whose records showed that Nick and Vickie had checked in on Monday, September 21, 1978, and left the next morning. They had stayed in Room 104 at the Towne House Motel, and paid $37.80. They often stopped at the Towne House, and no one—staff or guests—had heard or seen anything unusual during the night.

"One thing, though," manager Steve Nord added. "One of our maids found a box for a gun and some bullets. There was a receipt there, too—from J.C. Penney."

The receipt showed that Nick Notaro, six feet three inches, age thirty, weighing well over two hundred pounds, had purchased a Smith & Wesson .38 Special, .38 double action revolver for $156.75 and a box of bullets *on September 21*!

Chapter Nine

On July 18, 2007, Ben Benson obtained the complete criminal history of Nick Notaro. He found that Notaro had been a suspect in a child rape case in Tacoma in 1994. There was also a statement in the file from a woman named Janet Blaisdell* who said that Notaro had told her about killing his first wife in Alaska in the late seventies. Janet was the witness mentioned in the more recent child molestation charges against Nick. Benson wanted very much to find her.

The Pierce County detective sergeant found it tantalizing when he first heard that Nick Notaro had told a woman named Blaisdell that he had killed a man in Tacoma and had buried him at Nick's mother's house on Canyon Road.

Benson left a message on Janet Blaisdell's answering machine. He also received a copy of a 1978 murder investigation file involving Vickie Notaro from the Alaska State Department of Public Safety's Records and Identification Unit in Juneau, Alaska.

Not one—but two—homicide cases were opening up like morning glories in bright sunlight. Either this was too good to be true—the suspects were stupid—or they had been very, very lucky for almost thirty years!

Jeanne Slook of the Alaska R. and I. office said she would mail Benson a copy of the Vickie Notaro case in Alaska, and Janet Blaisdell would be happy to fill Benson in on her conversations with Nick Notaro in Tacoma.

On July 23, 2007, Ben Benson met with her and taped her statement. Janet said that she had first met Nick Notaro in 1987 or 1988. He came to work at Winchell's Donuts as the night baker. They soon became casual friends. She met Lila May,* his wife, and Heidi,* his stepdaughter, shortly thereafter when they came in to wait for him to finish his shift.

"I'd get Heidi a glass of milk and a donut, and Lila May and I would talk," Janet said. "And then Lila May came to work for us, too."

The Notaros didn't have many friends, and Janet Blaisdell said she would invite them over for dinner at her house, or they would drop by to visit.

"After you became friends with Nick," Ben Benson began, "did there come a time where he told you about an incident where he had murdered his first wife?"

"Yes. Several months later—I'd say maybe even a year."

"Did you feel that he was trying to get it off his chest—or why do you think he told you?"

"To this day, I don't know why. I thought at the time he just wanted somebody to talk to, and he knew I was his friend—and he kind of unloaded. He asked me if I knew that he had been in prison, and I told him no, and then he began to tell me the story of how he killed his first wife."

"What exactly did he tell you?" Benson asked.

"He told me she was cheating on him while . . . I think he said he was working in Fairbanks, she [Vickie] was down here staying on Canyon Road in a house with his mother. He was sending all this money down here to her and his sisters. And so he came down here without any-body knowing and he found out that she was [cheating]. He went back to Alaska and, three weeks later, had her come up there for a visit. He was driving down a road and he confronted her with this other man, and they started arguing, and he reached down and took his loaded gun from under the seat and shot her in the head at point blank range. And then he took the body up to higher ground somewhere in Fairbanks and buried her. He said she laid [*sic*] there for a very, very, long time before they found her. Some animals had come down 'cause it was cold in the winter and they found her and kinda dug part of her up and were chewing on her limbs, and later some skiers tripped across it, and they put her face on the news and that's how he got caught."

"Did he tell you who recognized her face on the news?"

"His boss . . . He had taken her and introduced her to his boss and when they showed her as a Jane Doe and a number you could call with information, he did."

"And then did he tell you about coming down here to Tacoma and looking for the guy she was having the affair with?"

"Yes. After he killed her he came down to the Tacoma area and found the guy and killed him. His mother knew he was coming down, his sisters knew, and he got him and killed him—and then brought the body back to his mother's house on Canyon Road, and he told me his sisters helped him dismember the body, put it in bags, and buried him under his mother's front porch. I asked him if his mother knew—and he said yes, and his sisters and him had made a pact never to tell anybody . . ."

Janet said that Nick Notaro had threatened *her* sometime later—after she helped his wife Lila May and Heidi get away from him because he was clearly molesting Heidi sexually.

"I moved them in with me."

Lila May Notaro agreed to talk with Benson at her apartment in Tacoma. She told Ben Benson that she had married Nick Notaro in Marshfield, Wisconsin, in 1987. She was a dozen years younger than Nick.

"How did you meet him?"

"We both worked at Jimmy's Cafe in Marshfield," she began. "He was a cook and I was a waitress. I took him as being a kind gentleman. He treated me like a woman at the time . . . I saw his good side, him being a friendly, respectable person."

Lila May was raising her six-and-a-half-year-old daughter alone. She and Nick Notaro dated for about six months, and she was happy when he asked her to marry him. She knew virtually nothing about his past—not until the night before their wedding.

"Did you know he had been to prison?" Benson asked.

"Nope. Not until he said he was feeling guilty that he

had done something wrong, and he thought he should let me know before we got married—to see how I would react or if I would go through with getting married."

"Okay. And what did he tell you?"

"He told me he killed his first wife and someone else. He said they had an argument and they were fighting, and she fell between the tub and the toilet, and then he took her and put her in the car—and went to a ditch. And she got out of the car and he went after her and shot her. Killed her."

"Did he tell you why he did that?"

"Because of her having an affair."

"Did he say anything about the person she was having an affair with?"

She shook her head. "Just some guy who lived here in Tacoma. Nick said he cut someone up and put him in a pipe in the backyard."

"All right. So then you went ahead with the wedding?"

"Yes."

"How long were you married to Nick?"

"Just about six years. The first three years were wonderful. He was dressed decent, he worked, and I didn't have any problems until the last three years."

Lila May Notaro said that Nick had kept working at Jimmy's Cafe until they had moved to Tacoma. He had moved out west a month before she did, and he got a job right away at Winchell's Donuts.

But their marriage wasn't as successful once they moved to Washington State.

"He just didn't want to be bothered," Lila May said. "He was starting to tell me that we should separate because it wasn't working out—I guess it was because of the way he was treating Heidi. He didn't want me to interfere."

Lila May said Nick would get mad at her seven-year-old daughter and make her sit still for long periods. "He wasn't really disciplining her for the right reasons. I mean, he just took it out on her [because] of his actions."

"He eventually started molesting Heidi?" Benson prompted.

"Yes—when she was the age of nine it started."

"When did you find out?"

"It was a while. One night he got up and I thought he went to the bathroom, but he went into her room, and I looked and he was kinda under the blanket. I kinda got the idea he was doing something, but you know, I didn't want to believe it 'cause I didn't think he was that type—"

A few weeks later, Lila May couldn't lie to herself any longer. She had to leave for work at 7 a.m. "And he took Heidi and molested her—penetrated her and everything. Two days later, Heidi told me everything."

Lila May had been horrified, but didn't know what to do. She first went to Geri Hesse and told her what Heidi had said about Nick. Her mother-in-law didn't seem shocked. She'd said only, "Then you better believe her."

Geri Hesse told Lila May that Nick had also molested another girl—a young female relative—but she didn't offer Lila May any solution to her problems.

Lila May Notaro wasn't a very brave woman; she didn't have the courage to confront Nick. It was her boss at the donut shop—Janet Blaisdell—who suspected something was wrong and urged Lila May to confide in her. When Lila May finally did, Janet went immediately to the phone and called Child Protective Services.

Nick Notaro was arrested and the case of child molestation went to court. Sadly, it resulted in a hung jury. The prosecutor wanted Lila May to go to court again, but she said she was too frightened.

"I had a bad feeling something was going to happen if I did it."

"What do you mean by that?" Benson asked her.

"I felt like he would've tried to do something."

"To harm you or Heidi?"

"I had such a bad feeling that I told [the prosecutor] just to get Nick on whatever he could. So he did."

Without the complaining witnesses, Nick Notaro drew a relatively short sentence. (The fact that he was a Level 2 sex offender in a Southern state wasn't known to the sentencing judge. His "victim" in that case was a developmentally disabled teenager with whom he had had consensual sexual relations.)

Nick divorced Lila May but she didn't know that until she was given some papers the night before Nick's trial, papers that said their divorce was final.

"When did you last see Nick?" Benson asked.

"Sometime back in the middle of the nineties. I didn't have a car, so I was taking a bus and I saw him sitting in the back. I turned my head away and didn't look at him."

Lila May said that her ex-husband had also told Janet Blaisdell about murders he had committed, and Janet had urged her to get away from him. Without Janet, she probably wouldn't have had the strength to leave Nick—and she felt grateful to Janef for having her back.

The two women had worked at the same places for a while, but over the years they had drifted apart.

Ben Benson was puzzled by the many versions that Nick Notaro had given when he decided to talk about the murder of his ex-wife Vickie. Was he trying to make it seem as though Vickie had been having an affair with Joe Tarricone? Or was he just making up details as he went along? Or was he a man who wanted to be the center of attention and told tall stories to achieve that?

One thing seemed certain; over a period of almost thirty years, Nick Notaro had admitted that he'd killed Vickie in every scenario he gave people.

Gypsy Tarricone told Ben Benson that she had talked to Renee on the phone a few times after her father disappeared, and Renee told her that she and her mother, Geri, felt that Joe had met with foul play. But they were emphatic in their denials that he had vanished from their rented house in Puyallup—even though Renee acknowledged that Joe *had* left his Mercedes, his pickup truck, and a camper at the house.

According to Renee and Geri, Joe had been in Alaska when he went missing. When Gypsy told Detective Jerry Burger of the Des Moines, Washington, police department that, he forwarded a copy of the information the missing man's daughter gave him to Alaska State police trooper Roy Holland, and to the Anchorage Police Department.

In talking with Joe Tarricone's family, Renee continually edited her recollections of the last few times she'd seen Joe. Whether it was Gypsy, Gina, or Dean Tarricone who called her in their desperate search for their father, Renee was friendly—but seemed completely mystified about whatever might have happened to Joe. She insisted she had no idea where he was and seemed surprised that none of his family had heard from him.

As he read through the thin files on Joe Tarricone, Benson saw that about a month after Gypsy Tarricone filed the first missing report on her father, Des Moines detective Jerry Burger had received a call from Renee Curtiss. Even though the Des Moines police had closed their case on Joseph Tarricone, since he hadn't gone missing from their jurisdiction, Renee had had something more to tell him.

She said she now remembered that Joseph Tarricone *had* come to her house in Puyallup sometime in August or September of 1978. She wasn't sure which month it was. "He said he had a surprise for me," she began. "Joe showed me two tickets to Italy, and he asked me to go on a trip there with him—a honeymoon. He wanted to marry me.

"I didn't want to go," Renee continued. "I didn't want to marry him—not at all. That made him very angry and upset. He threw those tickets on the ground and walked off. That was the last time *I* ever saw him."

"What happened to the plane tickets?" Burger asked.

"When he didn't come back for them, I cashed them in at a travel agency. He also left his 1978 Mercedes 240D at my house," she said. "He had already signed his pickup truck with the camper on it over to my mother. He likes my mother. I think he financed the Mercedes through some credit union in Anchorage."

"Was he drinking that last day you saw him?"

"No."

Gypsy didn't believe that version of Renee's ever-changing memory for a minute. She told Burger: "I don't buy that he would walk away from her place in Puyallup and hurt himself because Renee rejected his proposal. I don't think he proposed to her at all, but they definitely were involved in some kind of a relationship. I believe that. I think Renee led him on because he had money. She was only in her twenties and she already had a boyfriend."

When Ben Benson read this old report years later, he shook his head. Why would a man *walk* away from the home of a woman he'd apparently been in love with when he had a brand-new expensive car, and, quite possibly, a truck and camper, too?

Sure, he might have been disappointed—even devastated—if he had, indeed, proposed marriage to Renee and shown her the tickets and reservations for their honeymoon trip to Rome—only to be turned down. But Joe sounded like a tough and rugged man, a man who had survived wars. He had taken hits before, and gotten up to regroup.

Renee Curtiss had offered a lot of information back in the late seventies, but it had come out in peculiar segments—disjointed recollections that seemed to contradict things she had told people earlier.

Even before the DNA match came in from the FBI, Ben Benson and his partner, Denny Wood, had no doubt that the remains found on the Canyon Road property were those of Joseph Tarricone. Any reasonable person would feel the same way. And they believed that any reasonable juror would agree. It seemed completely implausible that Tarricone would *walk* away from the semirural property and abandon his Mercedes and the rig he used for his meat delivery business.

More than that, from what the detectives had learned so far, Tarricone was an excellent father, one who kept in touch with his children and grandchildren. And he was the son of aged parents who depended on him, lived for his phone calls, and looked forward to his visits to New York every year.

It would have been totally against his grain to disappear into the moonless night, leaving behind his obligations and those who loved him, no matter how besotted he'd been with the mysterious Renee Curtiss.

Over the last part of 2007, the Pierce County detectives were almost positive that he was the homicide victim. However, they had to wait for the FBI lab tests to come back.

And the more they investigated Renee, the more suspects they uncovered.

By that time, they had learned a great deal more about the violent background of Nick Notaro, Renee and Cassie's adopted brother.

Chapter Ten

Nick Notaro, who was thirty at the time, had had
a remarkably busy week in late September 1978. If he
had been all the places people said he had, his activities
between September 18 and September 23 would have
required a superman. Nick was a huge man, well over
six feet, and closer to three hundred pounds than two
hundred. The old records from Alaska showed that he entered the Fairbanks Memorial Hospital on Monday—the
eighteenth—to have his festering appendix removed. Dr.
J. K. Johnson was the surgeon who operated, and Nick recovered without incident. He was released earlier than the
hospital advised, on Thursday, the twenty-first.

And Nick was also one of the family members who
witnesses remembered being at the birthday barbecue
Renee threw on Saturday, September 23.

Ben Benson traveled far in his search for Joe Tarricone's
last moments: New Mexico, Maryland, Oregon, and
now—Alaska. The Alaska State Police in Anchorage had

assured him on the phone that their old records on Nick Notaro still existed, and they believed there was physical evidence, too.

When Ben Benson arrived in Anchorage, Alaska, on August 28, 2007, he had practically memorized the 1978 homicide case in which the Jane Doe victim turned out to be Nick's first wife.

Not surprisingly, most of the Alaska investigators of Vickie Notaro's homicide had long since retired. Luckily, Benson found Marjean Denison in the state police office, and she was of immeasurable help in locating contact information for the former troopers.

Benson found the Alaska State Police detectives quite forthcoming in talking with him about Vickie Notaro's bizarre murder. The original investigators agreed to talk with him, recalling that her body was discovered twelve miles north of Nenana along the Parks Highway on October 15, 1978.

"How long had it been there?" Benson asked retired Alaska state trooper Detective James McCann. (McCann had been on the force from 1972 to 1999, and he was one of the first investigators into Vickie Notaro's murder.)

"Probably two—maybe three weeks," he answered slowly. "But it gets cold early here, and there was some snow on the ground already, so it's hard to tell. Her body was frozen."

McCann said that his memory had become vague in the thirty years that had passed since Vickie was murdered, but he did recall going to the crime scene and that there was one of many "gravel barrel pits" there where the

Department of Transportation loaded up gravel for road construction and repair. "Someone may have stopped to relieve himself, climbed up the gravel—it was higher than the road—and down into a depression and he found her there."

McCann said that he and other Alaska detectives had photographed the scene, measured it, and taken some physical evidence—which they bagged and tagged.

Here, James McCann had a sore spot. He had always believed that evidence should be preserved forever, but their headquarters were very small in 1978 and there was barely space for an evidence room.

"Some of our commanders took it upon themselves to destroy evidence prior to a case being solved—and then some cases *were* solved—and I guess it was just taking up room . . ."

Earlier, Benson had called the 2007 evidence supervisor, Diane Lindner, and she had searched, but she had to tell him that they no longer had physical evidence on the murder of Vickie Notaro in their property room. It had been purged. Since Nick had been convicted of murdering his wife, this news came as no surprise to Benson.

Before the computer age, a lot of the old records in police evidence rooms disappeared. It is something that makes homicide detectives shudder, particularly in the twenty-first century when so many cold cases are being solved with DNA residue that has clung to physical evidence for decades—useless until now.

Lindner had, however, been able to locate some photographs from the case.

One photo showed Nick Notaro's tennis shoes; they were spattered with dried blood. After he read about how Vickie died, Benson thought that her blood wouldn't necessarily have been on Nick's tennis shoes. But maybe those spatters had come from sawing up Joe Tarricone's body?

Ben Benson pressed on with his questions about Vickie's murder, which almost certainly had happened within the days before Joe Tarricone disappeared.

"Do you recall if the gun in the case was ever located?" he asked.

McCann tried to recall, saying he thought it had been a revolver.

Benson nodded. "He bought a thirty-eight Special from Gary Tellep when Gary worked at Penney's up in Fairbanks. Notaro told some of your guys that he threw it in the river?"

"Yeah. We never did recover that gun," McCann said.

"Okay," Benson said, waiting.

"Our rivers—our rivers here hold a lot of guns," McCann said with a sigh.

Benson talked next to retired Alaska State police detective Bradley Brown—who had been with the force from January 1973 until March of 1999.

Brown remembered Nick Notaro very well indeed. Brad Brown had been the sole trooper assigned to the Healy, Alaska, post. Healy is a small town just outside McKinley National Park, a popular tourist spot in warm months. The park and Healy are roughly 120 miles south of Fairbanks.

Benson grinned at the thought of a single trooper handling such a relatively large area.

"So you were like a one-man show at that time—back in 1978?" he asked Brown.

"Yeah, I had an office in Healy alongside the Parks Highway at the intersection of Healy Road. I knew Nicky—that's what I called him."

"Did you know his wife, Vickie?"

"Yeah, she was kinda like a maid or worked housekeeping at the Healy Hotel and several other places around here. From my understanding she did some odd jobs on the side, like laundry, just to make ends meet."

Although Healy was surrounded by natural splendor, the Notaros weren't exactly living high on the hog.

In the late seventies, Nicky Notaro worked as a cook at Jerry's Healy Service, a gas station/restaurant/store/gathering spot owned by Jerry Hamel. Brad Brown said he had often dropped into Jerry's late at night when the rest of Healy had pretty much rolled up the sidewalks.

Even the Road House and the Auto Lake Lodge, the two bars in town, were closed.

"Maybe there were only one or two clientele inside Jerry's," Brown elaborated. "So I would talk with Nick because he did most of the nighttime work. I would just be friends—like everyone was [in Healy]—with him."

In the frigid hours before dawn when Healy was mostly dark except for the neon sign glowing at Jerry's, the trooper drank hot coffee and watched Nick slap burgers or eggs on the grill, scraping it clean when he was finished. Nick Notaro wasn't a particularly scintillating conversationalist, but he was a pleasant enough guy to talk with when the rest of Healy was asleep.

"Did you know him on a personal level?" Ben Benson asked Brown.

The retired trooper shook his head. "No—not per se. When we speak 'personal,' I think like being close to him, like going to his house for dinner. No, it wasn't anything like that. I knew him as far as his general demeanor. He was a hard worker behind the grill, and he would always talk and communicate, [with a] smile on his face. That's kind of how I knew him."

Like almost everyone else in Healy, Brad Brown had been surprised when he heard that Nick Notaro was the prime suspect in the murder of his wife. Nick had seemed like a "gentle giant."

"Did you participate in the investigation?"

Brown nodded. "Yeah, I did." He remembered the details quite clearly. There had been nothing gentle about Vickie Notaro's death.

There were many longtime residents who still lived in Healy. Ben Benson found Shirley Hamel, Jerry Hamel's widow, and her daughter, Geri Lynn Lucier, who both recalled Nick working at Jerry's Healy Service. Shirley said she and Jerry had arrived there in 1978 and bought the business. They hadn't had a large staff—just two or three of their children, and perhaps the same number of unrelated employees. Jerry was the one who had hired the mountain of a man who cooked at the Healy Hotel and seemed to have good references as a fry cook.

"But Nick was a strange sort of person," she said. "After I heard he'd been arrested, I felt nervous about the fact that I'd often let my kids go to town with him."

Benson asked Shirley Hamel if she had ever heard rumors that either Nick or Vickie was unfaithful.

"Not at all," she answered, surprised.

She explained that the Healy Hotel had been located in "Old Healy" in 1978. Later, the railroad bought up much of the property there, leaving it a virtual ghost town: Shirley told Benson that even the Healy Hotel had been physically moved the four miles to the new part of town.

"They call it the Stampede, now," she said.

"Did your daughters tell you any stories about any weird behavior on his part?"

"Geri Lynn used to say he made her nervous. She didn't want to have him go to town with her when she was carrying a bank deposit. I guess he never did much to help her, although he was supposed to. He'd go to town and take care of *his* personal business."

Shirley Hamel recalled that Nick had had sharp pains in his abdomen one night in the fall of 1978, and she and Jerry figured it was probably appendicitis. She had helped Nick pack a bag, throwing in his cigarettes, and then given him a ride to Fairbanks because he was complaining about how bad his belly hurt.

"And do you remember him coming back to town after he had his appendix surgery?" Benson probed.

"I saw him the day he got out of the hospital. He stopped by the little shop in Fairbanks where I was working," Shirley said.

"He told me they were staying in town that night, and they were going to head to Healy the next day."

She knew that Vickie was with him, but she could not remember if she came into the shop or if she was waiting in the car.

Ben Benson hadn't found anyone else who had seen Vickie Notaro after the day she picked her husband up at the hospital—September 21, 1978. He didn't tell Shirley Hamel, but he suspected she might have been the last person to come close to seeing Vickie alive.

Shirley had known Vickie only slightly—from when she came into their business to wait for Nick. Asked if she had heard from Notaro after he was arrested and imprisoned, she nodded.

"He called me around the time he either got out of prison or was about to get out, and asked if I would reemploy him as a cook. I told him no. That was all but that was pretty final."

Benson talked next to Geri Lynn Lucier, the Hamels' daughter, who had been twenty when Nick Notaro had worked at her folks' place.

"Why don't you tell me where you were and what you were doing in 1978—as best as you can remember?" he began.

"In May or June of 1978, I left Tacoma, Washington, and returned to Healy with my child. I was going through a divorce and went to work for my father at Jerry's Healy Service. That was when I met Nick."

"What do you recall about him—when you met him?"

Geri Lynn grimaced. "I didn't like him. He was a weird guy. He made me very nervous. He made suggestive comments and I didn't like being around him—so I tried to avoid him, except if my father asked me to run to town with him on a grocery trip. Otherwise, I basically stayed clear of him."

There had been only two or three times when she couldn't get out of a shopping trip with Nick. As her mother had said, he hadn't helped at all with carrying groceries, but had gone off on his own to do whatever he needed to do.

"You said he would make suggestive comments. Would he be making passes at you?"

"Sometimes passes—sometimes just lewd comments, of a sexual nature. I knew he was married . . ."

Geri Lynn was certain that Nick had wanted to have an affair with her, if she had shown any interest at all. She said that when he was arrested for his wife's murder, she wasn't the only one in Healy who had been glad to see him go. She said she hadn't known Vickie well at all.

The Pierce County detective sergeant found someone who had known Vickie Notaro very well—her friend and fellow employee at the Healy Hotel, Cheri Mueller. Cheri was also twenty in 1978, and she had lived in Healy since 1971. She and Vickie had liked each other from the first time they'd met in the summer of 1978. Employees had a free room at the hotel as part of their pay. Nick had a small room initially because he came to Alaska first, to work on the pipeline. Then he sent for Vickie, who was down in Washington State living with his sister. Not with Renee, but with her older sister, Cassie Martell.* As they were a married couple, the hotel gave them a larger space.

"Vickie and I spent time together—like hang out after work and stuff," Cheri said. But she shook her head when Ben Benson asked if Nick Notaro had joined them. "No, we'd just see him at the [hotel] café when we went in to eat or whatever . . ."

"Okay. Throughout this investigation that the Alaska state troopers conducted, there were allegations from Nick—in the statement he gave them—that Vickie was having an affair, was seeing another man. Were you aware of anything like that?"

"No." Cheri bristled. "She would never do that."

"Okay, on the flip side of that, how about Nick? Are you aware of his having any relationships with other women?"

"No—I don't remember hearing anything," Cheri said, adding that Nick had been jealous of Vickie. "He didn't trust her. I always thought that was odd because she was just a nice, nice person, and he just seemed like one of those jealous-type husbands, for no reason."

Cheri could not recall that Vickie Notaro had been afraid of her husband. If she was, she hadn't mentioned it.

"Tell me what you remember about Nick," Benson probed.

"I cleaned his room and I remember it was thick with cigarette smoke. And I remember he was big. And I thought he was kind of weird, kind of different . . . He had weird books in his room: books—magazines, really—about murders and how they were solved. I thought it was really weird that somebody would be obsessed with murder."

"How many of them do you remember being in his room?"

"He had a lot—he had them stacked up next to his bed and on shelves and stuff. Sometimes there were pictures in them—like graves, and crime scene photos."

Cheri recalled the last time she ever saw Vickie. It was the day she was going up to Fairbanks to pick up Nick at the hospital. "She asked me to go with her, but something happened. I can't remember why anymore, why I couldn't go, but I didn't end up going with her."

"What do you remember about that trip to Fairbanks?" Benson asked quietly.

"She never came back."

Chapter Eleven

Now Ben Benson had a new question: If Nick Notaro was released from a hospital in Fairbanks, Alaska, on Thursday, September 21, after undergoing an emergency appendectomy two days earlier, and claimed to have killed Vickie somewhere along the way back to Healy the next day, could he then have flown to Seattle to murder—or help to murder—Joe Tarricone in Puyallup, Washington, sometime in the next week? With a fresh appendectomy incision, would Nick have been in any shape to murder his wife on the way home, and then board a plane for the long flight to Seattle?

That seemed unlikely—at first.

Most people would have still been dealing with post-surgical pain and in no mood for a plane trip. Benson didn't know much about Nick. Apparently he was very close to his sisters and defended them if anyone dared threaten them or said a bad word about them. They were reportedly much sharper than Nick was, but they still doted on him. It looked as though Nick had always run to them—especially Renee—when he was in trouble.

The infant boy that Geraldine Hesse adopted in 1948 had grown into a grizzled mountain of a man. He was once the baby who was slow to develop sitting, walking, and talking skills. He had polio as a child and that might have delayed some of his physical and mental growth.

Nick Notaro was termed "slow" by most people who dealt with him in his life. He was a great fry cook, but outside of that and driving souped-up cars, he seemed to have no particular ambitions or hobbies.

Back in 1978, Geri Hesse had explained to the Alaska state troopers who were investigating Vickie's homicide that Nick "lived within himself" and was a "dreamer" and somewhat of a loner. She nodded when asked if her son was slow.

"He *is* slow, like people say, but he isn't retarded or anything like that; Nick does everything slowly and never seems to be in a hurry. He's very quiet. He's Scandinavian, or mostly Scandinavian. He's not talkative. He's very slow to anger."

Considering that Nick was rapidly becoming the prime suspect in the murder of his wife, this hardly sounded like an apt summation of Nick Notaro.

Geri had continued painting her only son with a loving and rather strange brush. "He never dated in high school, but he ran with a bunch of boys I didn't approve of. He wasn't doing well in school, so I gave him a choice: either stop running with them or join the service."

Nick had chosen the second option. Three days after he turned seventeen, he joined the army. He went AWOL soon after because he was homesick. The army meted out a relatively mild punishment, and he was sent to Vietnam.

"He was there for three tours of duty," Geri said. "The first time he was assigned there, but he volunteered to go back two more times."

Geri Hesse shook her head when asked about young Nick's interest in guns. "We didn't have any [in our home]. We never had any. My husband was no sportsman—he didn't even like a picnic! So we had no firearms. Nick never had a BB gun. He didn't play cops and robbers like most youngsters do. He was content with games. He'd sit and read a little in his room, so he was a dreamer. He really loves his family."

Asked how Nick and Vickie met, his mother said Vickie had moved to the Spokane, Washington, area from a little town in Montana. Nick's sister Cassie had taken Vickie in as she had no other place to go.

"That's where Nick met her. As I say, she was a very good girl—but anything she learned was after she came west and lived with Cassie."

Geri's opinion of Vickie was somewhat ambivalent. She admitted that she hadn't wanted her son to marry her because she was too young and had no experience in life. "He was twenty-seven and she was barely eighteen."

But the two of them had gone to Coeur d'Alene, Idaho, and gotten married on November 16, 1974. The Notaro women had to accept the surprise wedding and made the best of it, although they would tsk-tsk over Vickie's talents as a wife—or lack thereof.

According to Geri, she and Renee, Cassie, and Nick had been quite poor as the three children grew up. She gave no hint of her expensive tastes as she piously said,

"Nick always had clean clothes and a neat house. We may not have had much, but we always had clean things."

Her mother-in-law's disapproval of Vickie's house-cleaning and cooking was evident. According to her, Vickie didn't even know how to separate laundry, and their small trailer was a mess most of the time.

Yes, Geri had agreed, Nick had come down to Washington State right after he left the hospital, arriving on about September 23. She and her daughters had picked him up at Sea-Tac Airport. All of them felt sorry for him, she said, because Vickie had left him, just run off with another man without leaving a note. Nick had been very sad and brooded about his lost wife. As always, though, he didn't talk much about Vickie—nothing beyond his recall of her picking him up at the hospital in Fairbanks, their night at the hotel, and then his discovery the next morning that she had left him. She hadn't even taken her clothes with her. Nick gave one of her friends her wardrobe—including the green evening gown she'd worn when they'd gotten married.

"He was having a lot of pain when he was down here that week—his back hurt, he couldn't really walk, and you could tell it was from his surgery," Geri said. "He spent most of his time lying on the davenport at Renee's and my house."

Nick had asked his mother to come up to Healy and take care of him. With Vickie gone, he had no one. At first she said she couldn't—because she had Renee's daughter, Diana, to care for and because Renee needed her.

"But Vickie was going to be gone," Geri said, "and I thought Nick needed me more than Renee did. I thought,

'Well, I could go there just as easily as be at Renee's until he was over being lonely and found someone else.'"

Poor Nick. He'd told his mother he'd finally gotten all his bills paid up and he was ready to start a family—and then Vickie had abandoned him for another man. He believed that this man was older, could buy her more things, and had even promised he would take her on a luxury trip to Europe. He didn't mention the seducer's name, however.

It was a familiar scenario. As Sergeant Ben Benson read over the old homicide file on the death of Vickie Notaro, he wondered at the coincidence that *both* Renee and Vickie were having "affairs" with older men with money who offered them trips to Europe, specifically Rome, Italy.

Nick had had a number of run-ins with the law for minor offenses, and he never had been particularly clever about coming up with convincing alibis. But until September 1978, Nick Notaro had never been known for being violent.

And then he was suspected of having been extremely violent. But it wasn't Joe Tarricone for whose death he was the prime suspect.

It was his first wife: Vickie Notaro.

Chapter Twelve

Vickie Notaro had felt very insecure in her marriage to Nick. In December 1977, she wrote a letter to a friend while she was living with Nick's sister Cassie in Anchorage—just before she went to Healy to join her husband. They had separated over the summer months. Cassie liked Vickie and once again had taken her under her wing.

"I can't say what's going to happen to Nikkie [*sic*] and I yet," Vickie wrote. "I doubt very much that our marriage will work out. I'd like it to, but he'd rather be by himself than with me."

Perhaps looking for someplace to land if Nick dumped her, Vickie wrote that she had casually dated a few men when she was down in Washington, but her preference, clearly, was to save her marriage. Ambivalent, she was both in love with and afraid of Nick Notaro.

"Oh my God," she wrote, worrying that Nick was talking about getting her pregnant, "I think I'm going to be dead. And I don't know really about our marriage or not . . ."

Her words were tragically prophetic.

*   *   *

The news that the dead body in the gravel pit had been tentatively identified as Vickie Notaro had not yet spread when Nick Notaro faced two Alaska state troopers at 7:15 a.m. on October 21, 1978.

Nick Notaro listened to his Miranda rights, and agreed to be interviewed by Alaska troopers C. Roger McCoy, Brad Brown, and Glenn Flothe. He knew Brown, of course, and seemed comfortable with him. The troopers began with small talk and then asked Nick about his life with Vickie. He said he'd met Vickie Schneider in Spokane, where he lived at the time, and that she had recently moved west from her family home in Kalispell, Montana. They had been married for four years but had no children.

"When was the last time you saw Vickie?" McCoy asked.

"The twentieth of September—in Kalispell."

That was a surprising answer and didn't jibe with what Nick had told others in Healy, but none of the investigators commented on it.

"And she was all right?"

"Yes, she was."

"Did she tell you what her plans were?"

"She left a week prior to that—and she left a note," Nick said haltingly. "She didn't really explain why or anything. I wanted to find out and I figured she would head for home—to Kalispell. I went there—I had just gotten out of the hospital, and I hadn't gone back to work yet. So I went down to Seattle to see my relatives. My mom, and—"

"Where did you see her [Vickie] in Kalispell?"

"At the airport. I went over to Kalispell to see if I could find her, and, ah, then I saw her at the airport. She told me about her and another man. She told me his name was Richard. They had plans of going to Rome, Italy, and she said I should go ahead and get the divorce."

It was obvious that Notaro was making it up as he went along. He said he'd had no idea that Vickie was seeing another man.

That was one version.

"You mentioned something about being in the hospital," Brad Brown interjected.

Nick changed his story in a fumbling attempt to make the dates match. He now recalled that Vickie had come to the hospital to pick him up on September 21, and they had stayed at the Towne House Motel in Fairbanks.

"We checked in about four in the afternoon. Vickie went in to take a bath, and I turned on the TV and lay down on the bed and fell asleep. Probably about eight, we went out for dinner, and got back to the hotel about ten."

Nick said that, once again, he'd fallen asleep. When he woke up in the wee hours of the morning, Vickie was gone and he found the note. He was scrambling to make it all fit. It was after that when she had gone to Montana, and he'd followed her there. Again, he spoke of the mysterious Richard who was going to take Vickie to Rome.

"Did she have luggage or anything?" McCoy asked.

"She must have," Nick said quickly. "Because we're missing one big suitcase and an overnight bag."

"You didn't see them in the car when she picked you up at the hospital?"

Nick shook his head.

"How were you financially set? I mean—can she afford a ticket to Rome? Or can she afford to go 'outside [out of Alaska]'?"

"She couldn't, herself, no. She probably had three or four hundred dollars that I know of. Evidently, it was Richard—"

"Did you ever see airline tickets lying around the house?"

"No, I didn't."

Nick was no longer wearing his wedding band and the troopers asked him about it.

"I've been working on my car, and—ah—I took it off to clean my hands."

As for Vickie, Nick was sure she had been wearing her wedding ring the last time he saw her.

McCoy tightened the screws more. He told Nick that a dead woman had been discovered in the gravel pit outside Healy; he even drew him a map. But Nick denied any knowledge of that area.

He grew nervous, however, when McCoy said that they had made moulages of tire tracks found near the body.

Yes, Nick said he *had* told a few people who he knew in Healy that Vickie had left him. He could not recall how many.

"Did you report her missing to anybody?"

"No. The reason for that is because she left the note, saying she was going to see her relatives and that she'd get in touch with me later."

The tape was coming to an end. McCoy asked Nick if there was anything else that he might not have told them.

"On the night of September twenty-first, I purchased a thirty-eight Special from J.C. Penney in Fairbanks. The last time I saw her, Vickie said she had pawned it—that was when I saw her in the airport in Kalispell."

"Why did you purchase it—the gun?"

"For the restaurant—not just for myself. Jerry [Hamel] said that if somebody came in with a gun and robbed you, give him the money. But this one morning, Jerry—*we*— were discussing about buying a handgun, I told him I already had one. But that Vickie had it."

The more he talked, the more Nick entangled himself with statements that didn't make sense, but he hadn't seemed to notice that yet.

"Do you still love your wife?" McCoy asked softly.

"Yes, I do."

"Have you always loved your wife?"

"Yes, I have—ah—until, ah, this happened, I didn't know how much I did."

"In other words, you wish she was back, then?"

"Yes, I do."

"Well," McCoy said, "I'll be honest. I think it's your wife. The woman we found. Really do. I brought the gold ring here. I'll turn the tape off, and show you the ring and watch that we brought down."

Nick looked at the wristwatch and ring and at the artist's drawing of the dead woman's face. It was difficult to read his emotions, but he seemed either saddened or frightened. He said he thought the woman might be Vickie, but he could tell better if she had glasses on.

"You know how to cook, don't you?" McCoy asked.

Wary, Nick said only "Yes."

"And you know how to do your job well?"

"Yes."

"I don't know how to cook," McCoy said. "So I can't do your job. Right? My job is to talk to people. And I feel that I can generally tell when someone's lying. I think you're lying to me. I'm just going to be very frank with that. I'm not gonna beat around the bush and I hope you don't. If you're gonna lie to me, I'd rather not have you say anything to me . . . I think you killed your wife. You never saw your wife in Montana. Your wife died September twenty-second. What I don't know is *why*. Did you have a fight? Was she whoring around? Did you catch her? Did she try to kill *you*? I don't know. That's what I got to get from you. You've never seen me before. I've never seen you. And your wife is dead.

"You've known Brad for some time, and I hope you regard him as a friend. I hope you regard me as a friend. All I'm asking is tell me *why* it happened. Don't lie to me."

"I didn't—" Nick stuttered, poleaxed. He'd thought he was doing so well in the give-and-take, and suddenly the power shifted and he was losing.

"There's too much that doesn't add up, Nick. That just blows your story all apart. She never went to Montana. She was lying up there in the gravel pit, dead. You knew it, but you had to have some kind of cover."

The three troopers balanced the questions expertly. Their dialogue with Nick might well be taken from a movie script—but this was real, and their quarry now realized he was in deep trouble.

In the time-honored style of interrogation, Brad Brown talked to him as a friend, and McCoy was colder as he deftly described the degrees of murder. The thought of first degree wiped all color from Nick's face. "In the heat of passion" wasn't so bad—only second degree. Vickie might even have died of an accidental shooting, McCoy suggested.

Even a casual observer could see Nick Notaro's mind darting from one choice to another. At length, he sighed and told them that it had been an accident. McCoy offered to leave the interview room and let Brad Brown take a statement, but Nick shook his head.

He was ready to talk, to tell the truth.

Perhaps.

"Well," Nick began, describing the drive back to Healy on September 22. "I bought the gun at J.C. Penney, and I wanted to do some target practicing. I went up to the side road there, from off the highway. Vickie went up to set up some cans and some beer bottles that were lying around back there. The gun was loaded and it was lying right up by the windshield of the driver's seat. I heard somebody talking on a CB, and I laid the gun down on the hood of the car [and got back in]. I wanted to listen because it sounded like an emergency call. I wanted to see what happened. And when I sat down in the car, the gun fell off the fender—and it went off."

"Where was your wife when it went off?"

"About ten feet in front of it."

"Where did it hit her?"

"It hit her in the head. I got scared."

"You drug her body down through the weeds?"

"I knew she was dead."

"Normally, when you're hit in the head with a thirty-eight, you're dead. No question about it," McCoy said drily.

"I just panicked and drug her off into the side—and I left."

Nick said he at first meant to go to Nenana and find a trooper and tell him what had happened, but he was "really scared" that he would not be believed. So he threw Vickie's purse out of his car window and headed toward Healy.

The second tape ended. Once more, the troopers read Nick his rights, and he said he knew he could have an attorney—but he waived his rights to one.

With a new tape rolling, the four men studied the map of the area where Vickie's body was found, but Nick wasn't able to remember just where he had thrown her purse away.

"Why didn't you contact me, Nick?" Brad Brown asked.

"Like I said before, Brad, I was scared. I'm still scared."

And he was still lying, too. Asked if his car was running when the gun slid off the fender, he said it was.

"Did you see her hit the ground?" McCoy asked.

"No—I heard it. By the time I saw her, she was on the ground. From the way she was laying [sic], she looked like she had spun around. It was a distance within five feet."

But he had told them Vickie was ten feet away from him. And Nick had overlooked other elements that would pin him to the wall.

"Nick, you're lying to me," McCoy said. "Are you familiar with hand guns? I want to explain a couple of things to you. And, after I tell you this, I want you to tell me the truth. Number one, a Smith and Wesson thirty-eight will not go off when you drop it. Number two, your wife died and she had *two* bullets in her. Both thirty-eights. One in the head and one in the back. How do you explain that? Did the gun fall twice?"

Nick was silent. He couldn't explain that.

"Why did you kill your wife?" McCoy asked, his voice louder.

"It was an accident."

"Accident, my butt. The gun doesn't go off by dropping it. And you didn't drop the gun. It doesn't bounce two times and hit her once in the back and once in the head. And it was about two feet away from her head. It doesn't happen, Nick," McCoy said firmly. "You aimed the gun at her, and you pulled the trigger. Did you get in an argument with her? Over Richard? You told me she told you that Thursday night, the twenty-first. And it angered you?"

"I don't think it was anger as much as hurt."

"Of losing her?"

"Right."

"You lived with a woman for four and a half years, and you loved her. And she finds another boyfriend. And tells you, 'Nick, my darling, I'm leaving you forever.' That would hurt you?"

Nick nodded.

"Am I correct in saying, If I cannot have you, no one will have you? Is that what you thought?"

"Yes."

"You went to the gravel pit. She starts running. You shoot toward her. Did you know you shot her in the back?"

"No."

"But she fell down, didn't she?"

"Yes."

"And then you walked up to her and you shot her in the head. Is that right? You're shaking your head yes?"

"Yes—more or less. I really didn't mean to. I was trying to scare her. And she started running and the gun went off. I didn't know I hit her. I just thought she went down on the ground to get out of the way. I walked up to her to lift her up, and I had the gun in my hand. And it went off. Approximately, like you said, probably within two feet . . ."

Once the door was open for him to confess to his wife's murder, Nick Notaro added numerous details.

He said he had flown to Seattle within a day to stay with his mother and sister. He denied having told them anything about Vickie's murder.

None of the investigators in Alaska ever located the man named Richard who Nick said was going to take Vickie to Rome. Nor did they find *anyone* who believed Vickie was cheating on Nick. When she wasn't cleaning hotel rooms, she was busy doing laundry for pipeline workers to make enough money for herself and Nick to get by. If he really found other men's clothing in their hotel room, it was laundry Vickie had done.

The state police detectives placed Nick under arrest. Initially charged with first-degree murder, he agreed to plead guilty to Vickie's murder. He was subsequently convicted of his first wife's shooting death. He began his sentence in the federal prison on McNeil Island, Washington, in June 1978. He stayed there a little more than a month and then was moved to another federal correctional facility in Englewood, Colorado, a low-security prison for male offenders with an adjacent satellite prison camp for minimum security convicts.

Nick obeyed the rules and built up "good time." He stayed in the Colorado prison until the spring of 1983. Then he was transferred to a federal prison in Oxford, Wisconsin, where he remained until he was paroled in January 1986.

Chapter Thirteen

During the week Ben Benson spent in Alaska, he located the assistant prosecutor who had handled Nick's case. Benson was curious why Nick had received only a short prison sentence for the cold-blooded killing of his wife.

The prosecutor said he barely remembered the Notaro case, explaining they had so many homicides to prosecute back then. "We'd make a deal with anyone willing to make a deal," he ended lamely.

Nick had been allowed to plead guilty to manslaughter, and that meant less than eight years in prison.

As Lila May Notaro, Nick's second wife, had told Ben Benson, Nick had lived in Marshfield, Wisconsin—working as a chef—until he moved back to Washington State in March 1989. He'd moved into an apartment with a fellow inmate with whom he'd shared time. They planned to open a janitorial service but it didn't work out.

When Ben Benson flew to Baltimore, Maryland, to interview Nick's former cellmate, the man talked to him willingly enough. He said he knew about Vickie Notaro's death, but he insisted Nick had never mentioned anything about a man named Joe Tarricone, or just plain Joe, or even some guy who was bothering his sister. They had talked about a number of things during the long dark nights behind bars, but Nick had been closed-mouthed about a second homicide. Benson understood the code of prison where cons don't "snitch" on one another so he couldn't be positive he was hearing the whole truth.

In October 1978, Vickie Notaro had her modicum of justice when Nick was locked behind bars. But none of the Alaska troopers had asked him about Joe Tarricone. Law enforcement officials in Alaska weren't aware of Tarricone's disappearance.

Puyallup was a world away. And the alarm bells about Joe rang very softly in the fall of 1978. Indeed, there was always the chance back then that Joe would show up with a good explanation about where he had been.

Ben Benson continually perused the thick Alaska State Police file on Vickie Notaro's murder. He came to know Nick Notaro, before they ever met, as well as—or better than—close friends he'd known for years.

He had already talked to Lila May Notaro and learned of Nick's life after prison. The Pierce County detective sergeant flew back to Seattle out of Anchorage. Now he needed to see what Nick was doing as the holiday season approached in 2007, or where he was living, or *how* he was living. He learned that Nick was still required to report to his probation officer once a week for failure to appear after the charges involving his stepdaughter, although records showed that his probation was soon coming to an end in June 2008.

Benson and his partner, Sergeant Denny Wood—who had returned from reserve duty—were ready to confront both Nick and his sister Renee. Renee's life over the past thirty years was not the open book that Nick's was.

And so they started with Nick.

The two Pierce County detectives arranged to meet Nick Notaro in his probation officer's office on March 24. Nick was living wherever he could. His current home was at the Bread of Life Mission on Skid Row in Seattle; he had been there since early September 2007. For the price of listening to a daily sermon and doing odd jobs around the mission, he could get a free meal and a bed. Sometimes, if the weather wasn't too bad, he lived under a bridge. And, apparently, Nick was still close to his sisters—Cassie and Renee—and would visit them often where they worked at the bail bonds company.

Seeing Nick in person was something of a shock. He had been fairly good-looking in his early booking photographs, but now Nick had aged tremendously. The skin on his face drooped; he could have been sixty or eighty. His thick white hair grew into sideburns down his cheeks and then became a brushy mustache and a beard, giving him the look of the fabled Sasquatch, the half man/half wild creature thought to ramble through Northwest forests.

When Ben Benson and Denny Wood spoke to Nick, they told him only that they were detectives who were checking on what his plans were once he was off supervision. They didn't say they were from Pierce County and he didn't ask why they wanted to know; he simply assumed that they were conducting a routine exit interview from his probation.

"I doubt very much that he would have talked to us if we'd said we wanted to talk to him about his dead wife and his sister's missing boyfriend," Benson said. "But it worked out perfectly."

The two detectives had different interview styles. Benson appeared pleasant and nonconfrontational; it was hard to read what he was thinking. Wood asked mostly hard questions. They were a subtle version of good cop/bad cop.

Nick spoke to them readily. He said he'd lived at his sister Renee's condominium before he moved to the mission. He said he also had another sister named Cassie.

"How often do you see them?" Denny Wood asked.

"Daily," Nick began, "but Cassie only works three days a week. I see Renee every day. When I have a travel permit, I go to Cassie's house in Federal Way."

Nick said that when his probation was up in June, he planned to move to Arkansas where he had lived recently. He had good friends there who were holding a place for him to live.

For a long time Benson and Wood asked Nick questions that they already knew the answers to. He was most forthcoming as he answered—even about the time he killed his wife. He had paid the price for that, and he knew that he could not be charged again for that crime because double jeopardy would attach.

He said he no longer drank alcohol, and he proved to have a remarkable memory when it came to his family. Although he didn't seem particularly intelligent, Nick recited their ages, where they all lived, and how he was related to them.

"Cassie and Vickie—my first wife—were working together in a nursing home in Spokane," he said. "They were sharing a house, and that's where I met Vickie. She lost her mother when she was ten. She became the mom because she was the oldest. She never got to be a kid, you know. The main thing my mother and Renee had against her was the way she kept house. To me, it was good—but they're clean freaks. My mom smoked, too, like Vickie, but there was no such thing as a dirty ashtray in *her* house."

Geri Hesse had never liked Vickie, and Nick felt it was because she thought no one was good enough for her son.

On the surface, they almost sounded like a typical family. If the two detectives didn't suspect the grotesque things they had done, they might have accepted the folksy meanderings. But they did know, and it seemed almost eerie listening to Nick, who became more voluble with every sentence. Oddly, he seemed to have no regrets about the sad and premature death of his first wife, even speaking of her with affection.

Nick said that he had always been closest to his sister Renee. Cassie and his mother had friction between them, and he often had to play the middleman.

"If I prefer one of those [sisters], the reason is because Cassie is Italian," he explained in a seeming non sequitur. "My dad and mom adopted me, but Mom left my adopted

137

dad not knowing that she was pregnant with Cassie by her lover. Cassie didn't learn about that until she was in high school. I believe it was my uncle who introduced her to her [real] dad—and she was the spitting image of him. He paid for DNA tests [that] proved he was her biological dad."

"So you say Renee is the sister you've always been the closest to?" Benson asked.

"I'm not so sure anymore . . . I'm finding now that Cassie and I have a lot more in common. Cassie is definitely opinionated, and Renee is a person that is easy to take advantage of," Nick said, adding how he treasured both his sisters. "You can do anything you want to me, call me anything you want, but don't mess with my sisters. And like Merle Haggard said, 'You're walking on the fighting side of me.'"

Nick was garrulous, emphasizing that he couldn't wait to get his life back and be a law-abiding citizen. He could afford to live in Arkansas on his disability payments—but not in Seattle. Still, he didn't want to move away from Renee and Cassie, so he'd been applying for local jobs—principally as a flagger on highway construction projects. So far, he hadn't been successful.

"I just wanna get this over with, and go back to my life. I just wanna be left alone—nobody mess with me and I ain't gonna mess with them . . ."

It seemed abundantly clear that Nick no longer thought about what had happened to Joe Tarricone. In his mind, he was in the clear. After all, Joe had been gone for thirty years.

The Pierce County detectives' questioning had begun to change direction so subtly that Nick didn't sense a shift in the wind. Ben Benson and Denny Wood were asking more about his sisters than they were about his plans for the future. Ben Benson told Nick that he'd done some "research" on his past.

"I believe you've been truthful with us to this point," Benson said. "I did review some of the case file from Alaska in your wife's case—that's all public information. The one thing that stands out in my mind in talking about Vickie is her having a boyfriend who wanted to take her to Rome."

"Oh. Okay. Yeah . . ." Suddenly Nick was wary.

"What was that about?"

"Okay. That was a gentleman that had a meat company and he delivered [meat], you know, to different places in Alaska."

"Uh-huh."

"And he was Renee's partner—business partner."

"What was his name?"

"Oh—Joe."

Nick Notaro's answers came haltingly now. He explained that he had seen this guy—Joe—down in Washington when he came down after he left the hospital in Fairbanks. Before that, Vickie had told him she was going to Italy with Joe.

"Where did this guy named Joe come into play?" Denny Wood asked.

"Well, he stopped in the restaurant there [in Healy] and sold some meat where I was working. He had good hamburger patties. And because he knew I was Renee's brother, he came over to the hotel where we were staying a couple of times."

"Talk about body language," Benson recalled later. "Every time we mentioned Joe, Nick involuntarily backed up his chair. He was halfway across the room when I asked him, 'Nick, where you going?'"

Nick hastened to explain that Renee and Joe had been only business partners and platonic friends. Renee had been seeing another man, a chef named Keith or perhaps Curt.

In the meantime, he sold his house on Green River Road and moved to the yellow rambler in Auburn. The 14th Avenue house wasn't nearly as imposing as the white stucco house Bob had built near the river, but it didn't matter; he didn't intend to spend much time in Washington.

"He was German. He's the one who got me a job up on the pipeline for Campo Pacific."

"What was Joe's last name?"

"I don't remember. Joe was Italian."

"Now, you did tell somebody that you saw your wife Vickie and Joe together down in Washington?" Ben Benson probed, seeing sweat bead up on Nick's forehead.

"I believe I did. I'm not positive, but I don't remember [if] I either saw them together or whether I saw just one of them."

Nick Notaro was stumbling over his own tongue at this point. He recalled that he and his mother had felt Joe was much too old for Renee—closer to Geri Hesse's age than Renee's. He thought Geri or Renee had told him that Renee traveled with Joe only for business reasons, and they stayed in separate hotel rooms. If they went out for dinner, it was also for business. He was positive that Renee had no romantic relationship with Joe.

"Now, you killed Vickie and you told people she went to Italy with Joe. Where did Joe go? Why wouldn't people still see Joe around?"

"I don't know. He could've gone back to Italy," Nick answered, and the detectives could almost see the wheels whirling in his brain as he struggled to make his story match up with facts.

"He was from Italy, and Renee mentioned one time that he had talked about goin' back. Their business was starting to peter out, and he was talking about goin' back."

Nick denied now that he had ever seen Joe Tarricone in Washington State. He had been wrong about that. He was sure he had seen him only in Alaska. Nick had backed his chair as far away as he could from the desk where Wood and Benson sat, far away from the digital recorder. Any farther and he would have had to go through the wall behind him.

At 11:43 on the morning of March 24, the detectives read Nick his Miranda rights and took a break while Nick went to the restroom.

Ten minutes later, Ben Benson looked squarely into Nick Notaro's eyes as he told him that he and Denny Wood were investigating the death of Joe Tarricone.

"Human remains were found on your mother's property on Canyon Road in Puyallup, Nick. DNA tests have been done and the bones are identified as belonging to Joe Tarricone."

Benson told Nick that he had been investigating the case for several months. "We have probable cause to arrest you—and your sisters—for the murder of Joe Tarricone."

Nick Notaro looked stricken. *When had the conversation gotten away from him? One minute he'd been talking about regaining his freedom, and now he was about to be arrested!*

"We need you to tell us what happened at your mother's house," Benson said.

"Renee—my sisters—weren't involved. Not one iota."

"Then tell me what happened there—because the information I have is that your sisters *were* involved."

Nick shook his head. "No. When I came down from my appendectomy, Mom told me she had shot him, and he was in the freezer. I helped Mom put him in the place where you found him. Renee was in Hawaii and she wasn't involved."

"Tell us what happened."

"We took him out of the freezer," Nick said slowly, "and me and Mom used a chain saw to cut him up, and we buried it [the bones] in the yard."

Geri Hesse was dead, and had been for eight years. Blaming her for the murder itself—if anyone believed that—would take suspicion off Cassie and Renee, and Nick apparently thought he would get a lesser sentence as an accomplice after the fact.

"I don't believe you," Denny Wood said. "How could your mother—at her age—shoot a man and then carry him downstairs to the freezer and put him in? I think you asked Joe to go downstairs and that you're the one who shot him. And that would have had to be a really big freezer to fit a large man into."

"Yes," Nick admitted, he had shot Joe Tarricone. "But Renee was in Hawaii when it happened."

"What happened after you shot him?" Wood asked.

"We went to K-Mart and bought a chain saw—and a tarp. Mom held the tarp while I used the chain saw. I cut off Joe's legs, his arms, and his head. My mother took the head away and got rid of it separately."

"How did you get to K-Mart?" Wood questioned. "You say you didn't know the area?"

"I don't remember. I buried Joe's legs, arms, and torso in the yard."

"But how did you get to K-Mart?" Wood pressed, believing that there was someone present that night other than Geri Hesse.

"I don't remember who drove me."

"Why did you kill Joe Tarricone?" Wood asked bluntly.

"He was always trying to get Renee into bed, and he wouldn't leave her alone. He kept asking her to marry him and wouldn't take no for an answer. My mother called me in Alaska and she asked me to come and take care of the problem. She said Renee had gone to Hawaii to get away from Joe. It made her mad when Joe kept showing up at the house."

"Did anyone tell you to kill him?"

"Nobody had to tell me to kill him."

Nick Notaro seemed almost proud to be the avenging

brother who took care of his sisters. When he was asked about where Cassie was on the date Joe died, he said she was in Anchorage.

"You can check her employment records up there, and you'll see she never left Anchorage."

Nick had given the details of Joe Tarricone's murder for an hour, but when he was asked to record his confession, he balked.

"I fell for that in Alaska," he said gruffly. "I'm not going to fall for it again."

He requested an attorney before they went any further. He was immediately arrested, taken into custody, and handcuffed. Detective Gary Sanders and Deputy Erik Clarkson transported Nick Notaro to the Pierce County jail where he was booked for first degree murder.

Chapter Fourteen

Beginning with a case that seemed certain to be a "loser," and after nine months of steady, cautious, and intuitive investigation, the avalanche had finally begun. Suspects were about to tumble like dominoes. Although it had been frustrating to wait until all of their ducks were in a row to make solid arrests, Denny Wood—and especially Ben Benson—were seeing it all come to fruition.

With Nick Notaro on his way to jail, they contacted Cassie Martell and Renee Curtiss (Renee never took Henry Lewis's last name) where they were both at work at Henry's Bail Bonds. Renee gave no sign that she recognized Ben Benson from the time he had dropped in the previous summer and asked her about bailing out his "nephew." She probably didn't; she must have seen a lot of faces come and go since Benson had been in the previous July.

Benson told Cassie and Renee only that their brother was in a little trouble, and that he and Wood needed to talk to them over at the Seattle police precinct.

"We can't both leave at the same time," Renee said, apparently neither surprised nor disturbed that Nick was in trouble—again. Cassie Martell said she would go first and then come back so Renee could talk to them.

From the beginning of the interview with Cassie Martell, it was obvious that she didn't know what had happened to Joe Tarricone; she had been living in Anchorage from 1977 to 1980, and had come outside to the lower forty-eight states only once.

"I came down for Christmas that first year I lived in Alaska," she said. "That would have been in 1977."

Asked if Nick had ever lived with her in Anchorage, she shook her head. She had really been closer to Vickie, who had lived with Cassie for two or three weeks shortly before Nick killed her.

"He never gave me a reason why he did that," Cassie said. "You know, I finally asked him just a few months ago. First, he said that he did it because our mother didn't like her. Then he said he was in the hospital with appendicitis and he believed Vickie was fooling around on him. I don't think she was. I knew that *he* was seeing someone else—a woman who had children—and he just wanted to get rid of Vickie."

"We think someone was murdered in that house where your mother and Renee lived in Puyallup," Benson said.

"That might have been where something happened. I think so. My mother and sister were not murderers—but there was a man my sister knew. I can't think of his name right now. I want to say Tony. I know he was Italian. He had a meat business in Anchorage. He came down to see Renee a couple of times, and he left a car there. But no one ever heard from him again."

"Do you think Nick is capable of murder?"

"I think he's a psycho," Cassie responded. "I know not to push him too far. He's my brother, and he comes to see me a lot, but I'm afraid of him."

It was clear that Cassie wasn't in on the family secrets, nor had she wanted to be. She thought the *victim* in Puyallup—probably the man she called Tony—was dead. She even allowed that he might have been murdered by someone she didn't know. She wasn't even convinced there had ever been a homicide on Canyon Road.

"How close are you to Nick?" Benson asked.

"Not close. He slept one night on the floor of my house in Anchorage right after Vickie was killed. Before that, I hadn't seen Nick for years."

"You didn't enter into a pact with Nick never to talk about the incident when the person was killed in Puyallup?" Benson prodded. "You and your sister?"

"I have never had a pact with him concerning murdering anybody!"

Cassie was upset, but she was more angry. She was furious that Nick had tried to draw her into a murder plot—something she knew nothing about.

Both Denny Wood and Ben Benson felt Cassie was telling the truth. She hadn't been part of the tight circle formed by Geri Hesse, Renee, and Nick, rarely being close to them geographically or emotionally.

NORTH TO ALASKA

Joe Tarricone had a thriving meat sales and delivery business that took him all over Alaska. His clients were glad to see him. He was a gregarious man and his life was good until he met a pretty and seductive younger woman.

Joe Tarricone at about 10. He's standing with his two sisters perched on the running board of their family's new car in the thirties. The Tarricones lived in New York, and they were a typical loving Italian family. Born in 1925, Joe was the oldest child and only son. He would always keep in touch with his parents no matter how far he roamed.

Joe Tarricone in 1953, when he was 28. He's wearing a "loafer jacket," very fashionable for men in the fifties.

Joe and Rose fell in love when they were in their teens in the forties. Even though Rose was not Catholic, there was no question that they would marry one day.

Rose and Joe on their honeymoon. She was sweet and pretty and wore her hair in a "Betty Grable" pompadour. Joe was handsome. The future stretched brightly ahead of them, and they were anxious to have children. Joe was a man with itchy feet, and Rose wanted a home in one place, but they didn't think about that then.

A teenage Joe Tarricone with his parents at a beach cottage in New York State.

Rose and Joe pose in a photo booth where pictures were four for a dollar. They had a lot of fun together and were so in love.

Joe Tarricone was a great cook and his fellow soldiers appreciated the meals he prepared. He loved to cook as a civilian, too, and devised a way to make giant pizzas for his whole neighborhood.

A very young couple—Joe and Rose Tarricone with their firstborn, their daughter Claire. Joe loved being a father and was thrilled when each of his seven children was born.

Joe Tarricone with his first four children. From left, Aldo, Joey, Claire, and Gypsy as a baby. The photographer was obviously focused on the children in this picture.

Joe wrestles with three of his seven children. He was always there for them—until one day he wasn't. They searched for him for three decades.

Joe and Rose Tarricone with their seven children: Claire, Aldo, Joey, Gypsy, Gina, Rosemary, and Dean. All the kids in the Tarricones' Albuquerque neighborhood followed Joe as if he were their own special Pied Piper.

Joe Tarricone was happiest when he was
cooking for his family and friends—
the more the better!

One of the last photos ever taken of Joe Tarricone.
He was an ebullient and magnanimous man who was
unaware of the danger he faced from a surprising source.

Rose Tarricone was Joe's high school sweetheart,
the mother of his seven children, but after thirty years,
Rose wanted to put down roots, while Joe was always
looking for the next place to move. Divorced, they
remained good friends.

Joseph Anthony Tarricone in a rare pensive mood.
There wasn't much that could get him down,
but the end of an affair did.
And then his eyes were opened.

Dr. Katherine Taylor demonstrates where some of the buried bones in Puyallup would fit into a human body. Many of the bones had been sawed in two, and a number of them were missing completely.

Dr. Taylor examined the shoulder blade and partial humerus bone of the nameless man found in Puyallup, Washington, and saw that a power saw had been used to dissect the body.

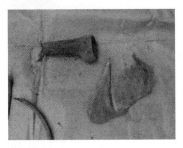

Dr. Taylor assembles the bones found on a deserted property in Puyallup, Washington. It was like a puzzle for her—where she put together parts that resembled a full skeleton. This was the first step in a very long and tedious investigation. Was the deceased male or female? How long had the bones lain undetected in a shallow grave? In time, all the questions were answered.

Renee Curtiss was in her twenties when she met Joe Tarricone.
She had a pretty, guileless face then, almost pixielike.
Joe loved and trusted her for a long time
and took her into his business and his heart.

Nick Notaro, Renee's adopted brother, would do
anything for his two sisters—anything. He had
many secrets in his past, but they came to light
because he was a very inept liar.

Nick Notaro's first wife, Vickie (left) and her daughter (right).
Nick lied about Vickie's sudden disappearance in Alaska.
The last time she was seen was when she went to bring
Nick home from the hospital after an emergency appendectomy.

Renee Curtiss, looking stunned, after she was arrested
in Henry's Bail Bonds in the Skid Row district of Seattle.
Pierce County sheriff's sergeant Denny Wood is on her right,
and Sergeant Ben Benson is on her left. She expected to bail
out of jail within hours.

Renee Curtiss was living in this condo in Seattle
with her husband, Henry Lewis, at the time she was arrested.
She had a lovely home, and Henry was quite wealthy. At last,
she seemed to have everything she wanted.

Benson in Baltimore, Maryland, with a Baltimore detectiv and that city's helicopter. Ben wa trying to find one of Nick Notaro's former cellmates.

The author and Detective Sergeant Ben Benson at a party to celebrate the finished manuscript of *Don't Look Behind You.*

Detective Sergeant Denny Wood, usually Ben Benson's partner, was on active duty with the reserves when the Tarricone case broke. He returned to the Pierce County Sheriff's Department in time to join Benson in interviewing two homicide suspects.

Dawn Farina, the Pierce County prosecutor who
faced two defendants charged with murder in the courtroom.
Gypsy Tarricone called Dawn "the little spitfire,"
and it fit her when she was cross-examining Renee Curtiss.

Gypsy Tarricone at her father's grave in Mount Calvary Cemetery. Joe's seven children chose this cemetery in Albuquerque because it is always "full of life," with families visiting, luminarias to light the pathways, and the laughter of children and old friends.

Chapter Fifteen

March 24 was turning out to be a very long day. Denny Wood and Ben Benson returned to Henry's Bail Bonds to talk to Renee Curtiss. She told them that she had an appointment with a doctor at the University of Washington Medical Center. "He's treating my husband—Henry— who is very ill with heart failure."

Henry Lewis was scheduled to have a heart pump installed the next day. The two detectives offered to accompany her and wait until she had talked with Henry's doctors, but she said she preferred to talk to them first. They then agreed to interview her at the bail bonds office rather than take her to the precinct.

As Benson already knew, the woman who spoke with them was nothing at all like her brother; she was expensively dressed in a black dress and matching sweater. Although she used thick makeup and had a hard edge to her, she was still attractive. If Renee and Nick had colluded in a plan to kill Joe Tarricone, that seemed bizarre. Benson and Wood could easily visualize Nick as a murderer. Indeed, they knew he had already killed at least once before Joe died.

Renee was calm and friendly. For the first minutes of this interview, they made small talk and asked easy questions. She gave her birth date as August 1, 1953; she was fifty-four but didn't look it. She seemed to feel that she was the one in charge of the interview.

"We're investigating a murder with ties to Alaska," Ben Benson said.

"Oh, yes," Renee said, "You mean my brother's wife—"

"No," the Pierce County sergeant said flatly. "We're investigating the murder of Joseph Tarricone.

"Okay, Renee," he began, "we've explained that we have your brother Nick in custody for his murder. We need to talk to you. I think I'll start with you explaining to us what your relationship with Joseph Tarricone was."

At the first mention of Joe Tarricone's name, Renee's demeanor changed. "First, she gasped," Benson recalled, "and then her chest and neck flushed scarlet. The redness rose up into her face and even her ears. She was shocked.

"Denny told me later that he expected her ears to burst into flames—she was that red. After thirty years, I don't think she expected us to be wondering about any relationship she might have had with Joe, or that anyone would come asking about him so long after."

Renee listened as Benson read her her Miranda rights, and she nodded that she understood them and signed on the bottom of the card. Recovering some of her composure, she agreed to have their conversation recorded after Ben Benson explained that he believed she might be guilty only of offering "criminal assistance" after Joe was murdered. And he did believe that. At the time.

"But that was twenty-nine years ago," Benson said, "and the statute of limitations for that ran out a long time ago. You can't be arrested for that in 2008."

In truth, Benson and Denny Wood didn't expect to arrest Renee Curtiss, at least not on this day. That was why they were interviewing her in the bail bonds office rather than taking her to the police station. Hearing that the statute of limitations had passed, she relaxed a little.

Even so, Ben Benson advised her once more of her rights so that the Miranda rule was on tape. Most Americans know the rights by heart—either from watching television or by reading a crime novel. And, of course, a certain number have actually had Miranda rights read to them.

"You have the right to remain silent," Benson began. "Any statement that you do make can be used as evidence against you in a court of law. You have the right at this time to talk to an attorney of your choice, and to have your attorney present before and during questioning and the making of any statement. If you cannot afford an attorney, you are entitled to have one appointed for you—without cost to you—and to have the attorney present at any time during the questioning and the making of a statement. You may stop answering questions or ask for an attorney at any time during any questioning and the making of any statement. Renee, do you understand each of these rights?"

"Yes."

"And is this your signature on the bottom of the rights form?"

"That's correct."

Renee Curtiss's position with her husband's bail bonds

firm had taught her a great deal about the judicial process; Benson had been impressed with her knowledge the first time he met her.

She began with a lie, saying that she had met Joe in Alaska when, in reality, she'd met him at the wholesale meat company in Seattle. Unfortunately for Renee, she had no idea how much of her background Ben Benson had uncovered.

Renee denied that she had ever lived with Joe; she said he had lived above his business in Anchorage where he had just a bed and a small space for his clothes and belongings; he had been on the road selling meat most of the time.

Her words came out haltingly, and she stuttered as she looked for answers. "My mother and I had a house—had a house on Jewel Lake."

"Okay. And that's where you were living when you met Joe?"

"You know, I don't recall if it was then or prior to that. It might have been when I was renting an apartment off of C Street."

"Now, you told us that you were a business partner with him?"

"He gave me part of his business, yes."

"Now, did you start out working for him initially, or did he bring you in as a partner?"

"No, I think he brought me—I mean, I may have started [by] working for him. I don't recall."

"Did you buy into the company, somehow?"

"No."

"He just made you a partner?"

"Yes . . . yeah."

"And was that while you were romantically involved with him?"

"Correct." Renee's voice was taut and her answers very short.

"At that point in time, had he started asking you to marry him?"

"No."

"So this was early in your relationship?"

"I—I, as I recall."

Renee said she had worked with Joe for over a year, and then she had broken off her relationship with him.

"But you did become engaged to him?"

"I did."

"And then what happened?"

"He wanted to move to Seattle and we did move, and he was still working up there in Alaska, and planning on coming down. And then something happened that he did—I broke that relationship off."

"Okay. Can you tell me what that was?"

Renee said that Joe had slept with one of her female relatives. When she learned that, she dumped him.

"Did Joe have any kind of relationship with your mother?" Benson asked.

"I don't—no."

"They were just friends?"

"Yes. She liked him."

"Was he paying for things up there in Alaska? I know he bought you a car. Was he paying for your rent?"

"You know," Renee said carefully, "I was generously compensated for working for him, so if you want to say he paid the rent—he was always buying stuff, always buying jewelry or buying my mother something or my daughter something. I mean, he was *always* buying something. I mean he was a hard worker."

After she broke it off with Joe Tarricone, Renee said, Kurt Winkler, the German chef whom she was dating at the same time she dated Joe, had proposed and they became engaged. She had continued to have a working relationship with Joe, although she knew he wasn't happy about Kurt.

Although Renee's answers often began with "I don't recall," she did remember that Kurt and Joe had known about each other, but she couldn't say if they ever had harsh words about it.

And then, in the midseventies, Renee said, she, her mother, and her daughter had moved to Kirkland, a suburb of Seattle.

"So when you moved down here to Kirkland," Benson asked, "did that end your working relationship with Joe?"

"It did."

"What did you do for a job when you lived in Kirkland?"

"I was working for a company called Elite Models." She acknowledged that it was an escort service.

"Was your mom working?"

"She might've been working in a nursing home."

Renee said she had broken her engagement to Kurt Winkler because he wouldn't leave Alaska either. After a year in their north end apartment, the women had moved to the Canyon Road house in Puyallup.

"Okay. Did Joseph Tarricone come and visit at that house?"

"Joe didn't know where to find me at first, but eventually he located me," Renee said. "He was there several times . . . several times. The majority of the time uninvited. I can't recall how many times."

Renee's face and chest were now brick red. She said her mother might have invited Joe over some of the time.

"He was, he was kind of obsessed. I mean he'd do almost anything to be around me."

Ben Benson asked Renee about the barbecue at her house in the summer of 1978. "Do you recall what month the barbecue would've taken place?"

"Summer . . . July or August. I mean it was warm. It could've been in August because there's probably three or four of us who have birthdays in August."

"Okay. But Joseph was there for that barbecue?"

"I remember him being there."

"Was Nick there?"

"I do not believe Nick was there."

"How about Cassie?"

"I don't know. I'm not sure."

"Did Joe bring steaks and meat to the barbecue?"

"I'm sure he would have."

"Do you remember having an argument with him at the barbecue?"

Benson was leading Renee into territory that could be dangerous for her, and she parried his questions thoughtfully. "Yeah," she finally answered. "It would've been something like [me saying], you know, 'I'm not interested in you. I do not wanna be romantically involved with you.' I don't recall anything more specifically, and I don't recall, you know, certainly there was nobody—there was no fisticuffs or anything like that. Would've been, you know, it was almost the same every time I saw him, you know, he wanted, would claim, 'Oh, can't we just be friends?' and then he didn't want just friendship. He wanted, you know, to—to somehow buy my love and affection."

Renee denied now that Nick had *ever* been to the Canyon Road house—until Benson reminded her she had told them early in their conversation that he *had* been there at least once.

"That I recall." She quickly recovered. "Yes."

"Let's talk about that more," Benson said easily. "In relation to when the barbecue happened to when Nick came down, do you remember how close that was?"

"I mean, I'm not sure that Nick wasn't there [at the barbecue], but I don't recall him being there. It could've been within days—it could've been within weeks—"

"But you're certain—you told us earlier that what happened to Joe didn't happen on the night of the barbecue?"

"Um-hum."

"Why are you certain?"

"'Cause I don't recall Nick being there."

She remembered that her brother had come to Canyon Road right after his appendix surgery. "I talked to him on the phone when he was in the hospital."

"Did you talk to him after he was out of the hospital?"

"Yes . . . I told him I could use some help and, you know, if he needed to come and rest, relax, and recuperate, it would probably be a good thing."

Renee's version of how Nick happened to come down to Puyallup changed with every answer. She did recall telling him that her mother was putting a lot of pressure on her, and Joe Tarricone was practically stalking her and pressuring her, too. He hadn't hurt her physically, but he'd pushed her, and threatened her.

"And what was the nature of those threats?" Benson asked.

"Everything from 'I'm not gonna stop—I'm gonna continue to make your life miserable.' He scared my mom at one point. He told her if I wasn't with him, I shouldn't be with anyone."

"Did you relay this information to Nick?"

"I don't recall." She didn't think she had *specifically* asked him to come down to help her with the Joe situation. "Maybe Nick could talk to him—I mean, I'm putting words in my head that I don't recall."

Yes, she knew that Nick had killed Vickie after he'd gotten out of the hospital—learned about it, she thought, a day or so before he came down to Washington. It could have been in her phone call to him. She couldn't recall. She'd been shocked that Vickie left her poor brother in the hospital with a "burst appendix" and never checked to see how he was.

"How did you react when he told you about that [killing Vickie]?"

"The same way most people would. A little bit of horror. I talked to him and he felt tremendous remorse. I think he turned himself in." (This was not true.)

"Was there anything to make him believe Vickie was having an affair with Joseph?"

"Wow, I don't know. Never heard that one before."

As Benson, Wood, and Renee Curtiss worked to bring 1978 into the present, they finally came to the night Joseph Tarricone died. Renee said she was at work when her mother told her to come home at once. It wasn't a request; it was an order. Geri Hesse had sounded *very* serious.

"Tell me what happened when you got home," Benson directed.

"I remember I was taken downstairs and shown a locked room; the door was unlocked and Joe was inside . . . dead."

"Who took you down there and showed you that?"

"Both of them. Mom and Nick."

Nick had blamed his now-deceased mother for Joe Tarricone's murder, and now Renee was putting the onus on both of them. She said that Joe was lying on his side, and that she'd been surprised that there was no blood. "I'm sure there had to have been blood, but I don't recall any blood."

She couldn't remember where her daughter, Diana, was. Renee knew that the ten-year-old wasn't in the basement with them. The three adults had locked the door where Joe was, and gone upstairs to discuss what to do.

"Tell me about that conversation with your mom and Nick about what happened."

"I don't remember. We just talked about how to get rid of the body. We talked about burying him in the backyard at the house."

Renee said that Nick had dug either two side-by-side holes or one very large one. She couldn't recall which.

"It took a long time."

"Prior to that, did you and Nick go somewhere together?"

"Either to a sporting goods section or a hardware store—someplace—to buy a saw."

"Do you remember what kind of saw it was?"

"Not a brand—but it was a chain saw."

"A gas-powered chain saw?"

"I can't—I don't, I assume so. I don't think they make electric chain saws, do they?"

Renee thought she and Nick had gone into the store together. She believed she had probably paid for it.

"And then what did you do after you bought the chain saw?"

"I used it on Joe."

Until this moment, neither Benson nor Wood had felt that Renee was anything more than an accessory after the fact; now they began to suspect that she had conspired with her brother to have him come down to Washington State to kill Joe Tarricone.

"You used it on Joe. Did anybody else use it on Joe?"

"Nick—I'm not saying that we, you know, we would, you know . . . Sometimes, you'd hold, you would hold him while Nick used the saw."

"So it was a joint operation? Was your mom helping as well or was it just you and Nick?"

Even for seasoned detectives—detectives who knew that Joe's body had been dissected cleanly with a power saw—the conversation was grotesque. They fought to hide their own feelings. With the spirit and image of Jimi Hendrix on the walls surrounding them, they listened to Renee as she brought back the scene in the basement of a now-destroyed house.

"Mom was down there as well. Whether she was holding him—I don't know, but I have the memory of the three of us being in that basement."

"What specifically was the chain saw used for?" Ben Benson asked.

"To make it so the body wasn't so heavy—"

"Okay. What part of the body was dismembered?"

"Arms, legs—"

"Did you cut his head off as well?"

"Oh, God, I don't remember that. I think so, I don't—I don't recall."

"Now, was this horribly messy?" Benson prodded. "Describe for me, were you cutting through his clothing or had you taken his clothes off?"

"The clothes were not off."

"So the chain saw went right through his clothes?"

"Correct."

"Did you ever hold the saw, and remove any part of Joe's body?"

"Possibly. I think I was mostly holding."

Even though the crime had happened three decades earlier, this interrogation sent chills through the detectives—and, possibly, through Renee Curtiss. It was a scene that almost anyone would want to bury deep in his or her subconscious memory. Renee described how each body part that was severed was put into black garbage bags. When they got too heavy, they were taken to the backyard where Nick Notaro had dug deep holes.

Renee was sure that all that remained of Joe Tarricone had been buried on the property; they hadn't removed hands or feet or head to take them to another disposal spot so they would be more difficult to identify.

The two detectives both thought about Nick Notaro's statement that his mother had killed Joe and put him in the freezer. That could not possibly be true. *Three* people could not move his body without dissecting it into pieces.

"Okay," Benson asked. "How did Nick kill Joe?"

"He shot him."

"And what did he use to shoot him with?"

"A gun," she said vaguely. Renee said she had no idea where Nick had obtained the gun. As she remembered, her brother had given her a handgun after the murder, and asked her to dispose of it. She wasn't sure how long she had it—but she had been on another boyfriend's boat on Lake Washington, just off Mercer Island, when she threw it in the deep water. The boat owner—also named Joe— hadn't seen her toss the weapon away.

As far as Renee knew, Joe Tarricone didn't carry a gun, although she thought he might have had one in his truck in Alaska. "So many people had guns up there."

"Okay, I've been told," Benson began, "that Joe was known to carry large amounts of cash with him. They say he carried a briefcase, and a lot of his business dealings were in cash?"

"That's correct."

"How much cash would he carry at any given time?"

"Oh—it could be upward of a thousand dollars."

That would have been quite a lot of money in 1978. Asked about which of Joe Tarricone's possessions were left at the Canyon Road house, Renee had a memory lapse again. She didn't think his yellow truck with the camper on it was there because she believed it wouldn't make the drive down from Alaska. (It *was* at Canyon Road after Joe vanished; Geri said Joe had signed it over to her.)

"The briefcase where he carried his cash?"

"You know," she said. "I believe there *was* a briefcase, but I believe that was put back in the office in Alaska. I don't know if Nick did that or if my mom did when she went up for Nick's trial [for Vickie Notaro's homicide]."

"Speaking of that, you and your mom mentioned several times back then that Joe's office in Alaska had been ransacked. Was that something to make it look like there was some kind of problem he had up there?"

"You know, I don't recall that . . . I wasn't up in Alaska, so I wouldn't have known his office was ransacked."

But, surely, Renee's mother—Geri Hesse—would have told her about finding Joe Tarricone's office a shambles after someone had trashed it? Benson thought that was something that Renee would remember.

Chapter Sixteen

Renee Curtiss's answers came more slowly, yet she didn't ask for an attorney or stop the questioning. When Denny Wood took over the questioning, she looked at him warily.

"How did you know the briefcase got back there—you said it was returned to Alaska?"

"Joe never went anywhere without his briefcase."

"You knew he was dead," Wood pressed. "Why would your mother return the briefcase? He didn't need it up there. He's not taking it anywhere. Why would anybody return a briefcase that had nothing in it?"

"I don't know. There wasn't anything in it."

"Well you mentioned—right?—that you sat down and had to come up with a plan?"

"Right," Renee said softly.

Wood outlined that their plan might have been to make it look as if Joe Tarricone had returned to Alaska alive and well, since they believed no one would find his body or prove that he'd ever come to Washington. If someone could have broken into his Alaska office, murdered him, and

163

then stolen the cash from his briefcase and ransacked his office, the false scene of the crime might look as though it occurred hundreds of miles from where he'd actually died.

His vehicles left behind in Puyallup warred with that explanation. And several people recalled that Joe was at the birthday barbecue—the last time *anyone* the detectives talked to had ever seen him.

What about the new Mercedes? Renee said that Joe had bought it for her, just as he had offered her the wedding trip to Europe. He was trying to buy her, and she wasn't having any of it.

"What did you do with the plane tickets he threw down—after you said no to his proposal?"

"I don't believe we did anything with them."

"You don't recall cashing them in for money?" Wood asked.

"It's possible. I don't remember—it was thirty years ago."

"But Joe didn't pick them up. He threw them on the ground and his heart's broken?"

"He threw them down. I believe he threw them down. He was very angry."

Renee said the Mercedes had been taken to her aunt's house. Joe had tried to give it to her in Alaska, and he brought it down to Washington. "I didn't want it—I didn't drive it. I had a new Alfa Romeo that I leased at the time."

How long had the Mercedes been there? Perhaps Joe had driven it down before his final visit; he couldn't drive both the Mercedes and his yellow meat truck and camper at the same time.

Denny Wood asked Renee about the wound in Joe's head. She didn't know what had caused it. Was it from a bullet, a baseball bat, perhaps a knife? She apparently had forgotten what she said about the gun.

"I don't know. It was just a head wound. I can't recall if there was blood," she said slowly. "It's almost as if—like it's in black and white."

"But you knew he was dead at that time?"

"Yes."

Renee Curtiss's memory was growing more and more clouded. She was fairly sure that they had kept Joe's body in the basement for a few days before they dissected his body and buried the pieces.

"Was he put in a freezer in the basement?"

"I don't recall."

"Well, think back. You were either working the chain saw or holding on to the limbs while they were being cut off. It's a huge difference if somebody's flexible and warm or whether they're stiff as a board and cold and frozen. Was he frozen when you cut him up?"

"I don't recall that."

"Was there a freezer in the basement?"

"I think there was a small chest freezer."

"Was there a freezer big enough to put a body into?"

"I don't think so. It was small."

Ben Benson and Denny Wood had begun interviewing Renee Curtiss at twenty minutes to five, and it was now sixteen minutes to six. By the time they finished, their subject's answers were mostly "I don't recall."

They had begun believing that she hadn't been present when Nick Notaro called Joe Tarricone down into the basement on the pretext of fixing the washing machine, that she wasn't there as Joe bent over, all unaware, and was shot in the head.

Now they were sure from both her answers and her failure to answer that she had been far more than a shocked witness *after the fact* of Joe's sudden, violent death. They believed that she had been there during his murder, standing beside her mother and her brother.

They also believed that she had phoned Nick in Alaska and asked him to come down and "take care of her problem" with Joe.

And Nick—who had always vowed to protect his sisters—had done just that. He had put the blame on his dead mother at first and then admitted shooting Joe himself. But he denied that either Renee or Cassie had been there. He said Renee had been in Hawaii—but she hadn't even mentioned Hawaii.

Well, Cassie hadn't been in Puyallup. She had been in Anchorage, Alaska.

But Renee had been there. She was shocked when Ben Benson informed her that she was under arrest for conspiracy to commit murder, which is basically a murder charge. Grim faced, the two detectives, with Renee handcuffed between them, walked out of Henry's Bail Bonds. Her expression was stoic. The new world she had fashioned for herself had come tumbling down.

Renee was going to jail, a thought that had probably never occurred to her.

Renee Curtiss spent the night of March 24 in jail. The next day she was led into court for her arraignment. Both Renee and her brother Nick were charged with first-degree murder. Despite the fact that both of them had admitted to the details of Joe Tarricone's murder, they each pled "not guilty."

Judge Susan Serko set bail for Nick at $2 million and for Renee at $500,000. She stipulated that Renee could not arrange bail through Henry's Bail Bonds because of "a conflict of interest."

Which was, of course, obvious.

But Henry Lewis was close to all the long-standing bail bonds companies and they respected him, so something was worked out between them. Renee was released from jail and returned to the luxurious condominium where she lived with her husband.

Nick was not bailed out; actually, jail was probably a much nicer place to be than under a bridge or in a mission. At least he knew where he was going to sleep and that he would eat every day. "Three hots and a cot," was the term veteran prisoners used. His plans to retire down South were no longer on Nick's agenda. He looked old, stooped, and tired as he left the courtroom.

With this arraignment, the Northwest media publicized the awful details related in the courtroom and the story of a thirty-year-old unsolved crime of monstrous proportions was at the top of television news and in bold headlines in newspapers.

Quoting Deputy Prosecutor Dawn Farina, most lead-ins began with: "Miss Curtiss, along with her brother, chopped up Mr. Tarricone's body and buried it . . ."

There were undoubtedly many men who had once been involved with Renee Curtiss who heard about that and heaved a sigh of relief.

Chapter Seventeen

Dawn Farina doesn't look like a hard-hitting criminal-prosecuting attorney. She is a slender, pretty woman with long blond hair, but dumb blonde jokes never fit Dawn. She was to be Renee's nemesis. Beyond Dawn Farina's expertise in prosecuting homicide cases, Pierce County prosecuting attorney Mark Lindquist made an astute decision when he chose her to face Renee Curtiss in a courtroom.

Before he gained fame as the "baby doctor of America," Dr. Benjamin Spock did some psychological studies while on duty at a military hospital. He found that attractive women who exhibit sociopathic tendencies are quite good at manipulating men. But they don't fool other women. (The reverse is also true; sociopathic males can delude women quite easily, but their real motives are transparent to other men.)

From the moment she took on the case, Dawn could see through Renee's ploys as clearly as if she had x-ray vision.

Dawn Farina would handle the prosecution of Renee and Nick all on her own. She would not have an assistant prosecutor to help her, but the massive preparation ahead didn't faze her.

Trial dates were set and set again. Delays in a major homicide trial are far from unusual. In September 2008, Dawn Farina asked for a rare "double" trial where both Nick and Renee would be tried—but there would be two juries. Renee's jury would be excused when evidence was introduced against Nick—but not her—and vice versa. The deputy prosecutor argued that this would be the most expedient way to try two defendants for what was, essentially, the same crime. And perhaps it was, but there was also the possibility that it could be confusing.

Defense attorney Gary Clower, representing Renee, argued strongly against a dual trial.

Farina's request was denied.

There would be *two* trials, one for Renee and one for Nick. After more delays, Nick's trial finally began on Thursday, February 12, 2009, in Pierce County Superior Court with Judge Kitty-Ann van Doorninck presiding. Judge van Doorninck would oversee both trials—but separately.

By Farina's special request, Ben Benson sat beside her at the State's table. He knew every aspect of Joe Tarricone's murder case by heart, and he was granted permission to sit with the prosecutor throughout both trials, even though prospective witnesses almost always are banned from the courtroom until after they testify. Dawn Farina didn't have a coprosecutor, but she had Sergeant Benson.

Gypsy, Dean, and Rosemary Tarricone were in the courtroom observing everything. They all noted how slow Nick's thinking was and felt he was a pawn for Renee.

Looking back, Gypsy sighed as she remembered Nick Notaro. "You could see that he was mentally disabled to some degree and he'd been manipulated by Renee. She probably paid him off all these years with money and other things. She really took advantage."

In her final argument, Dawn Farina had ample ammunition, gleaned from Nick's own statement. She showed jurors photographs of Joe Tarricone in life, immediately followed by pictures of his bones with the clean edges that proved a chain saw had cut through them.

"For the next twenty-nine years, Joseph Tarricone's five grown children and two minor children would worry and wonder what happened to their father," Farina said. "And finally, after thirty years, a family's worst nightmare came true. Not only had their father been murdered, but his body [was] brutally dismembered limb by limb with a chain saw and then discarded in large plastic bags—like a piece of trash."

Farina explained to the jury that they must find four circumstances true in order to convict Nick Notaro of murder in the first degree:

One: that on or about the period between the twenty-first day of September 1978 and the twenty-first day of October 1978, the defendant—as an accomplice—acted with intent to cause the death of Joseph Tarricone. Two: that the intent to cause the death was premeditated. Three: that Joseph Tarricone died as a result of the defendant's acts. And four: that any of these acts occurred in the state of Washington.

And then Dawn Farina pointed out with details and examples that each of these conditions was true. Notaro had had the opportunity, the means, and the motive to kill Joe Tarricone.

"The defendant himself said it best during the interview with detectives Benson and Wood. When they asked him who told him to kill Joseph Tarricone, Notaro responded, 'Nobody had to tell me to kill him. We went down to the basement and he leaned over [the washing machine] and I shot him in the back of the head. I shot him twice.'"

The jurors quickly found Notaro guilty of first-degree murder. Judge van Doorninck ruled that his sentencing would occur after Renee Curtiss's trial.

Renee's trial began in late March, almost exactly a year after Ben Benson and Denny Wood arrested her in Henry's Bail Bonds. She had been out on bail for that year, and remained free. Ironically, she would face a female prosecutor and a female judge, probably not her first choice.

No one was more elated to see Renee go on trial for first-degree murder at last than Gypsy Tarricone. Gypsy put a banner up on her fence marking the first anniversary of Nick and Renee's arrest, announcing her sentiments. When Ben Benson saw it, he told her to take it down immediately. The last thing the prosecution wanted was something that Renee's lawyer could use in an appeal. Chagrined, Gypsy obeyed. Ben had always told her the truth and she knew that he, along with Denny Wood, had worked many off-duty hours to make this upcoming trial happen. She had waited three decades to see Renee Curtiss punished for her father's death; she could wait a week or so longer to celebrate.

Renee dressed in expensive and flattering clothes at her trial. She was still free on bail and didn't have to sleep in jail when each day ended. Her hair and makeup were more appropriate than usual. Her sister, Cassie, other family members, and a number of women whom she identified as her friends were there each day to support her.

One trial spectator described these women as "hardened by age and experience, wearing a lot of thick makeup—much like Renee," while Gypsy Tarricone simply called them "the old biddy cheering squad."

Henry Lewis couldn't be there; his heart disease had progressed rapidly after Renee's arrest, and the strain of a murder trial where his wife was the defendant had accelerated the damage. His coronary artery disease had brought him to the edge of death.

Gypsy was there, of course, along with her brother Dean, her sister Rosemary, and occasionally other family members. The two camps stared at each other coldly as the trial progressed.

The defense had planned to call Nick Notaro to the witness stand first, but as the trial started, circumstances made it impossible for him to be in court on time, and Judge van Doorninck wanted the trial to move as quickly as possible without long delays. Had Nick testified first, Renee would have heard his version of their "facts," and tailored her testimony to fit. Usually witnesses are not allowed in the courtroom until after they have testified—to avoid hearing something that might change their testimony. But Renee was the defendant so she was allowed to hear every word witnesses said.

But Nick was late, so Renee began.

Renee Curtiss was determined to testify in her own defense, a choice that defense attorneys dread. By doing so, she was opening herself up to cross-examination by Dawn Farina, but Renee clearly counted on her own powers of persuasion and her ability to deny many things she had told Ben Benson and Denny Wood.

Renee's lawyer, Gary Clower, began the direct questioning of his client. Her affect was flat, unemotional, almost disinterested at times as she responded to his questions. If anyone in the gallery expected tears and emotion from Renee Curtiss, they were to be disappointed.

Renee gave her age as fifty-five and said her two children were now thirty-eight and thirty-nine. Gary Clower introduced Defense Exhibit #203, a picture of Renee at twenty-five. This was what she had looked like when Joe Tarricone was murdered—a sweet, almost innocent-appearing young woman. Would the jurors consider the young Renee as incapable of such a grisly crime?

"What was this photograph taken for?" Clower asked.

"For a makeup ad for our makeup store."

"Did you used to do a little bit of modeling?" Clower was obviously preparing for any questions that might come from the prosecution about Renee's escort and "modeling" career.

"Yes."

Asked to talk about her early life, Renee testified that she went to Alaska first in 1973, when she was the nineteen-year-old wife of a bush pilot. When the marriage failed, she said she was left alone with two children—alone until her mother moved up to join her. She recalled that she had been a bookkeeper for the Black Angus restaurant chain, a hostess at a Greek restaurant, and the night manager of an airport restaurant.

"Eventually, [I] went to work for Joe Tarricone for Alaska Meat and Provisions."

Did she not remember that she had met Joe in Seattle—not in Alaska? It was of no import, really, and Clower moved on.

Renee continued along the paths of her life—at least as she remembered. She testified that she, her mother, and her daughter moved to a northern suburb of Seattle in 1977. She didn't mention her son. The trio had lived in Kirkland, Washington, for about a year.

"Where were you employed?" Clower asked.

"I worked two different places—actually three—different places. I worked for Elite Models. I also worked for Frederick & Nelson. Then I went to work for the Griffin Group."

Renee had a precise memory for these details, odd, because her memory would soon fail her again and again. She believed that she and her mother had moved to Canyon Road in the summer of 1978, but she wasn't sure of the month. Shown the lease for the Pierce County house, she agreed that it must have been in June.

The defendant said she had lived in two rentals at the same time. One was the Canyon Road house, where she "spent weekends" with her mother and daughter, and the other was in downtown Bellevue some thirty-five miles away. Gary Clower didn't ask her why she didn't go home to her mother and daughter at night; the thirty-five-mile commute would have been on freeways all the way.

Nor did he ask her who—if anyone—she lived with during the week.

Renee remembered how ill her husband, Henry, was when Ben Benson and Denny Wood came to interview her a year before: "He was in late-stage heart failure and late-stage renal failure," she testified, omitting the fact that the Pierce County detectives had offered to take her to see Henry's doctors before they asked her any questions.

"When the police came to talk to you, they told you that they wanted to talk to you about Mr. Tarricone?"

"That's correct."

"How did that make you feel?"

"Um . . . my heart probably went to my stomach. Frightened. Worried about not being able to keep the appointment. Worried about the trouble I would be in for my actions."

Gary Clower could not erase his client's gory confession to Benson and Wood about how she helped to dissect and hide Joe Tarricone's body. But he needed to raise the doubt that Renee's Miranda rights might not have been given correctly and in time; he suggested that Renee had somehow been tricked into talking freely, believing that the statute of limitations on being an accomplice after the fact had run out.

Of course, he would hit on that. All he had going as a defense strategy was to paint his client as a vulnerable young woman at the time of the murder, and to do whatever he could to remove her as far as possible from the scene of Joe's killing.

Asked to recall her relationship with Joe Tarricone, Renee described him as a somewhat crass man, much too old for her. She said she had met him at the Cattle Company restaurant in Anchorage. "He used to come in and I repeatedly had to ask him to leave because he was trying to sell his salami and different things at the bar."

Despite her early distaste for him, at some point—she could not recall when—Renee said she had gone to work for Joe, answering the phone, keeping some of the bookwork straight, even delivering meat herself to the Kenai Peninsula.

She estimated that Joe had been in his mid- to late fifties, the same age as her mother, who, she commented, liked him.

"Was Joe a generous sort of person?" Clower stepped into more dangerous waters.

"Very generous. He'd buy me things, my mother things, my daughter things."

"Did he buy you a Mercedes?"

"He did."

"Did you accept it?"

"No, I did not," Renee testified. She had another car already—but Joe had persevered and practically forced the Mercedes on her, shipping it down to Seattle by boat.

Renee recalled that she and Joe had only dated about six months, although she still worked for him for another six months before she moved to Seattle. She was dating Kurt Winkler at the same time, and they became engaged.

"Kurt was planning on taking a job that was going to relocate him to Seattle."

"Did Mr. Tarricone ever ask you to marry him before you left Alaska?"

"More than once."

"What was your answer?"

"No."

Asked if she had told Joe Tarricone that she was leaving Alaska, Renee wasn't sure. Her memory was fading in and out. "I don't believe that we told him because he was—could be persistent."

Kurt Winkler hadn't followed them to Seattle after all, but Renee testified that Joe had come down to visit several times. She felt her mother had been on his side in trying to get Renee to marry him. But, when he proposed to her once more in Washington, she said he'd been very angry when she refused.

Renee Curtiss was adamant that she had never suggested to her brother that he hurt or kill Joe. "It was annoying," she said, "[but] I mean it wasn't annoying enough to have someone hurt over a situation like that. Not at all."

The prosecution believed Renee had asked Nick Notaro to come to Washington to get rid of Joe for good. His wife's blood had barely been washed from his hands when he flew to Seattle. Renee shook her head firmly. No, she was sure now that she didn't know that Nick had just killed his wife in Alaska when she talked to him after his appendectomy. Maybe she had told Ben Benson and Denny Wood that when they interviewed her in the bail bonds office, but once she thought about it later, she had realized *exactly* where she was when Nick told her.

"Where was that?" Clower asked.

"It was at the Canyon Road house, sitting in the kitchen nook, sitting there with my mom and Nick."

"And that was *after* Mr. Tarricone was killed, wasn't it?"

"Correct."

Renee stressed that she also learned that Nick had killed Joe Tarricone as they sat at their kitchen nook. Her mother had told her—quite urgently—to hurry home from Bellevue. Only when she arrived on Canyon Road had she learned that Joe was in the basement—dead.

Renee testified that the three of them had debated what they should do. She had been concerned about her mother and her brother. What would happen to them, she testified, if they were arrested for murdering Joe? Feeling "a little bit of horror," she described her feelings as she heard about *two* murders in a week. Even so, she had agreed with them that they had to get rid of Joe's body.

"So what did you do?" Clower asked.

"Nick was going to—we were going to buy a chain saw and cut him up and bury him."

No one in the courtroom envied Gary Clower; this had to be one of the toughest clients he'd ever defended. Renee evinced no emotion at all; her eyes were dry as she spoke of the cold-blooded disposal of a human being—a scene right out of a horror movie.

At this moment, she could not remember who had gone to buy the chain saw.

"What was your role in disposing of Mr. Tarricone's body?"

"We initially went down there—my mom, Nick, and myself—and he started the chain saw. I think we were holding a tarp, and I got—I got physically ill so I went upstairs. I came back down periodically, but Mom stayed down there, and I recall helping put body pieces in plastic bags."

Gary Clower needed to remove as many of the motives for murder Renee might have had as he could. Witnesses had told Ben Benson about the briefcase full of large bills, the Mercedes, Joe's gold nugget jewelry, even the yellow meat truck that Geri Hesse had. He asked Renee about those things of value.

She could not recall Joe's briefcase. She was sure she had kept nothing that belonged to the victim. She admitted disposing of the gun, simply because she had access to a boat trip some weeks later and she could toss it to the bottom of Lake Washington without arousing suspicion.

She hadn't wanted the Mercedes in the first place, and she had no idea what had happened to Joe Tarricone's jewelry.

"Since that day at the house, have you talked to anybody about what happened there—other than your mother and your brother?"

"No, I have not."

"And is it accurate to say that for the last thirty years, that you lied about the last time you saw Mr. Tarricone?"

"Continuously,"

"Why did you do that?"

"To protect my brother, my mother, and myself."

"Did the extent of Mr. Tarricone's attention to you cause you to hurt him or kill him?"

"No. Absolutely not."

"Did you ever ask your brother to harm him in any way?"

"I did not."

"Did you kill him?"

"I did not kill him."

"Were you present in the house when he was killed?"

"I was not."

"Did you do *anything* at all to encourage your brother to kill Mr. Tarricone?"

"No," Renee answered to this final question by her own attorney, "I did not."

She had done nothing to ingratiate herself with the jury; Renee Curtiss seemed offended that she had even had to answer her own attorney's questions.

Chapter Eighteen

If Renee Curtiss's testimony in her own defense had left jurors and court-watchers sick to their stomachs, revulsed by a side of life they might never have imagined, what would happen now as Deputy Prosecutor Dawn Farina rose to cross-examine her?

Renee eyed Farina warily as she faced questions not designed to make her look even marginally innocent.

"When detectives Benson and Wood contacted you on March 24, 2008, they advised you of your Miranda warnings? Correct?" Farina began.

"That's correct."

Yes, Renee agreed that it was her signature on the bottom of the rights form, and her initials after each warning. Yes, Ben Benson had offered to take her to see her husband's doctor. Yes, she had worked for Joe for over a year, and he had bought her many presents.

"He paid for your rent while you were in Alaska?"

"No. I told [the detectives] that I was generously compensated. If they wanted to consider that he was paying me a wage, that's fine. If they want to say he paid the rent, I was generously compensated."

Dawn Farina brought out the fact that Renee had been the business manager at Henry's Bail Bonds. She was no neophyte when it came to the justice system.

Renee's demeanor was frosty and unemotional. Most of her answers to Farina's cross-examination questions were, "I don't recall."

She could not remember meeting Joe's children or talking with them on the phone after he vanished. She agreed that she might not have told the Pierce County detectives that she lived at two addresses at the time Joe was killed. It didn't seem important.

"The only time that Nick Notaro came to the Puyallup house was the one time Joseph Tarricone was killed. Correct?"

"Correct."

Yes, Nick had stayed at the Puyallup house, and Joe had been there several times, although he didn't stay over.

"He came to the barbecue during the summer of 1978 and brought meat to grill for you and your family. Correct?"

"I don't specifically remember meat—but he could have."

"Do you recall him being there for the barbecue?"

"Yes."

Farina switched to Renee's invitation to her brother to come down and help her at the Canyon Road house. After repeated questions, Renee thought she might have mentioned that Joe was "harassing" her. "I mean that [Nick]

184

was well aware of Joe's harassment. Due to conversations with my mom and me."

"And you never called the police to report Joe's harassment of you while you were living in Puyallup or in Washington State?"

"Correct."

"Nick Notaro brought with him from Alaska the gun that was used to kill Joseph Tarricone?"

"I believe so," Renee said cautiously.

"And that was the same gun that was used to kill Vickie Notaro. Correct?"

"I believe so."

"And today you testified that you learned of your brother killing Vickie Notaro *after* he killed Joseph Tarricone, after he had already arrived here? Was that your testimony today?"

"Yes, it is."

"Isn't it true that you told the detectives not once—but twice—that you learned over the telephone that your brother killed Vickie Notaro *before* he came to Seattle?"

"I remember telling them that once, and then a couple of questions later, I corrected myself."

"You told them twice. You're saying you told them once?"

Dawn Farina was getting to Renee Curtiss, who hastened to insist that she had *not* known Vickie was dead before Nick came down, but her answers were becoming more and more jumbled.

"How did you react when Nick told you about that?"

"The same way I would assume most people would. I mean, a little bit of horror—"

That was what she had said to Benson and Wood, too. "A little bit of horror." Still, the defendant's face mirrored no horror at all. No emotion.

Now Renee's memory was failing her. She could not recall driving Nick to buy the chain saw. She wasn't sure if Joe's body had been left in the basement for a few days. She admitted that Joe could not have fit into the small freezer there. She just couldn't recall.

"You helped dismember Joseph Tarricone's body, didn't you?" Dawn Farina pressed.

"I was there. I was present. Absolutely."

"Do you recall taking a turn with the chain saw?"

"No—I remember [the detectives] telling me that. I did tell them I used it on him."

"Joseph Tarricone's arms were cut off. Correct?"

"Correct."

"Joseph Tarricone's legs were cut off. Correct?"

"Correct."

"Joseph Tarricone's head was cut off. Correct?"

"Correct."

Renee agreed that the victim's body parts were put into large garbage bags and carried to the backyard. She could no longer remember whether they were carried out the basement door or through the house. It was all so vague to her, but the deputy prosecutor was relentless. As distasteful as a retelling of the details was, it had to be done.

Renee was showing the first emotion in the trial; she was growing increasingly annoyed with the blond prosecutor.

"During the conversation you had with Jerry Burger of the Des Moines Police Department—who testified here—you told him that the last time you saw Joseph Tarricone was when he came to your house with two tickets to Rome, Italy. Correct?"

"I believe what he [Burger] said, yes."

"And that was a lie. Correct?"

"Yes, it was a lie."

"You told Detective Burger that Joseph wanted you to go to Italy with him. Correct?"

"I have no reason to disbelieve him [Burger]."

Dawn Farina had carefully compared all of the statements that Renee and other witnesses had made to the Pierce County detectives, and now her cross-examination was a juggernaut as she elicited answers from the defendant, answers that could not possibly match her earlier statements. Farina peppered Renee with questions that ended with, "Correct?" and, "And that was a lie, wasn't it?"

More than a dozen times, Renee answered, "Yes, that was a lie." More than three dozen times, she responded, "I don't know, I can't recall—I cannot recall specifically."

Often, she testified, "I have no reason to disbelieve him—or her," when faced with what others said she had told them.

Over three decades, she had lied to police detectives, her relatives, the men in her life, virtually *everyone* with whom she interacted. How could anyone—even someone as clever as Renee Curtiss—remember which things she had told to which people? She was desperate to convince the jurors that she had not planned Joe Tarricone's murder, enlisted her suggestible brother, or even been present when Joe was shot twice in the head.

Now each of Farina's questions brought forth another coil of untruths that trapped Renee in a cage of her own creation.

Renee admitted her statement to the Pierce County detectives, but she acknowledged only that she *was* present in the old yellow house on Canyon Road while Joe Tarricone's body was being sawed into pieces. She denied vociferously that she had asked her brother to help her get rid of the victim, who was "stalking" her. She insisted that she had never even suggested that. She had asked him to come visit in Puyallup solely because their mother was putting too much pressure on her. She had never said what kind of pressure Geri Hesse was exerting—whether it was emotional or just full of annoying demands.

"No. No. No." She was not present when Joe Tarricone was killed. Sarcastically, she asked the deputy prosecutor, "Do you really think I would not remember if someone was shot in my basement?"

As Dawn Farina zeroed in on the process involved in dissecting a six-foot-plus man into manageable pieces, the jurors listened carefully, some turning pale and others looking ill.

Gypsy Tarricone, who still calls Dawn Farina "the little spitfire," for her fearlessness in bringing her father's murder case to trial and for her incisive cross-examining of Renee, listened and watched avidly. She could see that Renee was no match for Dawn.

Renee clearly detested the prosecutor, answering her questions curtly.

Using Renee's earlier statement to Ben Benson and Denny Wood, Farina read aloud what the defendant had said on March 24, 2008—now fourteen months in the past.

"You first said that you didn't talk on the phone to Nick in Alaska before he came down here," Farina said. "And that was a lie, wasn't it?"

"Yes, that was a lie."

"And you said that you didn't know that Nick's wife, Vickie Notaro, was dead before he came down here. And that was a lie, wasn't it?"

"Yes, that was a lie."

"You said you didn't know where Joe Tarricone was when he disappeared, didn't you? And that was a lie?"

"Yes, that was a lie."

Renee's eyes shot daggers at Dawn Farina.

"You told Dean Tarricone [Joe's youngest son] that you had never spoken to the police about Joseph's disappearance. Correct?"

"I don't recall."

"And, in fact, you did speak to the police?"

"I spoke with Detective Burger and Detective Reinicke [of the Pierce County Sheriff's Office] about Joe's disappearance, correct."

"You told Dean, during that phone conversation, quote: 'Yeah. It was—it was before that. The last time I saw him, he wanted to go to Europe. And then when all that came about, I thought—well, maybe—heck, maybe that's where he went. Maybe he went to Europe.' You said that to Dean Tarricone, didn't you?"

"If that's in the transcript, yes."

"And that was a lie?"

"Yes, it was."

"You also told Dean Tarricone, during that phone conversation, quote: 'But, you know, or I kind of figured, well, finally, maybe he met somebody else, and you know, kind of attached his affections there.' End quote."

"Yes, that was a lie." This time, Renee hadn't even waited for Dawn Farina's question. She had plunged ahead and identified yet another lie.

On redirect, Gary Clower tried to defuse some of the damage Dawn Farina's cross had done. He pointed out that Renee had occasionally been confused on the tape of her interview with Ben Benson and Denny Wood.

"You were asked whether you made statements to the detectives regarding asking Nick for help with Joe; do you recall those questions from counsel [Farina]?"

"I remember the questions."

"Do you remember being asked the question by the detectives: 'How did you think he was going to help with the situation with Joe?' and you answering, 'I don't necessarily recall thinking he was going to help. Maybe he could talk to him. Maybe I'm putting words in my head that I don't recall, and I don't want to do that'?"

"The detectives had asked the question so many times, their questions were becoming my memories," Renee testified.

Could the jury give this bemused version of Renee's first interview more weight than her just-ended testimony about cutting up her former lover's body?

It seemed unlikely.

*   *   *

"Call Nicholas Notaro."

The tall, shambling man who had admitted to killing both his wife and his sister's former lover took the witness stand.

Had Nick Notaro testified first, as originally scheduled, and as the defense planned, Renee could have backed up his version. But, as it was, he came to testify *after* she did, and he was totally clueless about what she had said.

Nick took the witness stand fully intending to support Renee's version of how Joe Tarricone perished in 1978. But few of his answers matched hers. He wasn't anywhere near as cunning as Renee was, and he didn't make a good witness for the defense. He admitted killing his wife on Friday, September 22 after he got out of the Fairbanks hospital. He then testified that he flew to Seattle on the following Monday—September 25—intending to kill Joe. But he hastened to explain that it had all been *his* idea.

Nick said he had neither *seen* nor talked to Renee during the first four days he was at the Canyon Road house and believed that she was working in Hawaii. He said his long-dead mother—Geri Hesse—told him that. He had brought along the gun that he'd used in Vickie's homicide, but he said that was only because he wanted Renee to get rid of it for him.

Of course, it had come in handy since he had already decided—all on his own—to murder Joe Tarricone.

Nick said he didn't like Joe—never had—because he was too old for his sister, and that Joe was always "trying to get her in bed."

Renee had just testified that her mother liked Joe, but Nick testified that Geri didn't like him. Nick testified that Joe had shown up on Friday, September 29.

Over and over again, the witness took full responsibility for Joe Tarricone's murder.

"Do you remember when he arrived?" Gary Clower asked.

"It was early evening—or early afternoon. He came to the house and Mom said, 'Joe's here.' We were sitting at the table, and I went into the bedroom and got the gun and stuck it in my waistband."

"Why did you do that?"

"Because I was going to kill him. Because he was messing with Renee."

Nick's recollection was that Joe had arrived in his refrigerated yellow pickup truck.

"Is it accurate to describe," Clower asked, "that you asked him to go in the basement to help with a problem with the washing machine?"

"That's correct."

"So describe what happened then," Clower urged as Nick seemed to lose track of his thoughts.

"When we went over to the washer, Joe leaned over the washer, and I took the gun out and shot him."

"How many times?"

"Twice."

"What happened then?"

"Well, Mom was a little shocked and she said, you know, 'What'd you do? You didn't have to kill him.' And I said, 'I took care of a problem.'"

With Renee's defense attorney prodding him, Nick Notaro went into a long description of how he had driven Joe's truck to a strip mall and bought a "come-along" so he could lift Joe's heavy body up more easily. He needed to put him in the freezer.

"I put one hook in his belt and the other hook over a rafter, and ratcheted him up."

Nick said his mother was there helping him load a man over six feet tall and weighing more than two hundred pounds into a ten-cubic-foot freezer—"three, four feet long, three feet deep, two feet wide."

Anyone in the courtroom could estimate that the victim could not have fit into such a small space. Nick rambled on that he wanted to freeze Joe's body so that it wouldn't be so "messy" when he cut him up.

None of what he said matched Renee's testimony, but Nick didn't know that. With his misguided sense of loyalty, he continued to insist from the witness stand that his sister hadn't been there.

Gypsy and her sister Rosemary sat in the gallery, weighing every word of testimony as they had since the beginning of the trial.

"How could it suddenly be Geri who had complained about Joe Tarricone to Nick?" Gypsy asked herself. "Nick didn't know that Renee had just testified that she was there in the house helping to dismember my dad's body."

Gypsy and Rosemary studied the jurors' faces, trying to get some sense of who might be on their side.

"There was an older, kind of country-looking man in the middle of the front row," Gypsy remembers. "He had a rather large belly and he crossed his arms across it. He sat there, not moving during the trial, but when Renee talked about cutting my dad up, tears rolled down this man's face. I knew then that *he* was with us.

"Another juror would look at Rosemary whenever Renee would act aghast—sighing and shaking her head—as she sat next to her attorney. Renee seemed horrified whenever someone testified about what a monster she was. We felt we could count on two jurors. We weren't sure about the others."

While Gypsy Tarricone has never hidden her hatred for Renee Curtiss, she felt differently about Nick Notaro.

"Yes, Nick has a sick perverted mind," Gypsy says today. "That, no doubt, came from his upbringing by Geraldine—with her alcoholism and using men as well, and pimping her daughter to gain possessions and monetary gain. Geraldine was a piece of work.

"Funny thing, I really don't hate Nick. Truly, in my heart, I do not hate him. I feel nothing but the fact that his mind is twisted and something very wrong happened in his life, along with the fact that he is mentally slow. He didn't have the brains to come up with a plot to kill my dad—but he would do whatever his mother or his sisters wanted. Many of my family members think like me. We hate Renee. It's because of her that our dad is dead. I am not even too sure yet that Nick did it. Because they lied so much . . ."

Would the jurors believe the defense witnesses, or would they recognize what was true and what was obviously a lie—a plethora of lies? In final arguments, Dawn Farina said that Renee Curtiss was guilty as an accomplice to murder. She had asked her brother to kill the victim because she had grown weary of Joe Tarricone's romantic advances. *She* was the link between Joseph Tarricone and Nick Notaro. *She* had the motive.

Defense attorney Gary Clower gave his position that the prosecution had submitted no evidence that his client had solicited the murder of her former boyfriend.

"The crime here is murder," he pointed out. "Not anything else that she might have done. She isn't charged with disposing of the body or covering up the crime. She is guilty of lying about Tarricone's whereabouts for nearly thirty years—maybe even for helping dispose of his body."

It was time for Renee Curtiss's jury to decide her fate.

Appropriately, perhaps, it was April Fool's Day 2009 when the jurors retired at noon to review evidence and testimony and deliberate on whether Renee should be found guilty or innocent of first-degree murder.

Expecting that it would be at least a day before the verdict was handed down, Gypsy and Rosemary Tarricone left the Pierce County courthouse to keep a doctor's appointment in Olympia, twenty miles south of Tacoma. Throughout the trial, Rosemary had said, "Jacqueline, you know, she could get off and you'd better be prepared if that happens."

Gypsy didn't even want to think about that possibility, but she did know—she had known from the first day—that she had to be the one who held everyone else in her family together during both traumatic trials. In many ways, they were reliving the grief they felt for Joe back in 1978.

Although they thought they would be back in Tacoma to wait out the jury's deliberation in plenty of time, Gypsy's cell phone shrilled, making them both jump. Suddenly, only a little more than three hours after jury deliberation had begun, it was over.

As the sisters drove as fast as they legally could on the I-5 freeway back to the courthouse, Rosemary reminded Gypsy (whom she still calls Jacqueline) again that they couldn't fall apart—no matter what the verdict was.

But the next phone call obviated the need for that. Renee Ray Curtiss had just been convicted of first-degree murder!

When Dawn Farina called Gypsy, she told her that the prosecution team and the detectives were holding a meeting on the tenth floor of the courthouse, and they were waiting for Joe's two daughters to join them.

Ben Benson had observed Renee closely as the jury was polled. One by one, they had all said "guilty." She seemed to be stunned, and then her jaw set stoically. Perhaps she had really expected to return to her home and celebrate her acquittal. But she wasn't going home at all; she was going directly to jail.

After Gypsy and Rosemary parked in the courthouse's rear parking lot, they saw Cassie, Renee's sister, and "the old biddy cheer squad" coming out of the courthouse, most of them looking either dejected or angry. It was a tense moment; the air was full of electricity.

Gypsy didn't fall apart, but she could not resist shouting at Cassie, "Your sister got just what she deserved!"

If it hadn't been so serious, it might have been comical—a bunch of women well over fifty preparing to have what looked like a gang war. Cassie headed for Gypsy and she seemed to be very close to a physical attack on her when one of Renee's supporters grabbed Cassie by the arm, shouting, "No! Don't do that!"

And it was over as soon as it had begun.

Judge Kitty-Ann van Doorninck set Nick Notaro's sentencing for April 4, and Renee's for April 24.

Renee lost another privilege on April 16—one that paled in the face of what might lie ahead. The Washington State insurance commissioner, Mike Kriedler, sent her a form letter telling her that her insurance agent's license had been revoked.

"This order is based on the following: You have been found guilty of Murder in the First Degree, a Class A. Felony, on April 1, 2009. Revocation is therefore appropriate under RCW 48.17.530 (1)(g)."

It may have been a "whatever" moment for Renee. Where she was going, she wouldn't be able to sell insurance anyway.

Epilogue

When Nick Notaro appeared for sentencing on April 4, he was sentenced to life imprisonment. The future he had pictured in Arkansas no longer existed for him. Maybe it never had; he had a warrant waiting for him on sex charges there.

On April 24, Judge Kitty-Ann van Doorninck's courtroom was packed with spectators and media who waited to observe Renee Curtiss's sentencing. Sergeant Ben Benson got there too late to find a seat, and he stood in the back of the room with Denny Wood and his lieutenant, Brent Bomkamp.

Judge van Doorninck is admired for her grasp of the law and for her honesty, but she can also be crisp. She speaks her mind. As she sentenced Renee Curtiss to life in prison, she told the convicted woman that she was "appalled" that Renee had never showed one iota of remorse throughout her entire trial.

Detectives often go above and beyond their basic duties to their departments and the victims as they work unpaid overtime and sleepless nights. They cannot help but be involved in the lives of survivors and of the victims themselves. Still, standing at the back of the crowded courtroom, Ben Benson was surprised when Judge van Doorninck singled him out. She said that the case just ended had finally come to a successful conclusion "thanks to Detective Sergeant Ben Benson."

It was exceedingly rare for a judge to do that, and it was something Benson would never forget.

Joe Tarricone's remains had lain in the morgue for a very long time, and now they were released to his family for burial. There was no question that his seven children wanted his last resting place to be in Albuquerque, where they'd had happier days.

"My dad was buried three times," Gypsy Tarricone remembers wryly. "First—where his murderers put him, and second because of a mix-up in Albuquerque. My mom wanted to be buried at the Sunset cemetery, but that is such a boring place. I know it sounds strange to say it but the 'hip' cemetery is Mount Calvary. It's full of life and there's always something happening there. Families come for holidays, or just to visit. You see people you know.

"On Christmas Eve, there are luminarias, hundreds, maybe thousands of them. They're little paper bags with sand in the bottom and a candle in each. They light up the whole cemetery, and the paths are full of people. We knew my father would want to be at Mount Calvary."

And she was right. After thirty years in a hidden grave, Joe Tarricone, who always loved a party, belonged at Mount Calvary.

"Rose, Claire, Aldo, Joey, me, Gina, Rosemary, and Dean were all there at 10 a.m. on May 2, 2009, for my dad's graveside military services, all of us carrying flags," Gypsy says.

"And then we realized that they had put our father in the wrong grave. I had some choice sailor's words to say about that, but my sister Claire said, 'Let's just go ahead with it. They can move him later.'"

And so they did. At last, Joe Tarricone rests easy at Mount Calvary Cemetery where his family visits often.

Henry Lewis passed away fifteen days after Renee was sentenced to life in prison. He died without leaving a will. For the first time, Renee Curtiss was, technically, a wealthy widow—something she might have been striving for since she was in her twenties. None of the older men she'd lived with had married her. And now she fought to inherit Henry's estate. She wouldn't be able to use much money at the time, since she was in prison, and prisoners' accounts had limits, but both she and Nick planned to appeal their verdicts and sentences to the Washington State Court of Appeals and she would need money for attorneys.

Gypsy Tarricone supported Henry's grown children in their efforts to receive the estate their father had worked for his whole life. In the end, they prevailed. As it turned out, the Lewis family was granted everything. "We were all happy with that decision," Gypsy says.

Renee Curtiss's appeals challenged the admission of her taped confession, comments on her right to remain silent, and the alleged admission of improper opinion testimony. She also claimed she had been the victim of prosecutorial misconduct and an ineffective defense attorney, and insisted that the evidence introduced hadn't been sufficient to cause her to be found guilty and also accused the State of "crowd manipulation" to influence the jury.

On May 6, 2011, the Washington State Court of Appeals denied all of her claims and affirmed her conviction.

Nick Notaro, who had a substantial rap sheet going into his trial, fared no better. On that same day in May, the court of appeals also denied his request for a new trial. Nick may be handling being behind bars better than his sister; he had done quite well settling into prison life easily in his earlier incarcerations.

Renee, however, who is used to the finer things in life, has had to face a major adjustment.

The Tarricone family does not feel sorry for her. They still miss their dad. But they have some serenity in knowing that he is, finally, in Mount Calvary Cemetery, with its glowing luminarias and the laughter of happy family celebrations—while his killers face the rest of their lives behind bars.

Once again, Ben Benson has proven—as so many dedicated law enforcement officers have all over America—that getting away with murder isn't nearly as simple as it may look. With old-fashioned, dogged detective work and space-age forensic technology, scores of murderers have found they aren't as smart as they thought they were.

TOO LATE FOR THE FAIR

Readers often ask me, "Where do you get the cases you write about?" I hear about intriguing cases from many sources, including detectives, relatives of homicide victims, the rare victim who has managed to stay alive, my readers, the Internet, email, snail mail, newspapers, radio, and television news. Out of the some four thousand suggestions I receive each year, I can choose only five to seven cases at the most. I have some books that feature only one case. Books like this one—my Crime Files—give me an opportunity to write about several felony cases. Still, there is no way one woman could write all the mysteries that occur in America.

My criteria in selecting cases are quite simple: if I am fascinated by what happened and I want to know more, I assume my readers will, too. Every once in a while, homicide cases choose me—not just by tugging on my sleeve, but by figuratively blocking my path so effectively that I have to write them! The story of Joann Ellen Cooper Morrison Hansen is one of those. Each time I looked at it and turned away to write something that seemed easier,

I was contacted, reminded, and persuaded to return to it, by a number of people who didn't even know one another at the time. It happened only a five-minute walk from my home in the little town of Des Moines, Washington, where I lived off and on for about twenty years.

And yet I was unaware of this tragic mystery.

In 2010, I heard from two people whose feelings about this case had become obsessions. My first email came from a man who had gone to school with my older son. Only weeks later, it was another email that cemented what I had to do. Kathleen Huget's message sounded a lot like many I receive from strangers who write that they have unearthed an amazing story that should be a book—but they are wary about telling me the details through the Internet or over the phone.

Frankly, sometimes my response to these people I don't know ends up with my getting trapped by delusional personalities, or those who *think* they have discovered "a sure bestseller and a movie, too." There are usually a dozen reasons why they are wrong. Kathleen Huget was extremely cautious about approaching me until she knew she could trust me to be discreet, and I was just as cautious about meeting her in person. Considering the genre in which I write, that isn't unusual. I fear that if I met every stranger who contacts me, I would be opening a Pandora's box of problems. And I've guessed wrong a number of times.

But somehow I felt a kinship with Kathleen Huget, and this time I was right. Rather than opening Pandora's box I was opening a "hope chest" for many people who have sought to unveil fifty years of lies and bring some kind of peace to a beautiful young woman named Joann.

Chapter One

Kathleen Huget and her husband, Jeff, live in a gated community on a hill east of Kent, Washington. They belong to an elite country club, and they live comfortably. Kathleen was once a flight attendant and Jeff was a varsity football player at the University of Washington. They found each other when they were in their middle years, they're very happily married, and they share interests but allow each other to follow separate paths when it comes to hobbies.

Kathleen is an attractive woman with startling blue eyes, wildly spiky blond hair, and a flair for fashion. Her main profession is as an interior designer—but she's not afraid to get her hands dirty or tackle physical labor. She is also a frustrated detective. When she attended Eastern Washington University in Cheney, she took a number of courses in criminal justice and law. Her internship was with the Spokane County public defender, where her boss was Dick Cease. Cease spent twenty-four years as the public defender, serving as the first head of that office, which was created in 1970. Kathleen did a lot of background checks and research, and she felt she might have found her niche. But her life changed and went in another direction.

Her curiosity, however, did not.

I don't think she would disagree with me when I say she is also something of a psychic, or, more properly, a sensitive. All of us have the capability to listen to other voices in other rooms when there is actually no one there—but most of us don't want to tap into that or open ourselves up to ghostlike entities who have secrets to tell.

Kathleen Huget has a friend who is a Realtor, who has called upon Kathleen a few times to clean out houses where the owners have left abruptly. To make a house appealing to prospective buyers, someone has to sort through what is valuable, what can be donated to charities, and what is ready for a trip to the dump.

In the late summer of 2009, Kathleen—with Jeff's help—agreed to clean up a house in the Kent Valley so that it could go on the market. She had no idea who had lived there, but she was told that the owner had committed suicide on the property. She would have discovered that soon enough by herself; the double garage still had pipes, tubes, and other paraphernalia that had been used to direct carbon monoxide into a vehicle with no ventilation.

As she worked from room to room, she also found a book titled *Final Exit*. The author is Derek Humphry, who started the Hemlock Society, which supported an individual's rights to choose his own time and means of death. When the book was published in 1991, critics were shocked at the number of "recipes" for suicide it held.

In the copy Kathleen held, she saw that someone had used a yellow highlighter to underline several methods Humphry suggested: death by suffocation with a plastic bag, death by barbiturates—after first complaining to a physician that one could not sleep and asking for much milder sleeping pills to allay suspicion and then hoarding them—and, finally, asphyxiation with carbon monoxide using car exhaust.

The third solution was obviously the one the late home-owner had used.

Being in an empty house where a suicide had occurred didn't bother Kathleen Huget, but she was curious about the things that had been left behind. When the draft from an open door blew in, dozens of yellow notepad pages, tacked to every wall, fluttered. They were mostly reminders, scrawled words that she figured someone whose memory was faltering had written.

A man had lived here only weeks before; from the notes, she felt it might be someone who was in poor health and feared his mind was failing him, someone who had given up all hope.

The house where she spent her few weeks working was a nice house, a yellow rambler that was neither modest nor ostentatious. Other than the uninspired and neglected landscaping, the exterior belied the condition of the interior. The lawn and shrubs were neat enough, and there were several sheds and outbuildings at the rear of the home. The house was 1,490 square feet with three bed-rooms and two and a half baths, built on a fifth of an acre.

But the inside of the house on 14th NE in Auburn was

bleak. As Kathleen worked her way from room to room, the things she found were either well used or strange—or both. She realized that the man who had died here had purchased almost everything from thrift stores. Although the house itself was well built and upscale, she thought that the occupant must have fallen on hard times. That happened to a lot of people.

She had no idea that his estate was worth $5 million!

There were no signs that a woman had lived there; it was definitely a bachelor's pad, with no feminine touches to soften its rough edges.

The yellow notes were mostly prosaic: "I must be sure and stay hydrated," and "60 Minutes—Sunday, Channel 7, 7 o'clock."

A few seemed to reflect his state of mind: "I have had my share of trouble and sadness—Man has a [*sic*] astounding ability to survive lifes [*sic*] unhappyiness [*sic*]."

However, one was puzzling; it seemed to be a quote that the dead man had copied.

"Ty: 'I won't stop until I find her bones!'"

What on earth, Kathleen wondered, was that about?

Kathleen Huget learned the name of the dead man: Robert Hansen. A common surname—my mother's maiden name—and also the name of a television reporter who became interested in the story hidden behind the story: Chris Hansen.

Someone had been to the house in Auburn before Kathleen, and they had removed personal papers and anything that might have been of value. She learned that Bob Hansen hadn't been ill or incapacitated. In fact, he'd routinely walked the banks of the Green River for miles every day, picking up cans, bottles, and other garbage that marred the peacefulness of the river that had recently become infamous due to the murders committed there by the Green River Killer.

She wondered what might have caused the desperate depression that led to Hansen's suicide on August 4.

Being inside the yellow house too long could become oppressive, but the weather was nice and Kathleen began to meet neighbors as she carried garbage containers and donation bags out to her SUV. They were all quite open to talking about their late neighbor, although opinions differed.

Hansen's male neighbors spoke of him as being a good guy—a man's man—but the women who lived nearby didn't seem nearly as taken with him. Apparently he had seen females as second-class citizens.

The days passed, and Kathleen felt a presence in the house. It wasn't that someone was actually there, at least not any living entity. If she believed ghosts could harm her, she might have been afraid. She felt that someone was asking her for help, and another presence wanted her to go away.

"I was never frightened," she remembers. "But I felt a residue of rage, the sense that someone or something hated my going through the house. I actually found myself speaking out loud a few times, saying, 'I'm not afraid of you! You don't scare me, and you can't hurt me!'"

Edgar Smith,* the next-door neighbor, told her that he had found his neighbor's body.

"We had a kind of signal system," he said. "When he got up in the morning, he'd come outside and blow this horn he had. It was from an old car he had once, and it went, Ooga! Ooga! When I heard that horn go off, I knew he was all right. He wasn't that young anymore, and, of course, he lived all alone.

"This one morning—August 4—I didn't hear the horn. I looked over at his garage and the windows looked like they were fogged over with smoke," Edgar recalled. "I knew instantly what had happened."

His neighbor had been dead of carbon monoxide poisoning for several hours.

When she began cleaning out the house on Green River Road, Kathleen Huget had no idea of its history and knew nothing about the former owner's life. She and her husband, Jeff, knew the attorney who was representing the estate of the dead man because they belonged to the same country club, but of course he was not at liberty to discuss his late client's affairs, and the Hugets knew better than to ask.

Puzzled, Kathleen googled Bob Hansen's name and date of death on her computer. Hansen, like Olsen and Carlsen, was a common Danish name, and the Northwest is rife with Scandinavians. Finally she found the short video that investigative reporter Chris Hansen had done for NBC News. It was about a son who was suing his deceased father because he believed that his father had killed his mother.

Joann.

Joann Hansen had simply vanished almost fifty years earlier and had never been found—alive or dead.

That was unusual enough to be picked up by news services, and Chris Hansen's segment on it was only a few minutes long, but it was enough to make Kathleen want to know more about the circumstances.

Kathleen Huget felt a cold shiver when she looked at an area behind the house, not a pantry exactly, more of a toolshed. Part of it had a cement floor while another section was only hard-packed dirt.

As she sorted and cleaned to make the house more desirable to potential buyers, she noticed a small bowl of miscellaneous items, a catchall, like we all have, where we throw stamps, paper clips, marbles, pretty pebbles, and myriad things that don't belong anywhere else. The collection in the bowl included a small souvenir bell shaped in the form of the Space Needle, the soaring landmark built for the Seattle World's Fair in 1962.

Another item was a spent bullet—a slug with the hollow point "nose" mushroomed by some impact. It had been fired from a Winchester Model 70 rifle. The casing that had once held the slug was gone. This was a powerful rifle and the bullet would have gone clean through a human being and impacted the first hard surface it hit.

Kathleen also found a list of the guns Bob Hansen had owned, with their serial numbers. They ranged from handguns to rifles and shotguns. He had noted thirty-two guns, and crossed out twenty-two of them. Interestingly, one of the rifles he had either sold or traded—or otherwise disposed of—was a Winchester Model 70 rifle.

Family members had already taken what they wanted from the house and didn't want anything that was left. But for whatever reason, Kathleen saved the bell and the slug from the items in the bowl. She didn't know anything about ballistics herself, but she could ask someone.

An almost obsessive curiosity was growing in her. True, she had a job history as an investigator and freely acknowledges that she loves a mystery, and she felt there was a mystery of major proportions associated with this house full of junk, dust, notes, spiderwebs, and the lingering onus of death by a man's own hand.

There were others who knew what the mystery was, others who had struggled for years to unravel it.

And, thus far, they had failed.

Chapter Two

JOANN

The man who had died in the ranch house in Auburn had had three wives in his life, or rather, three women he considered wives whether their connection was legal or not. The first was Joann (Jo-Ann) Ellen Cooper Morrison,* who was born on July 19, 1932.

Joann and her three sisters—Maxine, Alice, and Glenna Rae—were raised in Auburn, Washington, one of the small towns in the Kent Valley that flourished when the rich loam of the earth there made small farms burst with life. All four of the sisters attended the Auburn Adventist Academy from the forties to the early fifties, and graduated from there. It was a strict, religious school and the Cooper girls lived rather sheltered lives. Joann hated the academy and couldn't wait to graduate.

Joann was a tall slender young woman with long dark hair. She was also quite beautiful. Friends who knew her in her twenties recall her as high-spirited and glamorous.

Her best friend, Patricia Martin—who has always called her Joan—says, "When Joann walked into a room,

215

everyone stopped and looked. She knew she was sexy and she had all the confidence in the world. Actually, she never *walked* into a room, she made an entrance!"

Joann and Pat met when they both lived on J Street in Auburn in 1955. Pat was married to Louie Malesis and Joann to Walter Morrison. Louie and Walter had gone to school together, and they discovered they lived only six blocks apart. Joann had a baby boy—Bobby—and Pat had a baby son, too, Michael. Both women were in their early twenties.

"Back then," Pat remembers, "young families only had one car so most days, when their housework was done, the wives visited, drank coffee, and smoked while our children played."

The two women became really good friends in the midfifties and they shared secrets, the problems of their second pregnancies, and how to make their budgets stretch. A year after they met, Joann and Pat both gave birth to baby girls. Joann named her baby Holly Lou and Pat called her daughter Patti Lou.

They often exchanged babysitting. One night when the baby girls were about a month old, Joann asked Pat if she would babysit for Holly Lou while she and Walter went to the movies.

"I don't know why I said no," Pat says, "but I did. I just didn't feel like babysitting. So Joann and Walter stayed home, and that night Holly Lou died in her sleep—of SIDS, sudden infant death syndrome. I felt so bad for Joann, but I was grateful I hadn't been looking after Holly Lou; SIDS happens, I know, but I would have always felt guilty if she had died at my house."

Walter and Joann Morrison buried their baby girl in a private ceremony at the Mount Auburn Cemetery, and they stopped at Pat and Louie's house that evening. Joann seemed to take the loss with a kind of tragic acceptance, and she and Pat grew even closer than they had been before. They spent almost every day together while their husbands were at work, and Pat did her best to comfort her best friend.

Walter and Joann were complete opposites; he was very laid-back and content to spend all their evenings at home, while Joann longed to go out. She may have been running away from the grief of losing her baby or she may have just been terminally bored with her marriage. One day she admitted to Pat that she had had an affair with a physician in the town where they lived.

Pat was shocked. This warred with everything Joann had been taught by her parents and by most of her teachers at the Adventist Academy. Not all of her instructors had adhered to the religion's tenets, however. Joann had also confessed to Pat that she had lost her virginity to one of her professors. No one else knew, and it had been a shock when the man seduced her.

As lovely as she was, Joann lived a conflicted life. She wanted to be a good mother and have new experiences and a relationship with a man who showed his affection for her. And she wanted to be a "good" woman. She had none of these things after Holly Lou died so suddenly.

The pressure of stifling her feelings backfired on Joann. One night she got up after midnight and went to her bathroom.

"She told me that when she looked into the mirror, her reflection was the face of the devil," Pat recalls. "She got all hysterical and that was the beginning of what we called a nervous breakdown then. Walter took her to a private mental facility in Seattle where they gave her shock treatments.

"When they brought her back to her room, she was still under the effects of sodium pentothal. That was called 'truth serum' in the fifties. Walter sat there and asked her questions. She answered all of them, and some were about whether she had ever been with another man. She confessed her affair with the doctor. When her husband found out about her unfaithfulness, their marriage was over. Right then and there."

Her psychiatrist told Joann that her breakdown had been caused by unresolved guilt. He felt that she wanted to live a different kind of life from what she had been taught was right, and she was fighting within herself. When she accepted that she deserved to be happy, her mental problems lessened.

When Joann was well and left the clinic, she moved into Pat and Louie's home and lived with them until her divorce from Walter was complete. She then found a job with the telephone company in Auburn and moved into an apartment with her son, Bobby.

She continued to date prominent men in the south King County area, including corporate heads and attorneys, but none of her relationships worked out. Some of the men belatedly admitted they were married, and the single men had no intention of settling down.

In time, Pat also found a job with the telephone company.

"Joann and I had so much fun," Pat recalls. "Many nights we went dancing, and Joann was always the belle of the ball."

In 1957, Pat became pregnant for the third time. "That stopped the partying," she remembers. "I quit my job and stayed home with my three children. Joann and I still saw each other every day. We were great friends, and I thought we always would be."

The two young women did remain close even though Joann got married, too; they got together whenever they could and continued to share each other's joys and sadnesses.

They could not know, as none of us can, what lay ahead in the future.

Chapter Three

BOB

According to Robert Milton Hansen, his early life was far more difficult than his first wife's. He was born on October 13, 1924, near Eugene, Oregon, to a family who lived on a dairy farm. Lester and Helen Hansen had to work hard to support their two sons—Kenneth and Robert—and their four daughters. Bob's first faded scrapbook has pictures of him and Kenneth from the time they were two and three years old, a photo of his family posing in front of a Danish Old People's Home in Oregon, others of their dog, the two boys on new tricycles, and as teenagers. From the pictures, Kenneth and Robert seemed to have had a happy life, but no one can see through the walls of someone else's home. There were no pictures of Bob's sisters.

As young teenagers, Robert and Kenneth had to get up before dawn to milk the cows. If they failed to do that or didn't do it fast enough, Bob later told people, their father beat them black and blue. However, the worst humiliation for Bob Hansen was that he didn't have time to clean up afterward and he often went to school with cow manure on his pants. The other students made fun of him and called him names.

"I made up my mind that no one would *ever* make fun of me again," he told a neighbor some sixty years later.

As America plunged into the Great Depression, making a living became harder, and the Hansen family had to move from Oregon to Washington State. Their parents separated—but only so their mother could find work in Seattle. Kenneth went with his mother, Helen, and their sisters, where they started a small bakery in the Fremont district of Seattle. Bob and his father, Lester, moved to the West Hill of Kent, which was mostly covered in old-growth timber. They started from scratch on what Bob called the "Stump Farm."

Bob hated it, and the work clearing the land was back-breaking, but Lester Hansen taught him the basics of carpentry, a skill that would be important to him in years to come.

Still, he felt he never pleased his father, who often asked Bob, "Why can't you be more like Kenneth?"

Bob Hansen recalled his childhood with bitterness. He was a boy and then a man who would always see a glass as half empty.

Beginning with his own father, Bob felt that people treated him badly, cheated him, and tried to get whatever he had away from him. He distrusted almost everyone, although he could put on a jovial mask that hid his real feelings.

He told the few people he confided in that he could not

wait to get away from the Stump Farm, but, most of all, he wanted to leave his father far behind.

Bob grew to be six feet four inches tall, much taller than Kenneth and their father, and he weighed well over two hundred pounds. In his baby pictures, his hair was very light—what the Danes call "towhead"—and it was cut as if a bowl had been put over his head. At eighteen, it was still blond, but thick and wavy, and it added to his tanned good looks.

As soon as he graduated from high school, Bob joined the army. It was 1943, and the Second World War changed everyone's lives. Bob was sent to Calcutta, India.

Although Bob saved the photos of his family that were taken up to the time he and Kenneth were about twelve and fourteen, there are far fewer family photographs as the years passed. And then, there are many pages of shots Bob took in India, usually of the natives who lived there, but occasionally he posed with the dark-haired Calcuttans while someone else took the pictures. One gets the sense that he really enjoyed his first trip outside the United States.

He was quite good-looking at twenty-one. Even so, none of his photos taken in India were of women, although he had dozens of pictures of dead poisonous snakes.

Bob Hansen was sent to the front lines, serving under General "Vinegar Joe" Stilwell, as the Allied Forces fought to regain access to the Burma Road, which was overrun by the Japanese army. Indeed, Hansen's scrapbook has snapshots of "Stilwell Road" and the town of Ledo. Indian, British, and Chinese forces combined to build the

Ledo Road, which would eventually intersect with the Burma Road. It was a project that was essential in defeating the Japanese.

It was also extremely dangerous, and Bob didn't enjoy his time in India as much as he had earlier. Many years later, Bob told one of his few close friends, Marvin Milosevich, that he escaped his frontline duty—but he didn't say how he managed that. He may have deserted; he may have only talked his way into a safer assignment.

When he left the army, Bob Hansen journeyed into the far North, and found jobs on fishing ships in Alaska. It was—and still is—a dangerous, exhausting occupation where ships and men are lost almost every year as they fight the violent sea and icy winds. But it paid well, and Bob Hansen felt he could withstand even the frightening storms that sent waves crashing over the bows of the ships he was on. As he would feel most of his life, he was invincible.

Today the television show *The Deadliest Catch* draws thousands of viewers. It accurately depicts the kind of life Hansen lived when he set out to sea in Alaska.

In the off-season, he spent time in the Seattle area. Bob was thirty-two before he married for the first time. He was certainly as attracted to women as they were to him—at first. But for some reason, most of his romantic relationships ended suddenly and permanently.

Even her best friends don't know exactly where Bob Hansen met Joann Cooper Morrison. But they began to date in the midfifties.

Bob seemed to be a good catch for a divorced woman with a small son. He was definitely single, he was tall and good-looking, and he obviously made a good living. He wasn't the most sentimental guy in the world, however. His view of women resembled attitudes held by men generations earlier. He saw them as less intelligent than men and felt their place was to be obedient and subservient.

At some point, Bob proposed to Joann and they got married. Just *when* their wedding took place is a matter of conjecture. Some legal papers set the date as April 13, 1956. It's more likely that they married on April 13, *1957*. Patricia Martin recalls that Joann was pregnant when they got married; Joann gave birth to her oldest child with Bob, Nick, in November 1957.

Whatever their legal status was, in the beginning the Hansens lived in one of the first homes Bob owned—in Des Moines, Washington. It was a small white house, located behind a veterinarian's clinic, and it had a bird's-eye view of Puget Sound three blocks west.

Joann spent fishing seasons alone with Bobby and the baby, Nick. Bob was still spending months away, fishing and crabbing in Alaska. But when Joann became pregnant with their second child—Ty—Bob realized that his Alaskan adventures were coming to a close. Despite its hardships, he had enjoyed the challenge of fighting the angry, freezing sea that gave up salmon, crab, and bottom fish only grudgingly.

Since his days on the Stump Farm, Bob Hansen had been interested in construction, and he began as an apprentice carpenter in the South King County area.

He had native intelligence and he was as strong as an ox. He set his sights on a career as a contractor. Gradually, he learned how to build almost anything, and he soon had all the good jobs he wanted with construction firms.

Bob had planned to build his family another—larger—home in the near future.

And he did.

He also began to look for cheap houses to buy where he could leverage his investments with low down payments and long-term contracts. As soon as he bought property, he found renters, and their monthly payments took care of his mortgages.

Former tenants recall that he wasn't an understanding landlord—to say the least. If they failed to pay the rent on time and were even a few days late, he banged on their front doors and told them to get out—at once. He wasn't concerned with thirty-day notices, or interested in their excuses. He was such a large man, and he intimidated most people.

Surprisingly, Bob Hansen couldn't understand why his evacuated renters left his apartments and houses in bad shape. His friends who were landlords—and who followed rental statutes dictated by the state—never had that much damage. Bob, along with his sons Nick and Ty, spent a lot of time painting and repairing empty rentals.

It was during this period in the sixties that Hansen was approached by a man named Milosevich who wanted to hire him to build a spec house. Bob agreed to the project, but he said he would need a helper.

That was when the elder Milosevich suggested that his son, Marv, who was about twenty, would make a good assistant in building the spec house.

"Bob Hansen was a nonunion employer," Marv remembers, "and I got paid a dollar fifty an hour when the union rate was three fifty, but he was a good teacher, and I learned everything there was to know about the construction business. My wife, LaVonne, would ask me why I kept working for Bob when I could get so much more money from a union contractor, and I explained that nobody else could train me to be a contractor myself the way Bob did. I was getting an education, even while I was losing money."

LaVonne agrees, after almost fifty years of marriage, that Marv's success in building and real estate started with his working with Bob Hansen. That is not to say, however, that LaVonne liked Bob. She tolerated him because Marv liked him.

Privately, LaVonne felt, "He was the poorest excuse for a human being I ever knew!"

Bob Hansen was a fishing and hunting fanatic. Blood sports. He often returned from his hunting trips on the eastern side of the Cascade Mountains with the still-bleeding bodies of the animals he'd shot roped to his truck fenders.

Everything living was eventually lined up in Bob's gun sights. His photo albums include scores of shots of Bob Hansen and the things he killed: deer, wolves, elk, bald eagles, strings of mammoth fish.

One time, Bob organized a hunting trip to Montana with nine of the men he knew, including Marv Milosevich.

"We went to the Silver Creek Campground," Milose-vich recalls, "and the fishing was great, but after five days, I think every guy there hated him. Bob had to control *everything*! He planned the menus, cooked the food, or told the guy cooking how to do it, decided when we'd eat, when and where we would fish—*everything*!"

None of the nine—except for Marv—ever fished with Bob Hansen again.

"I went fishing with him but I had to keep him at arm's length," Marv said with a grin. "I insisted on taking two boats. We'd keep in touch by radio or walkie-talkies, but we weren't on the same boat."

Hansen never questioned why the man he considered to be his best friend wouldn't spend even a few hours alone with him. Marv had had enough of Bob's controlling nature, but he still liked Bob and felt obligated to him.

Chapter Four

A SMALL-TOWN MYSTERY

It's very difficult for me to believe that even though we lived in the same town, it took decades before I learned about Joann Hansen's disappearance. And then suddenly information about her vanishing seemed to come at me from every direction during the same time period.

I was approached by both Ty Hansen, Joann's youngest son, and Kathleen Huget. They didn't know each other—they had never even met. *I* didn't know that Ty had gone to school with my older son, Andy, and had played baseball with him. Nor did I know that my other children had been acquainted with the three Hansen children.

By the time I finally heard of the tragedy, which had occurred the year before we moved to Des Moines, almost five decades had passed. I found myself feeling guilty and regretful that I hadn't been aware of it. With my background as a police officer and a welfare caseworker, I know I would have found some way to help Joann's children. Our lives crisscrossed so often in the intervening years that it seems impossible I *didn't* know them.

In the early 1940s, my in-laws purchased a beach shack in Des Moines for $700. When they retired to Southern California in 1963, my then-husband, Bill Rule, wanted to go back to the small town where he grew up. Even though that little structure had been remodeled over the years, our house wasn't exactly weatherproof. It was the first solid object windstorms blowing northeast over Puget Sound would hit. The walls were still stuffed with old newspapers for insulation, and in the winter the wind blew through a hundred cracks, making the windows facing the sound rattle. Indeed, there were even a few times when the single-pane glass blew out and our whole living room was left in shambles.

When Bill and I and our three older children moved in, I was pregnant with my youngest son, Mike. It was summer and we all loved to roam the beach below the sandbank and across the street from our house.

Des Moines had only 4,500 residents in 1963; the beach, a Covenant Church camp, and a number of church-sponsored retirement homes were the main attractions. Main Street was about four blocks long, with a supermarket on either end and a friendly, small grocery store in between. It was to be expected that we soon knew many of the people who lived in Des Moines, and most of the mysteries, folklore, ghosts, and unexplained happenings in town.

And there were many.

Sixth Avenue was haunted. It may still be, for all I know. Through the years, tragedy stalked the residents of Sixth Avenue. At the north end of the street, a hundred years ago, a minister named Daddy Draper once oversaw an orphanage in an aged structure. Its paint had long since worn off. Over the years, a number of motley tenants moved in and out of the building. Moving toward the south end, almost every home had suffered a tragedy. Old-timers could list more than a dozen heartrending events.

There was one home where my daughter Leslie wouldn't babysit after her first night there. When the sun went down, anyone in the house—including myself—could hear what clearly seemed to be the anguished sound of a woman weeping, her cries spreading outside farther and farther the darker it got. More than that, unseen hands seemed to push the mantel away from the fireplace in the home. Our dogs refused to go in the crawl space beneath the house, and, oddly, we heard glass jars rolling down there—even when there was no room for that to happen.

Across the street, a psychotic son—whose "episodes" invariably happened during the winter holidays—killed his mother and then cut her head off before setting fire to their house; the daughter of the family next door was shot and left a quadriplegic; another family close by had been in a horrible accident that killed their teenage son and crippled them; and one could only guess at some of the tragedies that had brought orphans to Daddy Draper's.

The odd couple who lived in a ramshackle house on the corner next to where the weeping woman cried kept old Christmas trees and a dead dog on their front porch. And when they shopped at one of the supermarkets, they literally had a layer of dust on them—even on their hair and clothing. All of us gave them a wide berth in the checkout line.

There were true stories of several people who had drowned in the sound at the southern end of Sixth, including a scrawny fisherman who gave a ride in his rowboat to an immensely fat woman. Her weight caused the boat to tip. While her fat insulated her from the cold waters, *he* perished from hypothermia. She caught pneumonia but she survived.

Below our house, Cliff Avenue, on the edge of the sound, had been the burial ground for Native Americans in the nineteenth century, along with their canoes, intricately woven baskets, blue beads, and other treasures. A lot of people believed that they, too, haunted Des Moines after their graves were disturbed. (My former father-in-law, the Methodist preacher's son, was one of the bad boys who saved souvenirs. As an adult, he gave them to the Museum of History and Industry in Seattle.)

Now Des Moines has dozens of expensive condos along the beach, and I doubt that new residents have any idea about the old folktales.

Near where Joann and Bob Hansen lived in their first home—on Eighth Street two blocks east—there was a fatal fire on Christmas Eve, and a triple murder, each of them on a separate Christmas.

One had to be a student of local history and immensely curious—as I was, and am—to know of all these events. But, as much as I search my memory, to the best of my knowledge I never met either Bob or Joann Hansen, although I'm sure we must have passed each other in the supermarkets, at Little League games, or at school events.

And despite my interest in local history, I had never heard of their story until Kathleen Huget and Ty Hansen contacted me within weeks of each other. And independently, some of Ty's friends also got in touch with me. This was in the late summer of 2010, and what they wanted to tell me about had happened *forty-eight years* earlier!

As a stack of albums, legal papers, narratives written by friends, and newspaper clippings were delivered to me, I was startled to see school photos identical to some I have saved in my children's scrapbooks. In one photo of Mrs. Rilda Moses's private kindergarten, my younger daughter, Leslie, is sitting in the front row, wearing the red corduroy and paper-doll patterned dress I sewed for her back when we were poor and couldn't afford to shop at department stores.

I recognized several of her friends in the 1964 group photo, but Joann and Bob Hansen's first child, Nick, was in the back row; I never knew Nick.

Chapter Five
A DOOMED MARRIAGE

Joann gave birth to Nick Hansen at Auburn General Hospital on November 7, 1957. He weighed six pounds, ten and a half ounces, and he had dark hair like his mother. Someone pasted the hospital card that identified his bassinet in the newborn ward into the same album with his father's earliest photographs. It was probably Joann; she loved being a mother, and she adored Nick as she did her older son, Bobby.

If Joann had any reason to regret her relationship with Bob Hansen, there was no way she could change the direction her life was headed. For three years in a row, like clockwork, she became pregnant each February. She had her daughter, Kandy Kay, in November 1958, and her youngest son, Ty, in November 1959.

She loved her children and she gloried in being a mother. But by this time if Joann Hansen could have escaped from her marriage, she would have. Things that happened behind the walls of her home were sometimes so awful that she didn't tell even Patricia Martin. But when the burden got too frightening, she confided in Pat, and her best friend had a horrifying glimpse of the invisible prison Joann lived in.

Of course Joann had brought her first son, Bobby Morrison, with her when she married Bob Hansen. She had hoped that they would make a happy blended family. But her hopes evaporated one day when she and Bob went shopping for groceries. Bobby was somewhere between six and seven then, and he pointed to some bottles of pop—cream soda—and asked Bob to buy them.

"What's the name of those?" Bob asked the little boy repeatedly.

Bobby couldn't read yet, and he had no idea what the brand and the name of the pop were. He cringed as Bob asked him over and over. He didn't know why that made his stepfather so angry.

"When they got home," Patricia Martin remembers, tears filling her eyes, "Bob took that child down to the basement and he beat him black and blue—just because he couldn't say the brand of the soda pop he wanted.

"Joann phoned me and asked me to be sure no one was at my house because she needed to come over, and she didn't want anyone to see what had happened. I was there alone when she drove up with Bobby. He was only six years old, and he was so badly injured that she had to carry him in. Naturally, I said he could stay with us.

"I wanted so much to raise Bobby. After what Bob Hansen did to him, he couldn't go back to that house.

"Joann was pregnant again, and she didn't know what to do. I kept Bobby at my house for two months, but finally, his own father—Walt Morrison—wanted custody of him, and we had to let him go. Of all Joann's kids, I sometimes think that Bobby was damaged the most, and that's saying a lot. Joann grieved over that terribly, but she felt that she had no other choice."

It hadn't taken very long before Joann Hansen realized that Bob Hansen was a cruel, controlling man. He was just plain mean, and he viewed her as a possession—not as an equal partner. With her children as hostages, she was afraid to leave Bob. She had no income of her own and she didn't know how she could take care of them, or if he would even let her go.

In his odd bullying way, Bob Hansen seemed to care for their three children. She didn't think he would hurt them physically, but she was sure he wouldn't let her take them with her if she left.

Bob had no such compunction about hurting Joann. She was a battered wife long before victims felt they could speak out about what was happening inside their homes. Bob was smart enough to hit her where it didn't show—on her belly, her legs, her breasts. And it didn't matter if she was pregnant or not. It was a miracle that she didn't miscarry any of her pregnancies.

The obstetrician who had delivered her children, Dr. Fred Hahn, was horrified when he saw her breasts were so bruised that they were black, and he took photographs of her injuries. Joann's beatings were not isolated events; she almost always had a bruise someplace on her body, but

Bob was careful where he hit her and her clothes covered most of her injuries.

Joann could never be sure *what* would make Bob angry, so she tiptoed around trying to sense what he would do if she said the wrong thing. He had a hair-trigger temper and he could explode without any warning.

"As I said," Patricia Martin began, "Joann and I had both worked for the telephone company, and once we were invited to a company dance—with our husbands, of course. It was a chance for Joann to go out for a change, and Bob said he would go along. She wasn't allowed to spend any money without asking him, but this one time before the dance, she and I were walking along in downtown Auburn and we saw these feathered earrings in a store window. They were very popular at the time. Joann had a red sequined dress she was going to wear to the dance, and there were these great red feather earrings. I bought black ones to match my dress, and I told Joann she should get the red ones. She said she didn't dare—so I told her to buy them, and we'd say that I bought them for her."

Pat remembers that Joann was so beautiful and sexy that it didn't really matter what she wore, but, given a choice, Joann almost always chose red.

"She walked like a model—she practiced with books between her thighs so she just glided instead of walking."

Bob and Joann had Pat and her husband, Louie, and another couple over for drinks before the dance that night. Joann was getting ready when they arrived. In a few minutes, she walked into the living room. She was a knockout in her red sequined dress, and everything seemed to go smoothly until Bob noticed the red feather earrings and asked her where she got them.

"Joann said, 'Pat bought them for me,' but he'd already found the sales slip," Pat recalls. "He called her into the bedroom, and we could hear him knocking her into the walls. We could hear Joann saying, 'No . . . please, no!' To this day, I don't know why none of us said anything or tried to stop him. I guess we were afraid of embarrassing Joann. And then—in those days—people, especially men, didn't interfere with other people's marriages.

"And to tell the truth, everyone was afraid of Bob Hansen."

After a while, Bob came out of the bedroom, shutting the door behind him.

"Joann decided not to go tonight," he said almost smugly.

When Pat saw Joann the next day, her face was purpled and puffy with bruises.

Bob was pathologically jealous, although it was doubtful that he had any reason to be. Joann had dated a lot of men when she was single, but she'd been really happy when she first settled down with Bob. She welcomed a secure relationship or, rather, what she believed would be a secure marriage. Beyond that, since she was pregnant for three straight years, with three small children to care for, she wouldn't have been able to cheat on Bob—even if she'd wanted to.

Her strongest reason not to stray, however, was that, all too soon, she was scared to death of him.

The Hansens' children were also terrified of Bob. As they grew, they learned that their father's moods could be unpredictable and often violent. They used to line up on the brown couch beneath a picture window in the new house Bob built and watch for his truck at the end of the day. It wasn't because they were happy to have their daddy come home; it was because they were afraid.

Like their mother, they were never quite sure what might set him off. He beat them regularly; his punishments were more than spankings. Nick, Kandy Kay, and Ty were so small, and he was a very large, powerful man.

Patricia Martin knew better than to visit Joann when Bob was home, but they managed to get together on afternoons when they knew he was far away on a construction job. One day Pat's son and Joann's oldest son, Bobby Morrison, were wrestling around and accidentally knocked over the Christmas tree.

"We all panicked," Pat remembers, "but somehow we got it back up and the ornaments on the tree just before Bob came home. He never knew about it."

Bob always wanted to have a big Christmas. He had his camera handy, and he took photos of everyone opening presents and of the many decorations Joann had put up. Her parents and sisters weren't invited, however. Bob didn't care for them, and he frowned whenever Joann wanted to visit with them. It is a classic ploy for abusive husbands and boyfriends: separate the women from their families and friends so they will have no one to run to.

* * *

There were so many times when Bob humiliated Joann.

On a rare occasion, Pat and her husband, Louie, who was a police officer in Auburn, Washington, joined a group of people that included Bob and Joann for a night of dancing.

The Spanish Castle, a dance hall that dated back to the twenties, stood on the corner of Pacific Highway South—"Old 99"—and the busy Kent Des Moines Road. The dusty yellow stucco structure was long past its glory days when big name bands played there, but it still featured local bands that drew crowds. It was only three miles or so from the brown house where Joann and Bob lived.

The group was having a good time on that Saturday night until Joann apparently said or did something that made Bob mad.

"He knocked her right out of her chair, onto the floor," Pat says. "She was hurt and very embarrassed. People stared for a couple of minutes, and then they went back to drinking and dancing."

Nobody reported it to the police.

Fifty years later, it's hard to imagine that women were considered chattel by some men then—that they could be savagely abused in front of witnesses and no one interfered. But the term "battered woman" had yet to be coined. Women were humiliated and—more often than not—afraid to come forward; the majority of wives didn't work and were dependent on their husbands financially.

Certainly, there are legions of abused women today but at least there are safe places and support groups where they can run if they have the courage to leave.

Joann Hansen had few options.

She was an immaculate housekeeper and a good cook who kept within the budget Bob allowed for groceries. But their house on the road to Saltwater State Park in Des Moines wasn't homey. The wood floors were dark; Bob liked the brown furniture, his trophies of dead animals mounted on the walls, and his cabinets filled with guns.

Both Bob and Joann lived behind masks, trying to keep their secrets from prying eyes. He wanted his friends and other people to view him as a good family man. Like his own parents' scrapbook, where he and his brother Ken smiled for the camera, the younger Hansens' album is full of photos of them and their children. Bob and Joann's "wedding" photo depicts a willowy bride with an orchid corsage feeding cake to her handsome groom. There are the birth announcements, the babies' nursery identification cards, baby pictures, family reunions, snapshots of Bob and the kids on one outing or another, all looking joyful.

They could easily have been chosen for the cover of the *Saturday Evening Post*.

No one who hadn't seen her cuts and bruises could have guessed that the beautiful Joann, who still made an entrance when she and Bob had their infrequent dates, was so afraid behind her carefully constructed facade.

Bob was very successful in real estate investments and in construction. He worked hard and he was shrewd when it came to buying property. Although he wouldn't allow Joann to buy anything without his permission, his family always had food and shelter. As obsessed as he was with hunting and fishing, their large freezer in the basement was well stocked with elk, venison, and all kinds of fish. Bob smoked much of the salmon he caught, and he made ground venison quite palatable by mixing it with beef fat.

Again and again, Joann tried to convince herself that somehow he would soften if she just tried harder or found the right combination that pleased him.

Sadly, the scenario she envisioned was hopeless.

One evening in the early part of 1962, Joann prepared some trout that Bob had caught. She, Bob, and their children were sitting at their trestle table with benches on either side. Joann, as always, sat closest to the kitchen so she could jump up and get whatever Bob wanted. She was afraid she might be pregnant again, but that was no guarantee that she was safe from physical abuse.

As they ate in silence, Bob noticed that she had peeled the skin off her portion of fish and pushed it to the side of her plate.

"Eat the skin," he ordered her.

"But I don't like the skin," she protested.

"Eat it!"

"I can't," she said. "It will make me sick."

Suddenly he swung one muscular arm and knocked her off the bench.

This was just one of many times when Joann had done something, all unaware, that tapped into Bob's boiling rage. Sobbing, she ran to the kitchen while Nick, Kandy Kay, and Ty sat, stunned and confused, at the table.

Bob left the table and returned with a two-shot Derringer pistol. "See this," he instructed his three small children. "This is what we're going to use to kill Mommy with."

The children would not remember this, but Joann heard it, and she knew he meant it. She told Pat Martin she was very afraid Bob might kill her.

Chapter Six
ESCAPE

It was too much.

When Bob Hansen left for the construction site the next morning—July 25—Joann gathered up her children and fled to Patricia Martin's house. Pat hid Joann's blue Chevrolet so Bob wouldn't know where she and the children were, and Joann got a restraining order that forbade his coming close to her. She believed that if he did, she could call the police and they would protect her.

She was adamant that she wanted a divorce, even though she was fearful of Bob's reaction. She and the children drove back to Pat's house.

Joann didn't know any attorneys or where to start. She knew a Realtor in Auburn who shared his office with an attorney named Luther Martin (no relation to Patricia Martin). As fate would have it, Martin was out of town for some time. But she saw another lawyer's shingle right across the street. Determined, she asked the Realtor to take her over and introduce her to Duncan Bonjorni.

If any attorney could have helped Joann, it was Bonjorni. A former justice of the peace and police judge, Bonjorni was both brilliant and fearless. He had paid his way through law school by working forty-eight hours a week, much of the time as a Capitol policeman in Olympia.

He studied Joann Hansen.

"I knew her husband," the now-retired Bonjorni recalls. "He was a mean son of a bitch. There's no other way to put it. He appeared before me once when I was a judge—he got into a shouting match with another driver at a place in Renton we called 'suicide corner.' I remember that he cut the other guy off, and they argued. When the other driver pulled away, Bob followed him, caught up with him, and took out a crowbar or tire jack and started hitting his car, breaking the windshield and denting the vehicle, and he was threatening the guy."

Police were called and Bonjorni sentenced Hansen to twenty-four hours in jail, knowing he'd made an enemy. "I was too dumb to be afraid of him, I guess. But I still wouldn't have wanted to meet him in a dark alley. His hands were as big as hams."

Now, in late April 1962, Duncan Bonjorni asked Joann Hansen: "Are there any marks on you?"

Without saying a word, Joann stood up, removed her sleeveless blouse, and lowered her pedal pushers.

Bonjorni had seen cases of spousal abuse before—but nothing like this. "She was covered with bruises. She had one huge bruise—as big as a saucer—on her left side. Her husband had hit her mostly on that side—her ribs, her breasts, her thigh," Bonjorni remembers. "She didn't have a mark on her face—or anywhere that showed."

Knowing how big Bob Hansen was, the attorney realized that Joann would have "looked like a small child" next to him.

"She was tremendously afraid of her husband," Bonjorni recalls. "But she had a lot of spirit. Even though she was frightened, she didn't come across as downtrodden or intimidated."

Duncan Bonjorni agreed to represent Joann in a divorce proceeding. They would talk about money later.

Now in his mideighties, Bonjorni's memory is impeccable.

Asked if Joann Hansen was attractive, he nodded. "Any man who still had a heartbeat would take a second look at her."

"Were you interested in her romantically?" I asked him bluntly.

He shook his head. "No. But she needed someone to help her get away from Bob Hansen."

With Bonjorni's help, Joann filed preliminary papers seeking a divorce. She said she'd been married to Bob for more than five years, and gave her wedding date as April 1956. She might have fudged a year or it could have been only a typo in the document; Nick was born in November 1957.

Joann had signed a sort of prenuptial agreement back in the midfifties. The early agreement specified that, if they ever divorced, Bob would retain ownership of the four houses he'd bought before their union.

By 1962, there were more than fifteen properties, and his wealth had grown considerably. Joann hoped he would let her have a house where she and their children could live, and that he would pay child support. She could get a part-time job if she had to.

Anything would be better than constantly living in fear, and worrying about how Bob's rages were affecting Nick, Kandy Kay, and Ty.

On May 2, Bonjorni filed Joann's divorce complaint. The first sections listed known facts—date of marriage, names and birthdates of children, and their assets, which mainly consisted of the rental houses that Bob had purchased over the years. She had the Chevrolet Biscayne, and he had two trucks and $2,500 worth of tools and equipment. Their furniture was estimated at only $500.

Their property, however, was noted to be worth over $300,000—a very large amount in 1962. They had no debt except for mortgage payments, which were covered by rental payments.

Joann didn't hold back when her reasons for seeking a divorce were presented to the court.

"[That] Defendant Robert M. Hansen has treated Plaintiff Joann E. Hansen with extreme cruelty, rendering her life burdensome, and making the continuance of this marriage no longer possible. That, in particular, Defendant has kicked, beat, and struck Plaintiff and threatened her life in the presence of witnesses. That Defendant regularly beats Plaintiff severely, and does so in front of the minor children of the parties hereto. That said beatings are without reason and provocation, and are severe enough to inflict large painful bruises, making it impossible for Plaintiff to sleep, and causing her to be in extreme pain and unable to perform her usual duties and move about normally. That further, said Defendant beat and abused Plaintiff's child by a prior marriage to the degree that she was forced to relinquish custody of said child to her former husband. That as a result of the actions of Defendant, Plaintiff has lost all love and affection for said Defendant, and it is no longer possible for parties hereto to live together as husband and wife, or at all."

For more than five years, Joann had managed all of the Hansens' rental properties and kept the books. Duncan Bonjorni told her that the original size of Bob Hansen's estate had undoubtedly increased greatly in value due, in large part, to her efforts. She deserved to have an equitable distribution of their assets in any divorce settlement.

She also asked for a "full, absolute, complete decree of divorce," custody of their children—with reasonable visitation rights for their father—support and education of the minor children until they came of age, the household furniture, her car, and attorneys' fees.

Since Joann had no funds, Bonjorni asked for a temporary order giving her the Chevrolet Biscayne to drive, support and maintenance, the furniture, and the use of one of the many houses the couple owned.

In response, Bob pleaded poverty, saying that after he paid all of his mortgages each month, he only had $400 left from the rentals. But Joann, who had kept the records, knew he cleared $1,125 a month.

Bob Hansen hired his own attorney and fought Joann furiously over division of their assets. He harassed her constantly and made her life miserable. To upset her, he gave lighted cigarettes to Nick, Kandy Kay, and Ty—even though they were all under five.

In that summer of 1962, she had no real place to live. She took the children and went to visit one of her sisters in Spokane for a while. When she felt they might be over-staying their welcome, she moved back to Pat's house.

Duncan Bonjorni helped Joann file a tougher restraining order meant to protect her if Bob should try to locate her. The order was issued on August 8, 1962, and Joann heaved a sigh of relief. Maybe she could get away from Bob and have a new life where she wasn't afraid anymore.

She almost believed that was true. Today we have learned that restraining orders aren't worth the paper they're printed on as far as safety for the person who holds them. Yes, they can cause a stalker or angry spouse to be arrested if they disobey the orders, but many of them aren't deterred. If a man—or a woman—is obsessed with someone, a court order doesn't help. Too often, they make the stalker furious and their targets are in even more danger.

Joann and the children stayed at Patricia Martin's house in Auburn for two weeks, weeks when she was able to relax a little. But it was a temporary measure. She knew she couldn't hide from Bob forever, and he was sure to fig-ure out where she was, anyway. Probably, he already knew. Joann wasn't close to many people, but Pat had always been there to help her when things turned rocky. He would guess that she had run to Pat for shelter.

Forty-eight years later, Patricia Martin still feels guilty that she couldn't do more to help her best friend. They sat at Pat's kitchen table, drank coffee, and smoked endless cigarettes, as they debated what Joann should do. Both of them were naive about restraining orders. Joann wanted so much to be back in her own home, and Bob owned plenty of houses where he could live.

The restraining order said she could go back to the large brown house in Des Moines. Bob was supposedly living in the smaller white house a few blocks away.

Pat urged Joann to go home—to live the way she deserved to live. "He's not there, Joann," she said. "You'll see. You have made the first move to be free, and now you can build on that."

Patricia Martin honestly felt that she was giving Joann the best advice possible. No one should live in hiding, afraid of shadows. After all, Joann had a restraining order.

One thing Pat has never forgotten—and it niggles at her. "Joann begged me to go home with her, and stay until she got the locks changed," Pat says. "But I was too afraid of Bob. I knew he resented me for taking Joann's side and giving her a place to run to."

It was Friday, August 10, 1962. Joann had made plans with her mother and her three sisters to visit the World's Fair in Seattle the next day. She really looked forward to being with them again. Bob had forbidden her to tell their three children that they *had* aunts and cousins and grandparents on their mother's side. Her world had grown smaller and smaller, without her realizing how confining it was—until it was too late.

As Joann prepared to leave, Patricia Martin hugged her and Nick, Kandy Kay, and Ty. They would be five, four, and three in three months.

"Joann had five dollars," Pat remembers. "I know she wanted to buy some hair dye and she didn't even have enough for that. So I gave her enough to make up the difference."

Pat asked Joann to call her as soon as she got home. It wasn't that far from Auburn to Des Moines. She watched them drive away, and then went inside to wait for Joann's call.

"It was about forty-five minutes before she called me, and she said everything was okay—that she was 'all right.' She even thought it was probably a good decision for her to go home. She was feeling not so scared, and beginning to relax. We were both relieved . . .

"Suddenly, Joann said, 'Pat! Wait a minute—'

"And then she said, 'Oh, Pat! He's in the basement! Oh, God—he's here, he's coming up—'"

Joann started screaming as if she was terrified, as Pat frantically asked her what was wrong.

"But then the phone went dead," Pat remembers, and it's obvious Pat is right back where she was forty-eight years ago.

Patricia Martin dialed Joann's phone number, only to get a busy signal. She kept redialing, but for half an hour, no one answered.

After so many calls, Bob Hansen finally picked up the phone, his voice calm. Pat asked to speak to Joann.

"Stop that crap, Pat," Bob said. "You know she's with you."

But, of course, she wasn't. Joann Hansen was gone.

Pat wanted to call the police right away, but her husband discouraged her, explaining that adults couldn't be reported as missing until they'd been gone for forty-eight hours. And she didn't know which department to call. The King County Sheriff's Office or the Des Moines Police Department.

As it turned out, even if she had filed a missing report on that Friday afternoon in August 1962, it probably would have made no difference.

Chapter Seven
AUGUST 11, 1962

Patricia Martin held the tiniest hope that Joann Hansen had escaped and found some safe haven other than her own house and spent the night there. That seemed highly unlikely; Joann wouldn't have let her worry all night without finding a way to check in.

And then there was the outing where Joann was supposed to meet her mother and her three sisters at the Seattle World's Fair on that Saturday after her Friday disappearance. Joann had really been looking forward to that, especially since she didn't get to see her family very often. Bob wanted nothing to do with her relatives, but the restraining order had given her the courage to arrange to meet them.

But they had gone to the designated spot where they were to meet on August 11. They waited and waited, and she didn't show up. In case they had the time wrong, they kept returning to the meeting spot, but she was never there.

Patricia Martin didn't know what to do. She called

Duncan Bonjorni and told him that she didn't know what had happened to Joann and she feared for her safety.

Duncan called the King County Sheriff's Office and persuaded them to send out an All Points Bulletin if Joann didn't show up in twenty-four hours. Adults who disappear often do so because they want to leave, and police departments set a time period before they will act on a missing report—*unless* there are overt signs that the person has been injured such as blood, bullet holes, or signs of a struggle.

The brown house showed no signs that anything violent had happened there.

Although Pat's husband was a police officer in Auburn, the last place Joann was known to be was in Des Moines.

Louie Malesis warned Pat that he doubted that any police department would investigate a case without a body.

She soon found that he was right. Indeed, the first time prosecutors in Washington State would win a case where there was no body of an alleged victim would be in 2000, almost forty years in the future. Even then, the victim had been missing for nine years before a gutsy prosecutor, Marilyn Brenneman, agreed to file murder charges against the husband of the missing woman. Brenneman won that landmark case. (See *Empty Promises: Ann Rule's Crime Files,* Vol. 7.)

Patricia Martin was a woman on fire who refused to stand by and see Joann Hansen's disappearance be ignored. She contacted the Des Moines Police Department, then located in the upstairs of an old wooden building owned by the Benevolent and Protective Order of Elks who occupied the first floor. There were only a handful of commissioned officers in the department in 1962.

When she tried to report Joann as a probable murder victim, she was told that the Des Moines police could not investigate a suspected homicide where there was no body to validate that a missing person had died of homicidal violence.

Next, she called the *Seattle Post-Intelligencer*, one of Seattle's two newspapers, a publication that was known for its probing investigative articles.

But Pat was stymied when a reporter told her that they could possibly write an "unsolved" murder case *if* there was a body. "Without a body, we can't write anything," he finished.

"I knew there was no place Joann could have gone," Pat says today. "She had no money except for about six dollars and fifty cents. She loved her kids so much that nothing could have made her abandon them—nothing beyond her own death. She would have been so worried about what would happen to them if they were alone with Bob."

Duncan Bonjorni was troubled when he heard from a young woman who had babysat with Nick, Kandy Kay, and Ty the night their mother disappeared. She and a girl-friend had looked through Joann's closet, admiring her clothes—especially a sparkling blue cocktail dress that had been one of Joann's favorites.

"When the babysitter looked for that dress the next day," Bonjorni recalls, "it was gone. I sometimes wonder if Bob put it on Joann after he killed her. No way to prove it, though."

There was another possibility; perhaps the self-made widower had deliberately removed the cocktail dress, hoping it would validate his story that Joann had left him to run off and live the high life with another man.

Belatedly, Bob Hansen filed a missing person report on Joann on August 15. Joann had been gone five days, and he may have realized that spouses who don't even attempt to find their missing mates become suspect in the eyes of law enforcement.

Chapter Eight

A NASTY DIVORCE—IN ABSENTIA

Weeks after she disappeared, Joann's Chevy Biscayne was located in the lower Queen Anne Hill neighborhood in Seattle. So there *was* something left behind, but it's doubtful it was Joann who abandoned it. It was filthy and cluttered with junk, food wrappers, cigarette butts, and empty bottles. The windows were open and the interior was covered with dust. All the tires had gone flat.

"Joann kept her car immaculate," Patricia Martin insists. "She would never have let it get in that condition."

There were no usable fingerprints in the Chevrolet, nor was there any physical evidence that might have given the Western Washington Crime Lab something to examine with the tools they had in 1962. The use of DNA in solving crimes or identifying people was more than thirty years in the future, and there was no nationwide clearinghouse for fingerprints, nothing like the AFIS (Automated Fingerprint Identification System) structure that exists now. In a sense, 1962 was in the dark ages of forensic science.

More than likely, the suspect(s) in Joann's disappearance had abandoned the car with keys in it, an open invitation to car thieves and/or joy riders.

Life went on in the brown house—without Joann. Bob hired the first of a series of babysitters to watch Nick, Kandy Kay, and Ty.

"There were so many babysitters," Ty remembers. "We had *tons* of babysitters, so many that I can't possibly remember them all."

Joann's divorce action against Bob was still on Judge Story Birdseye's docket, and November 21 was the date for hearing evidence.

By October 23, Bob Hansen had hired a new attorney and filed a cross-complaint for divorce. He signed an affidavit he gave to Duncan Bonjorni in which he disputed all of Joann's claims in her May divorce filing.

He asserted: "The Plaintiff served her complaint upon me on or about the eighth day of August, 1962, and I thereupon voluntarily vacated the family residence. Shortly thereafter—on or about the tenth day of August, the Plaintiff disappeared, leaving the three minor children under [my care.] To present times, the Plaintiff has not reappeared, and the minor children have been maintained by me.

"The Plaintiff, Joann E. Hansen had, for some time prior to her disappearance, been nervous, upset, and distraught, and seemed discontented with our life, including our marital relationship. I repeatedly attempted to reconcile any differences and maintain a wholesome and pleasant family relationship and environment. At no time did I give the Plaintiff any reason to be fearful for her well-being and safety, nor did I ever in any manner threaten the Plaintiff.

"The disappearance of Joann E. Hansen was most surprising and shocking to me. It was not until the preparation of statements of financial condition for the United States Treasury Internal Revenue Service that it came to my attention that the Plaintiff—who handled the collection of income from rental properties—had apparently withheld approximately $8,000, which funds were received and receipts written, but are unaccounted for in deposits made and were never in my hands.

"I believe that Joann E. Hansen is presently alive and upon her past actions, together with her emotional instability, I further believe that she chose to desert me and our three minor children for reasons known only to her to live elsewhere and not proceed with the divorce action."

Putting a halo on his own head, Bob Hansen ended his affidavit by saying that he had been managing all the property involved and that his "prudent business acumen" had retained and/or increased the property values.

Since no one knew where Joann Hansen was, or even if she was alive or dead, Duncan Bonjorni decided to proceed with the divorce in absentia. He arranged for Donald Eide to serve as Guardian Ad Litem to represent Joann's interests.

Legally, it didn't matter that she wasn't there to testify.

*　　*　　*

Superior Court Judge Story Birdseye said he found the divorce case between the Hansens interesting since Joann Hansen had disappeared shortly after she filed for divorce.

"Whether she is living or not, no one can say. If [Joann's attorneys] discontinue their motion, the parties would remain married, and if Mr. Hansen dissipated the present community estate, leaving nothing for Mrs. Hansen when—and if—she returns, they might be subject to criticism."

Judge Birdseye declared that he felt justified in concluding that Joann had suffered violence at her husband's hands, and "sufficient personal indignities" to establish grounds for divorce.

"Accordingly, I will terminate the marriage by awarding a decree of divorce to the plaintiff."

Bob Hansen had already withdrawn his cross-complaint for divorce.

The judge was in a difficult position. Since Joann Hansen was missing, he couldn't award custody or visitation to her. Neither did he deny them. He said that they must all wait to see what Joann's mental condition was if she ever came home.

As for the division of property, Judge Birdseye considered Bob's demand for every single piece of property, all contracts, all vehicles, and the used furniture they had owned.

Donald Eide, speaking for Joann, asked for the small white house behind the veterinary clinic, the Willows

Apartments with the ten small rental units, a $3,000 contract on one rental house, and legal fees of less than $1,000 owed to Duncan Bonjorni.

Judge Birdseye ruled that the community estate— minus the mortgages and encumbrances Bob Hansen presented—was worth $70,000. Since Bob was raising Nick, Kandy Kay, and Tyler, he got 60 percent of the estate, and Joann was awarded 40 percent. Her share was $27,740, and it came as a lien against certain properties if Bob should sell them. In essence, she got a small house and a barn that was located on the Green River in Kent, Washington.

If Joann Hansen never returned, her share was to be held in trust for her children.

Patricia Martin maintains that if she could have, Joann would have shown up to get her share of the Hansen estate so she could take care of her kids.

"Tracking her social security number," Pat said, "we found that she never took a job over all those years. Her social security number didn't show up anywhere."

When people choose—for whatever reason—to leave of their own volition, they invariably leave a paper trail: money missing from their bank accounts, applications for employment, driver's licenses, gas card records. It isn't that easy to just disappear.

Joann Hansen left nothing at all; she might as well have been abducted by aliens and whisked away in a spacecraft.

Although local gossip said that Bob had murdered Joann and hidden her body, he would have had to have done a clever job at that. No shred of her showed up.

There was never a real police investigation, only a haphazard missing complaint from a husband who didn't seem that disturbed that his wife might be in danger.

Although Bob had law enforcement acquaintances, he wasn't close enough for any of them to pull back on investigating him. Some of them liked him well enough and even felt sorry for the troubles he had. Still, most of his male friends were cautious around Bob and didn't want to get on the wrong side of him. His temper was legendary. He could do a lot of damage when he was blind with rage.

To the outside world, he was the guy whose wife had run off and left him to take care of three little kids alone.

And that, of course, was the image he wanted to portray.

Chapter Nine

COLLATERAL DAMAGES

For every victim of violent crime, there are almost always several more people who suffer from the fallout of the tragedy. No one can accurately predict what will happen to children who lose a parent, or who suffer from childhood abuse. Some can override their sadness and loss and become well-adjusted adults; others are traumatized forever after.

When Joann Hansen went out of her children's lives, they lost the key person who had always made them feel loved and safe. Nick, Kandy Kay, and Ty were only four, three, and two, and Bob had to hire babysitters. He didn't soften his answers to their questions about "Where's Mommy?" Rather, he cruelly told them that their mother didn't care about them—that she had run away from them and wouldn't be back.

Nick Hansen was the oldest, nearly five, and he probably missed his mother the most. Although he had precious few memories of her, at least he had a few; his younger siblings had none at all.

"I *can* remember being in a car with my mother, and she was crying. Another time, she was taking me to the ocean. But that's all that I recall—other than the feeling of being safe and warm in her arms—and her taking care of me.

"I recall asking my father where my mommy was—can see him clearly in my mind, sitting in his recliner chair. He didn't want to talk about her at all. He just said, 'She's gone.'"

Strangely, Nick's very earliest memory is not about his mother. Rather, Nick recalls an odd incident that he believes happened to one of the multitude of babysitters Bob Hansen hired.

"I don't remember how it happened, but she accidentally cut her wrist and she must have sliced into an artery because I saw blood spurting all over the kitchen."

What he really saw is a matter of conjecture. It's quite possible that Nick is remembering his mother's murder—but his mind would not allow him to recall Joann bleeding profusely.

After intensive therapy, Nick Hansen believes that his response to having his mother suddenly disappear from his life was to turn to "infantilism." He didn't want to be a big boy any longer; he wanted to wear diapers and eat baby food like Kandy Kay and Ty did.

He could not cope with his life as the oldest child in a home without a mother.

Kandy Kay and Ty felt the loss of Joann, too, but it was more diffuse. They were sometimes overwhelmingly sad, but they could not explain why. They were simply too young. When pressed, Bob Hansen told all three of his children that their mother had gone away and left them.

And they believed him. They had no other choice. With Joann out of their young lives, they no longer saw Patricia Martin either. Patricia had been like an aunt, even a second mother, but Bob would have nothing to do with her. All his children knew was that Bob was there; he cooked breakfast and supper. They still had Christmases, and their father sometimes took them on vacation trips. As always, he took dozens of photographs of himself and his children. It certainly looked as though they were a happy family— even though they didn't have a mother.

That wasn't remotely true.

It was almost as if Bob Hansen lived two lives. One was what happened inside the walls of his house—a life where he was cruel and abusive to his children—and the other was the world in the photographs he took, the pictures that showed a perfect little family.

After seven years passed, Joann Ellen Hansen was declared legally dead.

Ty Hansen remembers visiting at his uncle Ken Hansen's house and playing with Ken and their aunt Lorene's two daughters. "They had a real family—a real home. I always wished that I could be in a family like that. We had Thanksgivings and Christmases with them.

"Our life was, ah . . . *isolated* . . . that's the only way I can describe it. We weren't like other families at all."

Nick, too, has good memories of being in his paternal uncle's home for holidays. "They were all good to us," he says. "And they had a player piano. I used to love that."

Both the Hansen boys remember that their father took them and their sister on trips and vacations. "We were kids—we had fun on some of the trips," Ty says. "We stopped asking about our mother because he didn't like to hear anything about that."

Patricia Martin could not forget Joann Hansen, and she didn't want to. Every time she looked at the palm prints that Joann had pressed into the wet cement in the foundation of Pat's house, she felt the pang of loss—and of frustration. Pat was afraid to confront Bob, but she called him fifty times a day, only to hang up when he answered. If all she could do was make him nervous, she was going to do that.

"He figured out soon enough that it was me calling him. He called the police, and they called me and told me to stop, that he was dangerous."

If they thought he was dangerous, she wondered why they weren't out looking for Joann.

Bob Hansen was eager to take his boys hunting and fishing, and as soon as they could hold a light rifle or a fishing pole, he took them with him to his favorite hunting spots, mostly on the other side of the Cascade Mountains, particularly Banks Lake in Grant and Douglas counties. They camped out, sped around lakes on a boat Bob owned, and went waterskiing.

Bob always insisted that they take a camera with them, and he took myriad photographs—at their camp sites or of his small boys holding up their unfortunate, dead and bleeding prey.

Although his hobbies were violent, Bob bragged that his children enjoyed their hunting trips with him. He appeared to be the epitome of the loving father who was doing his best to spend time with his motherless children. Joann had long since become known as the heedless, selfish mother who had followed her own dreams—even if it meant abandoning her children.

Joannn's family, friends, and her attorney were convinced that wasn't what happened, and they did what they could to find her. They had no luck. Neither did the private investigators who Joann's parents hired. Bob wouldn't talk to them, and they found no other paths they could follow.

Nick, Kandy Kay, and Ty didn't know they had a half brother: Bobby Morrison. Nick and Kandy Kay might have had a vague memory of him from when they were toddlers, but Ty certainly wasn't old enough to remember him. They didn't know Patricia Martin. Nor did they know they had relatives on their mother's side who loved them. Bob had cut all ties with anyone connected to Joann. Their father filled their world—figuratively and actually. He was so tall, so big, and his voice rumbled. He didn't want them to bond with anyone but him.

In his way, he may have cared for them more than he cared for anyone else in his life—but Bob Hansen seemed incapable of any real sensitivity except how he himself felt. He acted without thinking, particularly when he was angry. He seemed incapable of empathy, never understanding how other people felt—even his own small children. He gave them everything material that he thought they needed—but, most of all, he lacked tenderness.

And they needed that.

When Nick, Kandy Kay, and Ty were barely out of Mrs. Moses's private kindergarten in Des Moines, they were pretty much on their own. They no longer had babysitters. Bob was making good money in the construction boom that hit America in the sixties and early seventies, and that meant long hours on the job. His three children quickly learned to fend for themselves.

"Nobody knew it," Ty says, "but we walked to Mrs. Moses's kindergarten class, which was in the basement of Des Moines Elementary. It was about seven or eight blocks from our house, and we had to cross Kent Des Moines Road first, which was a really busy street. Sometimes a babysitter would see us across that road, and sometimes not."

In the annual photos that Mrs. Moses had taken of her class, the Hansen children wore clothes that were neat and clean, their hair was cut, and no one could pick them out as children who were basically taking care of themselves. Nick and my daughter, Leslie, were in the same kindergarten class, and years later Ty and my son, Andy, were friends in junior high school and played baseball together.

Oddly, perhaps, none of my five children recall Kandy Kay. That may be because the Hansen children attended another elementary school in the Highline school district. Students whose addresses fell north of the Kent Des

Moines Road could choose between Des Moines Elementary and Parkside. All three of the Hansen kids chose Parkside, although they would meet up again with their friends from Rilda Moses's kindergarten when everybody went to Pacific Junior High School.

Kandy Kay was obviously her father's favorite, and he let her do what she wanted.

In 1967 Barbara Snyder (née Kuehne) moved to Des Moines with her family from their former home in Cleveland. On her first day at Parkside School, her third grade teacher asked for volunteers who would show "the new girl" around the school. Kandy Kay Hansen raised her hand immediately, and that was the beginning of a lifelong friendship.

"Kandy was so good to me," Barbara Kuehne Snyder recalls more than forty years later. "I missed Cleveland and my friends there, but I soon felt at home in Des Moines."

Barbara spent a lot of time in the brown house on Marine View Drive. Bob allowed his children to bring their friends home after school and on weekends and holidays. He himself was often working, but he laid down rules that they all had to follow.

Barb Snyder remembers that all of the Hansen children were very talented. "Kandy played the saxophone and I played the clarinet. Nick was a musical genius—a genius at almost everything, although he didn't spend much time with us.

"We had a band for a while," Barb said. "Kandy, Ty, me, and Greg Hardman."

Nick Hansen wasn't a member of their band; he got together with his own group of friends who enjoyed music.

Nick played all the woodwind instruments—clarinet, saxophone, flute, and bassoon. His prime musical skill, however, was as an arranger. When he was in sixth grade, he did his first arrangements for the school band, as he would for the bands of every school he attended.

"My dad really didn't want me to be a musician," Nick says. "When I wanted to go to Kent-Meridian High School—which was out of our school district—he didn't approve. But he was finally convinced when my teachers said that was where the best music curriculum was. They also had a good math program."

Kent-Meridian High School was more than a dozen miles from where Nick lived in Des Moines, and he rode his bicycle there and back every day, rain, snow, or shine. Later, he was able to find a bus route where he could get off and walk several miles to get home.

But Nick Hansen spent as little time at home as possible. He stayed after school in Kent often, or he went to his friends' homes to play music. Alan Hall's, Todd Froy's, and Jeff Barclay's parents all welcomed Nick and he often stayed for supper or overnight.

Nick knew that he was something of a disappointment to his father. "He pushed me into playing baseball, but I hated it and I wasn't any good at sports."

"It's kind of difficult to explain our relationships," Ty says. "Nick went to a different high school than Kandy and I did. He wanted to take advantage of the advanced science, math, and music courses offered there. In a way, it was always the three of us against my dad—just to survive. But when it came down to it, it was every man for himself. Nick just stayed out of Dad's way, Kandy Kay was his favorite, and, as I said, I got the brunt of his fists."

Of them all, Ty, who was not yet two when Joann disappeared, was the "target child." He was the one who irritated his father more than the other two. Sometimes he and Nick wondered if Bob Hansen really *was* Ty's biological father because he singled Ty out for the very worst physical punishment. Maybe their mother had been starved enough for love that she had been with another man.

That was really just conjecture because Ty had Bob's height, his chin, and his physical prowess. And Joann Hansen had been too panicked by her husband to do anything but simply try to survive.

"Dad didn't like Ty at all," Nick says. "He wasn't wanted. I don't know why."

One of Bob's most egregious punishments for Ty happened when he and his children were camping on the shore of Banks Lake.

"Maybe Ty didn't tell you about this," Nick suggests. "It was so awful I don't think he chooses to remember it."

Banks Lake is a twenty-seven-mile-long manmade reservoir with clear blue water, formed by the north dam near Grand Coulee and the Dry Falls Dam near Coulee City, and filled with water from Lake Roosevelt. Surrounded by rocky outcroppings—basalt cliffs and talus slopes—the land around Banks Lake looks like it belongs on another planet, or in a desert. It is a draw for vacationers and tourists, an unexpected oasis.

"Dad was trying to teach us to water-ski while we were camping on the beach at Banks Lake," Nick recalls. "Ty was about six or seven and he just couldn't seem to get up on his skis, and Dad got really angry. He got out of the boat, took the rope, and wrapped it several times around Ty's neck. Then he got back in the boat and revved it up."

Ty was almost strangled. If Bob Hansen hadn't cut the throttle when he did, Ty could have broken his neck—or been decapitated.

"That was the worst day of my life," Ty remembers today. "I really thought he was finally going to kill me."

"Kandy slept in our tent on the beach that night," Nick said, "but Ty and I were so shaken about what could have happened that we slept up on the hill—away from Dad."

Remembering the incident, Nick mused, "The only thing that ever kept us alive was that my dad wanted the public to see him as a great family man."

Unlike some of the other true cases I've researched, the mystifying story of the Hansen family was told to me by a score of witnesses who related it with almost identical memories and opinions. There was general agreement that Bob Hansen was an alarming man.

Attorney Duncan Bonjorni, perhaps, summed him up most accurately: "He was warped. I never saw a man so devoid of a real personality. He was an aberration all the way. Bob Hansen was evil personified!"

*　　*　　*

Kandy Kay's best friend, Barb Snyder, is not as vehement as Bonjorni is. She was more puzzled by the dynamics in Kandy's home, but she came to feel used to the way things were there.

"Who took care of the Hansen kids while their father was out on the job?" I asked Barb.

"They took care of themselves." She shrugged. "One time, I asked Kandy where her mother was—I didn't know any other family where there wasn't a mother. She told me her mother was hit by a train and killed. We were both eight, and I accepted that. She didn't talk any more about her mother."

Barb said she stayed at the Hansen house for supper many times. "Bob cooked, and he was pretty good. I was kind of scared of him, though. It was his temper. Something would irritate him and he got angry so quickly. It didn't last long, but it was frightening for me. His own kids got real quiet when he blew up. We were all afraid of him."

Although the Hansen children could do pretty much what they wanted if they didn't get in their father's way, there was one area that was forbidden to them. None of them was ever allowed in Bob's bedroom. Beyond his warning of what would happen to anyone who snooped in there, they couldn't get in anyway; he had deadbolt locks to keep them out.

Barb Snyder remembers incidents where Kandy's father acted inappropriately and she and Kandy were both embarrassed.

"Bob took us to the circus once when we were eleven or twelve. We were watching the elephants, and Bob pointed out that one of the elephants was mounting the elephant in front of him. We didn't even know what an erection was then, but Bob poked us and made us look at its penis. He said, 'Wow! Look at the size of that!' I was just mortified."

When they were older, Barb recalls that a man whom Kandy called "Uncle" told someone she knew that Bob was sexually molesting Kandy. Incest was something Barb had never heard of and, again, she was far too embarrassed to ever question Kandy. And Kandy had certainly never even hinted at that. If it was true, it wasn't anything the two girls could talk about.

"Kandy got whatever she wanted, and her 'uncle' said that was because Bob was messing with her," Barb said. "I never thought that. But, as we got older, she had so much freedom and Bob gave her so many expensive presents. I just thought it was because they were rich. My family was very ordinary, and we lived in an ordinary house. We weren't rich at all, but we were comfortable."

Asked if they ever suspected that their father had sexually molested their sister, neither Ty nor Nick is sure about that—but both have suspected it.

When Kandy was eighteen and nominated for Miss Des Moines in the pageant that was part of the town's Waterland Festival every summer, Bob beamed with pride.

More persuasive that Bob Hansen was molesting Kandy Kay were her statements to the beauticians who worked with her in her pageant days. The wife of a man on Bob's construction staff went to the same beauty parlor. When it was far too late to have helped Kandy, the hairdressers said Kandy had confided in them. She said her father *had* taken sexual advantage of her for many years.

Bob Hansen dated a number of women. He was a man in his prime and well-to-do; his dark hair was thick and had no gray at all in it. He had never liked his large chin, and he had gone to a plastic surgeon who surgically broke Bob's jaw, moved it back, and shortened it by about an inch. It made a big difference and Bob was now much handsomer. He was tall, in great shape, and tanned from being on construction sites or tromping through sun-washed fields in search of animals to shoot. And to the outside world, he seemed to be a perfect father to three adorable children. He had no trouble at all getting dates.

But he had trouble keeping a relationship going. He wasn't nice to women, and they sensed that beneath the surface he didn't really like them. This sometimes led to no third date, and often to no second date.

Although she no longer had anything to do with Bob Hansen, Patricia Martin learned about one of his longtime girlfriends when she attended a pinochle group she had belonged to for decades. She mentioned Bob Hansen that night, and the hostess's husband overheard her comments and took her aside.

"My first wife dated Bob Hansen," he told Pat. "Marge and Bob really hit it off at first. They got along fine for a couple of years, and Bob was building a house for her. He bought her a huge rock—I don't know how many carats that diamond was—and things seemed to be going great."

But the host said it all blew up on one night. "She was at Bob's house and they made dinner. She has a son from her marriage before ours, and he was fifteen then. Lonny* was down in the basement, and Marge called him to come up and eat. As kids will, he dawdled and she had to call him twice.

"When he didn't come right up, Bob went down there and beat the shit out of him."

Marge had been horrified. Her teenage son wasn't a big kid; he was actually kind of scrawny, and he didn't have a chance with Bob Hansen. Marge grabbed her battered son and left hurriedly.

"She would never go out with him again, naturally. She saw what a bully Bob was. Bob tried hard to get her back, but she wouldn't even consider it.

"Funny thing happened, though. Somebody cut her brake line one night. Luckily, she didn't get far before she realized it, or she could have been killed."

Not surprisingly, Bob's own children suffered years of physical punishment. Bob knocked out a couple of Ty's baby teeth when the little boy made him angry.

Asked if his father spanked him hard, Ty laughs, but only slightly. "He hit me with his fists, threw me down the stairs and against walls. He was very violent, and I was the one who got hit eighty percent of the time. He hit me with belts and any object he got his hands on.

"I'm still perplexed, all these years later. Why didn't anyone ask us about our cuts, scratches, black eyes, and broken teeth? We were young kids, and teachers and neighbors saw us—but no one ever asked us what had happened to us. The only person who noticed was once when I went to the dentist with my broken teeth.

"He asked me, 'Did your dad do this to you?' And I said yes. I heard him arguing with my dad in another room later, but nothing changed."

Ty and Kandy Kay were very close, while Nick lost himself in studying and music. Bob gave his daughter almost everything she asked for. Nick didn't get in his way, but Ty grated on Bob, and suffered for it.

Although they got minimal affection at home, perhaps the saving grace for Nick, Kandy, and Ty was that they could depend on their friends. Barbara Snyder loved Kandy like a sister and Ty met a girl at Pacific Junior High who was shocked and saddened to learn that he had lost his mother so early in his life that he barely remembered her.

Cindy Tyler and Ty Hansen were in either the eighth or ninth grade when they met. Although they were both good-looking young teens, they would never be romantically attached, but Cindy would listen to Ty as he talked about his problems. She thought it was terribly sad that he had grown up without a mother.

Ty was only two when Joann went away. It was clear that Ty was going to be very tall—like his father—but he was quite thin at that age. Even so, he was a good athlete—especially when it came to baseball. Even that didn't endear him to Bob Hansen.

*   *   *

Joann Hansen had once had wonderful plans for her children's futures. However difficult her marriage was, she loved all four of her children devotedly. They were extremely intelligent children with natural musical talent, and their mother had encouraged them in whatever they wanted to do. She had been forced to give up Bobby because she feared for *his* life, her first baby girl had died in the night without warning, and she was extremely grateful to have Nick, Kandy Kay, and Ty. She hoped to find a way to raise Bobby, too. He was her firstborn and she loved him so much.

She was a natural mother, ready to endure whatever she had to to keep them safe.

Any mother's greatest fear is not for her own life—but that fate will take her away from her children's lives. In both the human and the animal kingdom, there may be nothing stronger than a mother's love and her need to protect her young.

When Joann disappeared, her children suffered—as they would for the rest of their lives—even if they managed to pick up the shattered pieces and rearrange them into a semblance of normalcy.

Chapter Ten

KANDY KAY

All three of Bob and Joann Hansen's children had inherited their father's elongated chin and his height, but his daughter—Kandy Kay—looked the most like him. She had strong features like Bob, but hers were feminine. She had thick long brown hair and a slender figure. As she grew up, she became more and more beautiful.

Bob Hansen owned a number of horses, which he kept in rented pasture land a few blocks away. Des Moines was far more rural in the fifties and sixties, and there were several meadows a block or so from "downtown." Today, most of the fields are covered with sprawling apartments and their parking lots.

Bob bought Kandy her own horse—Poker Chips—and she loved him dearly, but she resented it when her father wanted to show off her riding skills to his friends. She longed to ride free with Poker Chips.

Kandy sensed early on that she was part of the facade that her father had contrived to impress other people, and she wasn't comfortable with it. The Hansen children all knew that the smiling glad-hander that their father was in public was very different when their front door closed behind them.

Bob still owned the Willows Apartments that he built at the bottom of the hill just below the brown house: red-brick, flat-roofed, small apartments surrounded by concrete. Because the town had long since dammed up a small lake unwisely, during heavy rains the Willows' parking lot flooded, and sometimes the units themselves were endangered.

When Kandy was just sixteen, Bob let her have her own apartment—the end unit to the west. Bob Hansen also moved his son Ty into the Willows Apartments when he was in high school. It appeared that Bob felt sixteen or seventeen years was long enough to raise any child. He had his own life to live.

Bob sold the brown house and moved to Kent, several miles away.

Nick Hansen was a genius. After high school, he joined the navy and studied nuclear physics; he was the top honors graduate in 1984 with a grade average of 98.43 percent.

Living in her own apartment meant far too much freedom for Kandy—a teenager in the eleventh grade. Bob Hansen also bought Kandy a new car. Since they were old enough to have licenses, the Hansen teenagers had shared the use of an old station wagon, each handing it down to the next youngest when they were able to buy their own cars.

Bob bought Kandy her own car when she got her apartment. It was white and detailed with orange, yellow, and red bursts of fire.

A sixteen-year-old girl with an apartment of her own was an easy target for men who were attracted to her. Kandy didn't have the protection and parental concern she needed, although it may be that she had *never* had that. Underage students could drink in Kandy's small apartment as well as smoke marijuana or experiment with other drugs if they wanted to.

Barbara Snyder was very upset when she heard rumors that Kandy was "easy." She tried not to believe that her best friend since third grade was promiscuous. But Kandy had no adult supervision or anyone to turn to with problems.

And the whispers grew louder.

Kandy gravitated to men who were five to seven years older than she was, and she didn't mind if they were married. Amateur psychologists might say that she was looking for a father figure who would really look after her, but her life was far more complicated than that. Did she really believe that her absent mother had been hit by a train, or was that a lie she told herself so that she didn't have to believe Joann had abandoned her?

Bob Hansen was boorish and kinky when it came to sex; he apparently had no inkling of what was appropriate whether he was talking to peers, women, or even children.

In the spring of 1976, when it came time for Kandy and Barbara's big prom, Bob insisted on cooking dinner for several of the young couples before the dance. At that time, he lived in a new place he'd built, right across the street from the Green River. It was white stucco with high arches in the front, and much nicer than the house in Des

Moines. There were flowers in the stucco planter boxes on his front patio—but they were all artificial.

One selling point about Bob's new place was a ringside seat to a drive-in movie just beyond the river. He didn't have sound, but it was free, and the theater often showed pornographic films that didn't need any dialogue.

The prom dinner was an embarrassment and a disappointment for the girls, who were dressed in lovely gowns, with the matching corsages their dates had given them. This was supposed to be a time for teenagers, and Kandy Kay's father didn't fit in at all. It was almost as if he was usurping a special, memory-making evening that belonged to *them*.

Whether Bob Hansen knew beforehand that the drive-in was showing a pornographic movie—however soft- or hard-core it might be—or if it was a surprise for him, he quickly called the boys over to the window and pointed out what was on the screen.

"It was kind of like when he took us to the circus," Barbara remembers. "We were all humiliated, and it ruined our evening. The guys were glued to that window, we girls ate dinner alone, and we were really late for the prom. It seemed like Bob had planned it."

Kandy worked from the time she was old enough to get a job—first at Baskin-Robbins selling ice cream, and then at the Sears Outlet store. But she had had to grow up too fast, without anyone to guide her. In many ways, she seemed far older than she really was.

Saltwater State Park on Puget Sound is about five miles south of Des Moines. A very handsome—and very married—ranger worked there, and Kandy had a huge crush on him. He was at least seven years older than she was—a long stretch when she was seventeen. It was easy for him to seduce her, and they began an intense affair.

"He drove us wherever we wanted to go," Barb Snyder says. "He seemed as though he wasn't married, but both of us knew he was. Kandy wouldn't listen to good sense when I tried to warn her. She was madly in love with him."

When they were seniors at Mount Rainier High School, Barb decided to run for Miss Des Moines of 1977, a precursor to the Miss Washington pageant. The first prize was a $700 scholarship, and Barb urged Kandy to enter, too. It was something they could enjoy together as best friends, and she thought it might help Kandy turn her life around. At first, Kandy wasn't interested, but Barb kept plugging away and finally convinced her.

But Barb's plan backfired.

"Once she decided to enter, she *really* wanted to win— even at the cost of our friendship," Barb Kuehne Snyder remembers.

Bob Hansen was all for it. It was one more opportunity to show off his family—especially his daughter. He paid for Kandy's preparation for the pageant. He saw to it that she had the most expensive dress, the best pageant coach, the most talented beautician.

Like all fledgling beauty queens, the Miss Des Moines hopefuls attended breakfasts, lunches, teas, charity events, parades, and anything else that local boosters could come up with. The contenders got little sleep, but it was all so heady and exciting that they didn't mind.

The Des Moines Junior Chamber of Commerce sponsored Kandy, and the Wind Drift Restaurant sponsored Barbara. They both were chosen among the twelve finalists.

Kandy Kay Hansen won. It was a serious coup d'état for Bob. Wearing a white tuxedo, he stood proudly next to his daughter while photographers took their picture, knowing that they would be on the front page of the local weekly, the *Des Moines News*.

Bob Hansen had traveled far from the boy who had to wear manure-stained pants to school. He didn't give a second thought to whoever had fallen in his path along the way. Bob never had pangs of conscience that anyone could see.

Kandy was soon caught up in the whirl of the Miss Washington competition. Preparing for the state pageant on June 22 to 24, 1978, she had handlers and chaperones and they watched her closely. She had never had chaperones before but she did what they told her to do. She stayed away from her married lover, alcohol, and marijuana. For a time, she almost had mother figures, although it was far too late by then.

If she could only win Miss Washington, Kandy would be on her way to Atlantic City and the Miss America pageant in September. She was pretty enough and she certainly had talent enough to win, and her father was pushing hard and spending freely to help her surpass all the other young women.

"She wanted to be Miss Washington *so much*," Barbara says. "It meant everything to her."

In the end, Kandy Kay Hansen came in as third runner-up to Miss Washington. It was difficult to tell who was more disappointed, Kandy or Bob. She was his shining star and she had failed him. He let her know that, seeing, as always, only his own side of it.

With her dream lost, Kandy Hansen changed. She would be twenty in four months, and it seemed that she had aimed for—and failed to achieve—the most important goal she would ever have. She didn't want to go to college, and she didn't want to take another boring job. She was depressed, and the future seemed to hold no hope for her.

It was 1978, and it wasn't long before Kandy was back with the park ranger, back on marijuana, and probably on stronger drugs. She dated several men. Barbara saw the bruises and the cuts on Kandy's lips; her lovers were abusers—just like her father had been with her mother.

Kandy grew skilled at applying makeup to cover her battle scars, but it broke Barbara Kuehne's heart to see how men had physically hurt her. Their paths were diverging as Kandy and Barbara's lifestyles were no longer in sync. Barb wanted to have a husband and a family, and Kandy wasn't sure what she wanted. As much as they tried to pretend things were still the same between them, they both knew they weren't.

Barb Kuehne wasn't the only one who was angry at men who hurt Kandy. There was one man Kandy tried in vain to break up with; he wouldn't let her go and he trailed her everywhere she went. She finally told her father that she was afraid of what the guy might do to her.

Bob laughed later when he told his friend Marv Milo-sevich that he had instructed Kandy to invite the stalker into her apartment, and told her that he would handle things from there.

Kandy did let the obsessive ex-boyfriend into her apartment. When the unwanted suitor walked into the dark apartment, Bob was waiting—with an iron plumbing pipe. He swung it as hard as he could against the man's head.

"What happened to him?" Marv asked.

"Let's just say that she won't have to worry about him ever again," Bob said grimly.

He wouldn't reveal whether the man was dead or alive, but Marv suspected the former.

Barb was engaged to be married a year or so after graduation, and she asked Kandy to be her maid of honor.

"She said she would," Barb remembers, "but she couldn't seem to get it together enough to order her gown, or try it on. She always had something else to do, or I couldn't find her. In the end, I knew I had to leave her out of my wedding."

But Kandy did come to her longtime best friend's wedding.

"She came with the park ranger, even though he was still married," Barbara remembers sadly. "She was making bad choices."

Bob soon moved Kandy into one of the other houses he owned in Des Moines. It was only a few blocks north of the brown house behind the Willows. It was, in fact, the house he and Joann had lived in when they were first married. One or another member of his family lived in it over the years when Bob didn't have it rented out.

*   *   *

Kandy was not quite twenty when she began dancing in the disco night spots that popped up close to the highway and army and air force bases around Seattle and Tacoma. She hadn't gone to college and she was bored and sick of jobs in fast-food restaurants. She was, of course, very beautiful and a natural as a cocktail waitress and then as a scantily clad dancer.

She was dancing in Tacoma when she was attracted to a new man. He was a bad boy and exciting. His name was Ron Wakefield. Kandy married him.

Wakefield introduced Kandy to heroin.

"He was charming and good-looking," her brother Ty says. "But he was a junkie. Once Kandy hooked up with him, she went down fast. He dragged her down with him. They were both just junkies looking for heroin wherever they could find it."

Barbara, too, saw that Kandy's drug use had escalated, and Barb feared she was almost certainly using heroin. She also knew that Kandy was making her living as a topless dancer and sometimes stripping entirely. She even heard rumors that Kandy was working for an escort service.

"One of the last times I saw her," Barbara Kuehne Snyder remembers, "it may have been the very last time—this was in the eighties, and we were in our early twenties. I went over to her house to see her. She excused herself and came back with a syringe and some heroin. I couldn't stand to see that, and I told her so, but she didn't stop. I had to leave."

Shortly after that, Kandy and Ron Wakefield were in trouble for some kind of incident in a state liquor store.

Ty thinks Ron robbed it. Her brothers were never sure just what happened, but they believed that it was Wakefield who pulled it off and that he somehow involved Kandy.

"At any rate," Ty says, "they left town in a hurry, and on the run. They planned to head south and then drive cross-country."

They were in Wendover, Utah, when their car broke down.

Wendover sits on the Utah-Nevada border and each state claims half the city. It is a gambler's paradise.

"The cops stopped to help them when they spotted Ron's car beside the road," Ty continues. "They checked on Ron and found he had a warrant out of Washington for his arrest, so they handcuffed him and took him away in the back of their squad car.

"Kandy was left alone in the broken-down car, strung out and broke. She hitched a ride into town and managed to get a job as a cocktail waitress in a casino there."

Tom Yarbrough was the manager of the casino, and he was also the "go-to man" in Wendover. He had numerous friends and a reputation as a good guy. Tom was much older than Kandy—close to her father's age, near sixty—but he was quite handsome; he looked very much like the actor Omar Sharif.

Yarbrough noticed Kandy in the casino and they began talking, then dating. It was probably the first time in her life when a man had unselfishly wanted to do what was best for Kandy Hansen. Tom truly cared for her. She was only twenty-five, and still had a chance to change her life.

In time, Kandy moved in with Tom. With his help, she managed to get completely off drugs. Although it was a painful struggle, Kandy escaped her terrifying addiction to heroin. She was the picture of health in photographs taken of the couple at Caesars Palace in Las Vegas. They looked like two movie stars. Kandy wore a one-shouldered black sequined dress, and Tom was dressed in a white suit, wine-colored shirt, white satin tie, and a chunky gold bracelet.

"Tom was a prince," Ty Hansen declares. "He was a good influence on Kandy. He wanted to marry her; he even asked my dad for permission to marry her, and my father saw that she was clean and happy, and he said yes. But they never did get married."

Ty Hansen had suffered the most physical abuse over the years, and he had the scars to prove it. From the time he and Nick were in first or second grade, they started working with Bob Hansen on his construction jobs. One of their jobs was picking up endpieces of wood and debris around the construction sites.

Marv Milosevich thought Bob was too hard on the boys. "They were just little kids, and they would play with the scrap wood—making cars and boats. That made Bob angry.

"He had different kinds of punishment for them. If he thought Nick and Ty were deliberately sloughing off when they should be working, he would get out his hatchet. Then he made them put their hands flat on a stump, and he'd raise the hatchet. He'd stop just before he hit them, but they were scared to death. So was I—afraid he would miss and actually cut a hand or some fingers off."

Milosevich also saw Bob discipline the boys at home. If they watched too much television, or it was something he didn't want to watch, he simply cut the power cords in two, and the screen went black.

One positive thing Ty says about his father is that Bob Hansen was an honest businessman. "He never cheated anyone, he built good houses and buildings, and he didn't cut corners."

Nick agrees. Whatever his father might have kept hidden, or however cruel he could be, Nick, too, says Bob Hansen delivered solid buildings for a fair price.

It's interesting—but sad—that both of his sons tried for a long time to please him, to somehow have a father who was proud of them, even though he took "tough love" to extremes. Eventually, they realized there *was* no pleasing Bob Hansen.

Until they finally walked away from him, they kept trying.

There was the summer of 1980 when Bob spent three months with Nick building a house in Westport, Washington. It was a plain one-story house that was more a cabin than a house with frills—but it was solid. Bob wanted it for himself—so he would have his own place at the ocean.

He and Nick had time to fish while they were building the cabin. Westport, in Grays Harbor County, is one of Washington State's top harbors for deep-sea fishermen.

"It wasn't a bad summer," Nick remembers, "and I learned a lot about building—but I didn't see my future there. In the end, my father accepted that I wasn't cut out to be a blue-collar worker; I was probably more white collar, and he dealt with that."

Nick Hansen had so much going for him, just as Ty and Kandy Kay did. All of them were very intelligent and physically attractive. They were fairly adept at hiding the wounded places inside them. Nick graduated third in his class at Kent-Meridian High School, he was working toward a degree in math at the University of Washington, and his naval career drew many accolades. He was a handsome young man, and he had a pretty blond girlfriend, Melissa.

But Nick knew he was living a lie. And it ate at him like acid.

Still, there was no one he could talk to, no one to help him sort out his life. From about the age of five, he had more secrets than Bob Hansen or his siblings knew, and he had lived in torment trying to deal with his confusing emotions. His dilemma began—probably more than coincidentally—when his mother vanished. Nick cannot recall a time when he didn't want to be a girl instead of a boy.

It was a secret he felt he couldn't reveal to anyone.

Nick wasn't attracted to men; he was intrigued with what women thought and did. At parties, Nick always gravitated to circles where women were holding conversations.

Bob Hansen may have suspected what was going on with Nick—but he refused to acknowledge it. Of all men, Bob Hansen was the last one who could accept that his son was what was referred to as a "sissy boy."

Bob was all man, strong, virile, powerful. But he once caught his elder son trying on some female clothes. And he was enraged.

Ty recalls seeing his father burn a dress when he and Nick were in junior high, but he knew better than to ask questions.

Although Nick didn't suffer from beatings nearly as much as Ty did, this incident brought him a bruising.

Bob Hansen wanted sons who were athletes, sportsmen, and hunters. He wanted them to be womanizers, as he was, and took every opportunity to impress upon them that women weren't as good as men and never could be. He would have preferred to have both Ty and Nick follow him into the construction business. Neither of them did, despite all the years that he trained them in every aspect of buying land, carpentry, painting, and how to treat tenants.

Bob had also wanted his daughter to be Miss America. But, tragically, when she failed to get to the top of the pageants she entered, Kandy Kay had turned to drugs.

In the end, Bob Hansen's determination to have absolute control over his offspring only drove them away from him.

He had expected them to burnish *his* image, and found that they had dreams of their own.

Chapter Eleven
COSTA RICA

The part of the marital estate Joann had been awarded in the divorce proceedings where she had never appeared was supposed to be kept in trust for her children. It would have helped all of them when they came of age at eighteen. They needed it to pay for their educations, to find housing where they didn't have to bend to their father's will, and/or to start businesses.

But Bob Hansen met with lawyers who cleverly prevented the release of those trust funds. Kandy Kay might have received some property—but his sons got nothing. Somehow Joann's share of the estate came back to Bob. His first attorney, James Gooding, was later shot to death in his Kent office by an angry tenant in one of *his* properties.

At that time Bob had already regained possession of the barn on the Green River and the Valley Apartments, built with the same plans as the Willows. The units sat next to the new freeway in Kent and ended up among

Bob's assets along with the other properties. They were literally a stone's throw from the river.

In his fifties now, Bob Hansen had a lot of money—some estimated his wealth at more than $5 million. As far as anyone knew for sure, he hadn't remarried after Joann went out of his life, but that may be inaccurate. In the late seventies and early eighties, he was extremely interested in dating. He joined Parents Without Partners and met a number of women there. Of course, they didn't suit him because he didn't want any woman with an independent streak. He was annoyed to find that even the loneliest and least attractive of the single women in PWP seemed to be buying into equal rights for women.

Bob Hansen's hair was still thick, and it was gray only at the temples. He was in shape. His three kids were out of his house and he felt free; he was ready to begin to enjoy life. He joined a number of social clubs in addition to Parents Without Partners, including the San Juan Club. Good-looking men were exceptionally popular at PWP; there were far more single women than men.

But Bob's reputation preceded him. As handsome, tall, and rich as he was, most women still didn't care for him after a date or two.

Bob Hansen did, however, meet other middle-aged to elderly men, his "wingmen" at PWP, who told him that there were countries where pretty women—*young* women—were looking for well-to-do American men to marry. And they weren't bossy or demanding.

Bob was intrigued by the possibilities.

He had done a great deal of traveling in the continental United States: hunting, fishing, backpacking on horses and mules, and visiting many of the top tourist attractions.

In January 1980, he was fifty-six when he signed on for a seventeen-day luxury sailing trip on the barkentine *Polynesia*. The ship was 248 feet long and traveled to the Leeward Islands in the West Indies: St. Maarten, Anguilla, Saba, St. Barts, St. Kitts, and Statia. Bob was even allowed to steer the craft on a calm day and received a huge, flowery certificate memorializing his prowess.

From the West Indies, Bob went to Cancún, Mexico. As always, he took dozens of photographs, and posed for as many, filling still more scrapbooks. He felt comfortable in tropical climates, and he thoroughly enjoyed the many trips he embarked upon. The staff of the *Polynesia* served food, hors d'oeuvres, canapes, and liquor—anything he wanted—all free.

To the surprise of his children, Bob also began to organize Hansen family reunions, planning all the details, sending out invitations to even distant relatives. He even dug the roasting pit and oversaw the slow baking of large hogs.

He had never been a particularly social man but he now seemed to be trying to surround himself with people. Maybe he was softening, although Ty, particularly, doubted it.

"I think he realized that he didn't have many friends and that his kids were pulling away from him," Ty tried to explain. "But all of a sudden, he was into finding all of our relatives—not my mother's family, of course, but Hansens. Our immediate family was so dysfunctional—maybe he was looking for a family."

In their early twenties, Nick, Kandy, and Ty sometimes accompanied their father to the Hansen and Danish reunions in eastern Washington. Bob posed for photos with everyone there and took pictures of people who may or may not have been related to him.

The picnic tables were groaning boards filled with both picnic and Danish food: whole roasted pigs, fried chicken livers, little Danish open-faced sandwiches (*smorrebrod*), chicken and dumplings, pies, cakes, pastries, and peaches and grapes.

One of Bob's favorite parts of these reunions was the magnificent rolling wheat fields of the Palouse on the far eastern side of the Cascade Mountains. A distant cousin grew acres of wheat, and Bob was enthralled by the giant threshing machines needed to harvest it. Ty and Nick also enjoyed driving the combines in the golden fields.

Bob Hansen seemed somehow to be starting over, trying to create an extended family where he actually belonged, perhaps even trying to draw his children closer as they struggled to be free of him. They had been burdens for him, but now he was facing old age and he had no one close to him.

Marv Milosevich was the closest person Bob knew in terms of friendship, although Marv didn't realize it at the time. He himself had dozens of good friends and family members. It would be a long time before Marv came to the realization that he was probably Bob's *best* friend. He hadn't known how isolated the older man was.

Marv tried to see a good side to Bob because he was grateful for all that Bob had taught him.

"Some of the things he told me," Marv says with a laugh, "I didn't want to emulate. LaVonne and I had about fifty-two rentals by then and they were quite a bit nicer than Bob's rentals. He told me, 'Don't get close with your renters! Don't be friends with them, whatever you do.' But we chose to treat our renters well, and it worked out fine."

Bob was dealing with being alone. Nick was far away in the navy, Ty was selling used cars on Old 99, and Kandy was living with Tom Yarbrough in Wendover, Utah. Bob Hansen didn't hear from any of them very often.

He'd lost his brother to kidney cancer in February 1981, when Ken died in his sleep. Ken Hansen was only fifty-eight and his death made Bob realize that life was shorter than it had seemed when he'd been a young man.

Nick Hansen had gone to see his uncle Ken less than a week before he'd died. The retired police officer advised him to do and be what he wanted in life, and it made an impression on Nick. Ken Hansen had had a fulfilling life with his law enforcement career, and Aunt Lorene and Nick's cousins had made Ken's home life happy, too.

Nick wanted so much to live the life he only imagined, and Ken's kindness helped him.

*　　*　　*

Bob Hansen continued his travels throughout the eighties, searching for a place where he could live in the sun; he was tired of the rain that fell on Seattle most of the winter. He looked for a country where his money would last longer, as well as a place where he could find a lovely, docile woman to live with. He informed Ty that he would keep a small "pad" in the Northwest, but he didn't intend to spend much time there.

After all his searching for a spot he could truly call home, it was Costa Rica that called out the most seductive siren song to Bob Hansen. He found it was indeed true that many young women there wanted to be married to wealthy Americans.

And so, in the mideighties in Costa Rica, Bob Hansen discovered what, for him, was paradise.

He met a number of beautiful, dark-haired women in their late teens and early twenties.

"He brought home a different girl every year for four years," LaVonne Milosevich says. "They were very young and pretty. I remember there were *two* Cecilias."

Most of the young women chose to return to Costa Rica, but Bob eventually settled on the second Cecilia, who was twenty-one, slender and petite, and quite lovely. They were married and he took her home with him. They traveled extensively in America: to Alaska, Montana, Glacier National Park, Yellowstone National Park, and scores of attractions in Washington State. Everywhere they went, Bob had Cecilia pose in front of whatever oddity or scenic view was displayed—from looking at livestock at the state fair in Puyallup to standing high atop the windmill on

Bob's barn. He rarely identified her by name, but when he did write something in the scrapbook of Cecilia's era, he scribbled simply "MY Beauty."

Cecilia was so tiny that even with her black hair piled atop her head, she could stand under Bob's outstretched arm.

There are few people who can give details about what happened to Bob's second marriage. It lasted only a few years, and Cecilia returned to Costa Rica. She divorced Bob.

Chapter Twelve
THINGS FALL APART

In the spring of 1986, Kandy began to dabble in prescription drugs, thinking that she was in no danger of sliding back into addiction. She told herself that amphetamines and tranquilizers couldn't hook her the way heroin had. When Tom found out, he was very concerned and they argued. She had gone through hell getting straight, and he couldn't bear to see her slip.

Their disagreements were strong enough that she told Tom she was going back to Washington for a while to visit her brother. She wasn't leaving Tom; she just needed time to think and get her head together.

She called Ty and arranged for him to pick her up at Sea-Tac Airport on April 2.

As far as Ty could see, his older sister was clean and healthy when she returned to Des Moines. They stopped to eat dinner at a small, popular restaurant on Old Highway 99, and they had a good time talking and catching up. Ty hoped that Kandy intended to go back to Tom and weave together the tears in their relationship, but he didn't preach. He listened.

"We made plans to get together the next day," Ty recalls. "And I dropped her off at the Three Bears Motel on the highway at S. 216th Street."

The Three Bears was a familiar stopover near Des Moines for decades, but by 1986 it—along with several other moderately priced motels on the highway—attracted young prostitutes and their pimps.

And the Green River Killer was active along Old 99 then, too. His targets were teenage girls, many of them who stayed at the string of motels from S. 142nd to S. 240th Street. Ty wasn't really concerned; Kandy was in her hometown, she was twenty-seven, and she was quietly self-confident. Nevertheless, he updated her about the serial killer who roamed anonymously up and down the highway and reminded her to check the peephole in her door before she let anyone in.

When Kandy didn't call Ty by noon the next day, he was a little worried. He'd expected that his sister would sleep late; she'd been tired after her flight from Utah, but now it was afternoon.

Wondering if she might have turned her phone's ringer off, Ty drove the short distance to the Three Bears Motel. He saw a few police units outside, but didn't think much about it; they could be meeting for coffee. He began to feel a cold chill only when the front desk attendant at the motel gave him a peculiar look. He answered Ty's question about which room Kandy was in and pointed down the walkway.

Ty walked faster down the corridor. As he approached Kandy's room, he saw several police officers standing in the doorway and in the hall. He identified himself as he maneuvered into a position where he could peer into the room.

And he saw the sister he loved, the sister for whom he'd held out so much hope, lying perfectly still on the bed.

The police officers and paramedics shook their heads when Ty urged them to save her. It was far too late.

Kandy Kay Hansen had been clean and straight, and yet samples of body fluids taken at her autopsy for testing indicated that she had died of an overdose of black tar heroin. It had been administered subcutaneously. It wasn't hard to find along the Sea-Tac Strip, and being back in that milieu may have tempted Kandy. After years free of heroin, she had succumbed to a fatal temptation.

In the end, it didn't seem to matter how Kandy had gotten the heroin. She was dead and nothing would bring her back. Kandy was hours beyond saving when a maid had discovered her body.

Ty Hansen cannot even remember what he did when he was in that first numb grip of shock. He thinks he notified Tom Yarbrough, or, at least, had someone else let him know that Kandy was gone. (He did call Tom, who sent a mass of flowers and a note of everlasting love for Kandy Kay to her funeral services.)

Ty wasn't sure what to do next. He managed to contact his brother Nick who was on board the U.S.S. *Enterprise* as part of his navy tour. The *Enterprise* was halfway around the world, and even though the navy was willing to fly Nick back to Washington State, it would take several days.

Their father was in Costa Rica, as he often was.

"He didn't come back for weeks," Ty remembers. "We had Kandy's services in Kent."

The brothers had different recollections of the event, not surprisingly, as both were in shock.

Actually, Nick Hansen says he made Kandy's funeral arrangements. And their father *did* get back to Washington State in time to attend her services, although Nick said Bob already had reservations for that day and made no special effort to rush home.

Neither of his sons recalls Bob showing a great deal of grief during her funeral. Nick, however, went with his father shortly after Kandy's services to see two of his friends— brothers—who owned a truck stop in Algona, Washington.

"I was shocked to see my dad cry in front of them," Nick says. "I'd never seen him cry before. I know that Kandy put him through a lot when she was involved in drugs when she was younger. Some of his friends in Kent—where he went to have coffee—had talked to him then about getting her some help, but he didn't agree with them. I remember one of his closest acquaintances had lost his daughter in an accident. This guy was the mayor of Kent at the time, and he tried to get my dad to do whatever it took to get Kandy off drugs—but my dad said he believed in tough love."

In Kandy Hansen's case, toughness wasn't what was missing in her life. She had needed soft, nurturing love all of her life and rarely found it.

Ty feels that he was the one who missed Kandy the most after she died. They had always been close, about the only family members who were always there for each other. And with Kandy gone, Ty felt all alone.

Ty was doing fairly well painting used cars and repairing rental cars at a garage on Pacific Highway. But an acquaintance talked him into moving on and having his own business at a "great spot" further south that was going to be for rent.

Ty was twenty-six when he got his dealer's license, and he was selling used cars and making good money when a stranger out of Arizona walked in one day and said he wanted to join Ty as a partner. It sounded promising at first. Phil Hallop* said he would handle the books and come up with all the ads, publicity, and whatever stunts might be needed to bring in customers. And Ty, who had attended community college in a nearby town, taking auto mechanics courses, would be in charge of all the car maintenance and mechanical problems.

One of the Arizona glad-hander's ideas was to have Ty dress in a white cowboy suit, mask, boots, and ten-gallon hat so prospective buyers would see his resemblance to the Lone Ranger. This wasn't an original idea with Hallop; he had seen a car lot use it effectively in Phoenix. He figured that he could steal the gimmick since Washington and Arizona were far apart.

So Ty Hansen—not experienced with glib con men—agreed. With his height, he was a natural at portraying an honest-looking Western hero. His schtick was his nickname: "the Loan Arranger."

Ty soon became a semicelebrity in the Seattle area, and small children gazed at him in wonder as their parents shopped for an almost-new car or truck.

But Ty got in too deep when he trusted his partner's handling of the books. He was shocked to find that they didn't have anywhere near as much in the bank as he'd been led to believe. Within a few months, Ty Hansen's business was in trouble, and he fired Phil Hallop. A month later, someone broke into the car lot office and stole all of Ty's files. He realized it was Hallop when he later threatened to blackmail Ty.

"I'd bitten off far more than I could chew," Ty admits today.

He lost his business license and felt he had little choice but to leave Washington and start over. He moved to California and then Oregon.

In Oregon, Ty soon started seeing a young divorced woman who had a small daughter, Sylvie.* His new family changed his life. They married and soon had another daughter, Brigette.*

Nick was still dating Melissa. He loved her, but he remained torn by his sense that he should have been born a female. Before he asked Melissa to marry him, he knew he had to be totally honest with her.

"I told her everything," he remembers. "And she accepted me as I was. I married her because she was the only one I'd ever known who gave me unconditional love—who didn't judge me."

TOO LATE FOR THE FAIR

Robert Milton Hansen (left) and his older brother, Kenneth, pose for a Eugene, Oregon, photographer in 1926. The two brothers grew up to be total opposites.

Lester and Helen Hansen pose with their sons in front of the Danish Home in February 1929. Robert is sitting on his mother's lap, and Kenneth sits between their parents. During the Great Depression, the couple separated—but only in order to survive. Robert went with his father to the "Stump Farm" in Kent, Washington, and Kenneth with his mother and sisters to Seattle.

Bob Hansen in Ledo, India, assigned to the Burma Road project. He hated his long chin, hid it when he could, and later had plastic surgery.

Bob Hansen in the army in 1945 in Ledo, India, working under the command of General "Vinegar Joe" Stilwell on the Burma Road.

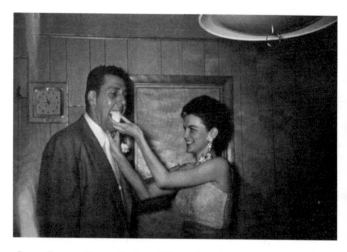

Joann Cooper Hansen feeds wedding cake to her groom. This probably happened in early 1957, although some believe they weren't legally married until 1962. She had great hopes for the marriage—a safe place for her first son and, hopefully, more children.

Joann Hansen with her first two babies with Bob Hansen: Nick and Kandy Kay (in bouncy chair).

Joann and her fourth child, Ty, on a camping trip.

Patricia Martin and Joann Hansen were best friends for years, and Patricia tried to save Joann. It was she who heard Joann's last horrifying words over the phone: "Pat! Oh no! He's in the basement . . . he's coming up—" Then there were only screams.

Christmas at the Hansens' house in about 1961.
They look like a happy family, and Joann had done
her best to decorate the way Bob preferred,
but the holiday was tense. Joann (left), Nick, Bob, and Ty.
Kandy Kay has her back to the camera.

Left to right: Ty, Kandy Kay, and Nick
no longer had their mother, and babysitters came and went.
"One thing I never understood," Ty said. "Why didn't someone
notice our black eyes, broken teeth, and bruises?"

Ty, Nick, and Kandy Kay show off the
fish they caught. They went on scores
of hunting and fishing trips with Bob,
and tried to smile as he snapped their
pictures with the dead animals.

Mrs. Rilda Moses's kindergarten in Des Moines.
Nick Hansen is in the top row, third from left.
My daughter, Leslie Rule, is in the front row, fourth from right.
And yet, I didn't know the Hansen family at all.

Kandy Kay was a Brownie in
a North Hill troop. She told
friends that her mother had
been hit by a train. None of
them knew the truth.

Kandy Kay was her father's favorite; Bob
bought her Poker Chips, her own horse, and
urged her to show off her riding skills to his male friends.

Kandy Kay was crowned Miss
Des Moines in 1977.
She went on to compete in the
Miss Washington pageant.

Bob Hansen was proud
as he escorted his daughter into
one of the Miss Des Moines
formal functions.

Miss Des Moines,
1977, in her royal robes.
Kandy had mother figures
in her chaperones for the
pageant, but it was too late;
she had grown up too fast,
without her mother.

Kandy Kay Hansen
was an absolutely beautiful
young woman. Bob Hansen
was full of pride when he
brought her to the Danish
reunions he organized.

Kandy Hansen and her best friend since third grade—Barbara Kuehne Snyder. Bob Hansen embarrassed the girls when they were younger, and ruined prom for them. Barbara fought to save Kandy from the evil that was permeating her life—and she failed.

Nick Hansen felt he had disappointed his father because he wasn't an athletic star—nor did he have much interest. In 1981 and 1982, he helped Bob build a cabin in Westport, Washington. That helped—but a bigger shock was coming after Nick married.

One of the last "family photos" with the Hansens. Left to right: Nick, Kandy Kay, Ty, and Bob share dinner at the Black Angus restaurant in Burien, Washington.

Bob Hansen was pleased when Nick married Melissa. Bob posed with his two sons: Nick (center), and Ty. It wasn't long, however, before Bob reneged on his gift of a house to the newlyweds. That ended their relationship—forever.

If anyone could have saved Kandy Kay Hansen,
it was Tom Yarbrough, who rescued her and loved her completely
after she hit bottom in a broken-down car on the border of
Utah and Nevada. Tom was old enough to be her father,
but he was very kind and caring. Tom managed a casino.
He wanted to marry Kandy, and, strangely, her father said yes.
But their wedding was never to be.

Bob Hansen, at 61, discovered Costa Rica and it seemed the answer to everything he wanted. He hadn't been successful in dating American women, but he discovered any number of dark-haired beauties in Costa Rica in their late teens and early twenties. He eventually bought a luxury condo there on March 7, 2007, for $250,000 and spent less and less time in the Northwest.

Bob Hansen's second wife, Cecilia, a lovely young Costa Rican woman who celebrated her twenty-first birthday in November 1987.

Ty Hansen, in his late twenties, was a master mechanic, and sold a few cars. When he moved to a new location, a fast-talking con man walked into his office one day and convinced him to become "the Loan Arranger." This was taken on his opening day in June 1988.

Bob Hansen, celebrating his sixty-fourth birthday in October 1988.

Bob Hansen expected to move into this plush condo, Los Amigos, in Rohrmoser, Costa Rica, and retire there forever. But he was denied citizenship and was shocked and disappointed.

Bob Hansen, 64, and his second wife, Cecilia, 21, in Costa Rica, posing next to a truckload of palm nuts.

Cecilia Hansen roller-skating in front of Bob Hansen's home on Green River Road. She was tiny enough to be a child.

Cecilia in the kitchen of the yellow house in Auburn. Her marriage to Bob Hansen was coming to a close. She felt like a possession and he called her "MY Beauty."

Flory Hansen, Bob's third wife. She felt she should marry him because she "owed" him for building her parents a safe and sturdy home in Costa Rica.

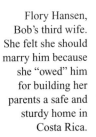

Flory Hansen, basting salmon that Bob caught. Bob wouldn't allow her to go beyond their property line without him. U.S. Immigration officers found out he'd brought her into the country illegally.

Flory standing in a burned-out forest on Blewett Pass in the Cascade Mountains in 2002.

Worth an estimated $5 million, Bob Hansen was alone now. He shows his age as he displays a king salmon in his yard in 2004. He was estranged from his sons and grandchildren, and he pinned his hopes on a new life in Costa Rica.

Bob Hansen's last home was this simple rambler in Auburn, Washington—and not the new condo in Costa Rica.

Cindy Tyler and Ty Hansen, friends since junior high, worked together to solve the mystery of his mother's disappearance almost fifty years earlier. The platonic friends cheered each other up when they ran into one frustration after another.

Kathleen Huget was helping a Realtor friend clean an empty house when she discovered eerie clues to a mystery of major proportions! She chose to fight for justice for a long-missing woman. (Huget Family Collection)

Left to right: Bobby (Joann's son by her first marriage), Ty Hansen, and Nicole Hansen (after her transgender surgery). Ty and Nicole didn't even know they had a half brother until Ty began to investigate his mother's disappearance. They were happy to finally meet him, but they have once again lost touch and are trying to find him.

Ty Hansen promised his mother's murder suspect, "I won't stop until I find her bones!" Forty years after Joann Hansen vanished, he literally moved tons of earth looking for her remains. Radar imaging indicated there was something buried here.

A photo of Joann Hansen shortly before she vanished in August 1962. The shape of her face is mirrored in the artist's rebuild of the woman's skull found in Suncadia, an area where the chief suspect once hunted.

The artist's reconstruction of the woman's skull found in Suncadia, a new resort east of the Snoqualmie Mountains of Washington. It resembled Joann Hansen a great deal.

Ty stood up as best man for his brother, Bob beamed proudly beside them, and Melissa made a lovely bride. Nick isn't sure what year they got married, but he knows it was in the late eighties or early nineties.

They soon had two daughters—Robyn* and Terri*— and they were both delighted with their girls. Like Ty, Nick adored his daughters.

"But the unconditional love from Melissa didn't last," Nick says. "It grew more and more conditional. I think Melissa might have thought I would change, but I couldn't. Being married didn't take away my fantasies. Loving my little girls didn't either. Inside, I still felt like a woman."

Nick never blamed Melissa, realizing that they each meant their marriage vows at their wedding, but they had both been naive about how they could work out the huge truth that divided them.

They were divorced, but they have remained friends and they share the care of Robyn and Terri.

Ty, too, feels that his marriage was responsible for a positive change in his world, even though they would eventually divorce.

"Brigette and Sylvie saved my life," Ty says. "They meant so much to me, and so did my wife, Jill.* I got clean and sober for them, and as they grew older, I wanted to tell my daughters about my family. The problem was that I didn't *know* that much about my family. Uncle Ken and his wife, Lorene, were gone, and I knew nothing about any relatives my mother might have had."

Ty decided to start with the court records on his parents' divorce—a divorce then thirty-odd years in the past. Ty himself was about thirty-three when he went to King County to ask about the divorce records.

He was shocked at what he found there. He'd never known about the physical abuse his mother had endured at his father's hands. But it was easy for Ty to believe—after the bruises, broken bones, and broken teeth he had suffered from Bob's punishments.

All he'd ever heard was that his mother hadn't wanted any of her children, that she had simply walked away from them without a backward glance. The woman he was reading about in the dusty divorce file sounded far different from the way his father had always characterized Joann.

The civil deputy at the counter evidently knew about the disappearance of Joann Hansen. He spoke confidentially to Ty.

"He told me that no one had ever found her, but then he said he had always believed my father had murdered my mother."

That revelation stunned Ty Hansen. He hadn't realized that many of the old-timers in the sheriff's department had long felt that his mother was a homicide victim; they just hadn't had any evidence to go on back in the day when no body meant no murder as far as the law and evidence went.

He knew his mother had vanished in August 1962. Ty wondered how many more people might still be around who would share information with him. Scarcely hoping that he could find his mother's divorce attorney—Duncan

Bonjorni—Ty thumbed through south King County phone books to see if Bonjorni was listed. Bonjorni might not even be alive, Ty thought, figuring that the attorney would probably be in his late sixties or seventies.

Bonjorni was alive, and quite willing to talk with Ty Hansen.

Ty took his daughter Brigette with him when he went to Bonjorni's law offices. "She took her first step there," he remembers. "In the rain at the parking lot, and she was so small. My wife and I were so blown away to see her walk!"

Bonjorni said that of course he remembered Joann Hansen. He had tried to help her, and then one day she had disappeared. Like the records deputy, Bonjorni was convinced that Joann was long dead and that she had been murdered.

He shared everything he knew with Ty.

Ty didn't know what to do with the information that he had finally stumbled upon; taken by surprise, he needed time to digest what he had learned, and he had no idea where to start looking for his lost mother. Bob Hansen had lived in a lot of places since 1962, and currently he was spending most of his time in Costa Rica. Ty doubted that his father would tell him anything about his mother even if he traveled to Costa Rica to confront him.

The barn in Kent near the Green River was gone, torn down when the road was changed, a road that now paved over where the white barn had once sat. But the Valley Apartments were still there.

Ty wondered if his dad might have buried his mother under the floors of the buildings Bob owned when she was last seen in 1962. Ty knew that Bob Hansen had cemented over part of the dirt floor in the barn not long after Joann had disappeared.

Had she lain undiscovered, deep in the ground that was now under a road?

That seemed unlikely at first; there were hundreds of places to hide a body around Washington State that were virtual wildernesses—impenetrable forests, deep lakes, and sere, sun-baked hills in eastern Washington. There was Puget Sound, just a block away from the last house Joann had lived in, that eventually emptied into the Pacific Ocean. Bob Hansen was familiar with the whole state of Washington. And he'd always had boats, boats seaworthy enough to traverse rough waters and tides in the Pacific Ocean.

"He could have hidden her body in many places. I left it alone for ten years," Ty remembers today. "I don't know why it took so long. Other things got in the way, but the mystery of my mother haunted me, popping up when I didn't expect it. I knew that one day I would have to face it head-on."

The millennium was approaching, and the last decade of the twentieth century was to bring more changes than anyone close to the Hansens' chaotic family could foresee.

Ty Hansen was in his forties when he told his old friend Cindy Tyler what he had learned about his parents' marriage and divorce: that several people he'd talked to believed Bob Hansen had killed his wife. Ty was ready to avenge his mother—if he could. Cindy was both horrified and captivated by this information.

"I had some free time," Cindy explained. "I decided that I would work with Ty to find the truth, and I told him, 'You know what, Ty? I'm gonna help you.' We didn't have much money; we sure couldn't afford to dig deep into places where Joann might be, but we hoped we could convince the county to help us."

Cindy agreed that there were so many aspects of Ty's mother's disappearance that hadn't been checked.

"Even though she had been gone for more than thirty years, I believed we could still find something."

The two old school friends made a good match; every time either one of them got discouraged about their seemingly futile search for Joann Hansen, the other was able to drum up enthusiasm. Cindy was more outgoing; she usually made the best cheerleader, and she was always able to get Ty to believe that they would find an answer—some day, some way.

Chapter Thirteen
AN IMPOSSIBLE CRIME

Given that many people who knew Bob Hansen through the years believed he had killed his first wife and gotten away with it, I wanted to be sure that Cecilia Hansen—his second wife—was alive and well. He must have been very angry when he realized that she wanted a divorce. She had been such a sweet and docile twenty-year-old woman when they met, and he had taken her to so many wonderful places.

Cecilia is alive, living in Costa Rica.

There was a second Cecilia, and they may or may not have been married. She abandoned Bob Hansen as soon as she got **her green** card. She, too, is living—in the United States—but, quite understandably, she doesn't want to discuss her brief relationship with Bob Hansen.

Although he was chagrined at how the two Cecilias had turned out, Bob was still entranced by Costa Rica. He wanted to settle there, and he kept his eye out for property to buy. In 1997, he also started sending checks and money orders to officials who he was told would make it easier for him to immigrate.

They accepted his money eagerly.

Bob was secretive about his Costa Rican connections. His old friend Marv Milosevich and his wife, LaVonne, suspect that Bob may have been married several times without announcing it. One photograph, with no notations on the back, may support that theory. Bob and an attractive American woman are standing together in front of an altar. She has an orchid corsage, and it certainly looks like a wedding photo. Who she is—or was—no one knows.

Bob approached several "possibles" in Costa Rica for his next bride. He took one young woman on a long hike, but he came back alone. Asked where his companion was, he explained, "She just went walking off and left me behind." Bob, however, was carrying the girl's backpack with all of her most valuable possessions.

The "disappearing" girl drew the attention of Costa Rican police, and they noted Bob as a possible suspect if she should have met with foul play. But despite the fact that the young woman was still missing, Bob wasn't arrested or charged with anything.

In about 1998, Bob met a beautiful girl named Flory Maria Villalobos-Perez in Costa Rica. She looked a great deal like the first Cecilia. The only bona fide way to tell them apart in photographs is to read the dates in Bob's scrawled writing.

Flory's birthday was June 27, 1974. That made her exactly—minus four months—fifty years younger than Bob Hansen. He was seventy-four, and Flory was twenty-four.

He found a way to win Flory's heart. When he saw that her parents were living in a broken-down house where a plague of bees had built hives, a home with few creature comforts, he offered to build them a new house.

He was still a skilled carpenter and soon finished a solid, weatherproof/bee-proof house. He was a hero to Flory's family, and she felt she owed him a great deal for being so generous with her parents.

When Bob asked Flory to marry him, she agreed. Despite his age, he was a tall, well-muscled man, but his thick hair was now snow white and his mouth hung half-open most of the time, a mien that old men often have.

Bob may have smuggled Flory into the U.S. from Canada, possibly using a bribe to get her out of Costa Rica. Once they arrived in Vancouver, British Columbia—years before 9/11 made border patrols more suspicious—it was fairly easy to drive across the northern Washington State border carrying a hidden passenger.

Bob's neighbors in Auburn, Washington, noticed the newest girl in Bob's house. She was very petite and had long dark hair, delicate features, a sweet smile, and a perfect body. She was, of course, young enough to be his granddaughter.

But nearby homeowners rarely saw Flory outside Bob's house, and when she was, Bob was always with her. Flory and Bob went hunting and fishing, and he taught her how to smoke salmon and dress game. She was lithe and lim-

317

ber, while Bob was stiff with arthritis, and age now forced him to walk stooped over.

Even so, Flory was loyal, and she was keeping her promise to pay Bob back for giving her family a livable house. If she longed for friends her own age or for some scintilla of personal freedom, no one knew. She really had no one to tell.

Once, an English couple who lived across the street invited Flory to go to the Washington State Fair with them. Bob was away for the day, and Flory shyly said yes. She wanted to go and enjoyed the fair tremendously. But Bob was outraged when he learned that Flory had gone to the fair without his permission.

"I own her," he shouted at his neighbors. "She belongs to me, and I say where she can go and who with!"

The neighbors knew better than to ask Flory to go anywhere with them again.

Surprisingly, Bob had notes in one of his many journals where he wrote about Flory's application for admission to Green River Community College's summer quarter, 1998. It is unknown if she ever went there.

Chapter Fourteen
AN EMPTY LIFE

Bob Hansen no longer saw his sons. Unaware of Nick's struggle with his sexual identity, he had been pleased when his older son married Melissa. As a kind of wedding present, Bob had offered to buy them a house down the street from his yellow rambler in Auburn.

It sounded too good to be true to Nick, and he was wary. Still, he and Melissa talked it over and decided to accept. Bob was gone in Costa Rica most of the time, and they could keep an eye on his place, and they couldn't really afford to pay for a house of their own at the time.

But there was a catch. They were on the verge of moving in when Bob informed them that there would be stipulations and "rules" they would have to follow if they accepted his "gift."

Nick and Melissa had two cats that they doted on, but Bob insisted that the cats would have to go. He wouldn't have them in *his* house. When he said that, Nick knew that his father had never meant to give them title to the house.

ANN RULE

Bob Hansen's extended list of dos and don'ts was much more controlling than the rules he had once set for his Montana hunting party buddies. He had the same overriding need for absolute control that he'd always had.

"We walked away," Nick says. "We weren't going to give up our pets, and it was pretty clear that the house wouldn't truly be ours, anyway. When he was in the States, living two doors down the street from him would be impossible."

That was the last time Nick and Melissa saw Bob. When their girls were born, they sent pictures of his granddaughters to Bob, but he returned the envelopes unopened.

Kandy Kay had been dead for about fifteen years when another of Joann and Bob's children shocked Bob Hansen. If Bob even suspected how determined Nick was to live another life in another body, he would have been furious and surely cut Nick out of his life forever. As it was, by the early nineties Nick was the only one of Bob's offspring who had any interaction at all with him, and that ended, of course, when he turned down his father's offer of a house.

Ty knew about Nick's longing to be a woman, but he hoped his brother would get past all that.

Just before Christmas, sometime shortly after the century turned, Nick Hansen called Ty. He wanted Ty to know that he was going to Thailand to have a series of operations performed by a transgender surgeon. When he came back, he would be "Nicole."

Ty was angry with Nick, and he begged him to think it over—but Nick was adamant. He had waited all his life to be the person he felt he was, and he would not be dissuaded.

A decade later, Ty still believes that no one is actually born in the wrong gender, and that those who have operations to change their sex are *choosing* to do that, and are in no way compelled. He argued, lectured, and pleaded with Nick not to take such an irreversible step as having all of his male organs removed.

It was like talking to a stone wall. Nick wasn't gay; inside, he felt he was a female. He went to Thailand and had the operations that would allow him to live like that.

Even so, the brothers are still close. Except for their four daughters, Ty and Nicole are, basically, all they have left of their secretive and often bizarre birth family. They did locate their half brother Bobby Morrison and had an affectionate reunion.

But now they have lost him again. They hope that he may read this book and get back in touch.

Nicole didn't tell her father what she had done; she hadn't talked to him in years, anyway. Bob probably found out. Melissa, Nick/Nicole's ex-wife, has an aunt and uncle who are longtime acquaintances of Bob Hansen's, and he undoubtedly heard of Nicole's surgery from them. It must have been a shock for him. The man who spent his whole life striving to be macho and the epitome of what he thought a male should be would not accept his oldest son as a woman, nor did he have the capacity to understand someone else's deep needs.

Nicole believes that her mother's sudden disappearance had a great deal to do with her very early confusion about gender. Along with her siblings, she experienced separation anxiety when her mother was ripped out of her life.

When that happened, none of Joann's children could completely trust or feel total serenity again.

Asked if she might have suffered so deeply at her father's abuse that she wanted nothing to do with being male, Nicole nods.

"I've considered that," she says. "I just don't know for sure. I've had a lot of therapy to help me understand it."

Ty had worked on many part-time construction jobs with his dad over the years, swallowing his feelings of anger when Bob belittled him. There were times when he simply needed the money, even though, on one roofing job, Bob Hansen threw him off the roof because he said Ty was tacking the shingles down wrong.

However, when Ty learned the truth about what had happened to his mother, he wanted nothing to do with the old man.

Bob began to sell off his rentals; in his third season in Costa Rica, he'd rented a nice condominium there and he was planning to buy a more expensive place.

Flory was living under "lock-down," and if she had ever felt love for Bob Hansen, she no longer did. She was a virtual prisoner, and neighbors along the street in Auburn felt sorry for her.

They chuckled when they saw official-looking cars drive up and Department of Immigration officers stride toward Bob's front door. When he opened it and started to argue with them, they wrestled him to the ground and put him in handcuffs.

He'd had no choice but to marry Flory to keep her in the country.

As I researched this case, no one knew exactly where Flory was. Fearing that she, too, might have vanished as Joann did, I checked with King County detective sergeant Jim Allen in May 2011, and he assured me that Flory was safe and living in Costa Rica. He had a recent telephone number for her and kept in touch.

Bob had never worried much about what law enforcement could do to him. But the immigration agents had worried him. His plan was for him to leave America and live in Costa Rica; he was willing to take whatever steps he needed to take to move there, and he needed to have as clean a record with the police as possible.

He had always felt invincible as far as the law went. He'd certainly been arrested a number of times for fighting and road rage offenses, but he'd only spent one night in jail—and that was the sentence Joann's lawyer, Duncan Bonjorni, had given him back when Bonjorni was a judge.

In March 1979, Hansen had been arrested for assault when he hit a highway employee with a shovel in an argument about the placement of a sign. Bob was working on one of his rentals and had placed a FOR RENT sign on the shoulder right-of-way. The state worker grabbed the sign and threw it in the back of his truck. Enraged, Bob confronted him and reached for his sign. The truck door hit him, and the state employee pushed him when he was off balance. Bob fell on his back. *Nobody could do that to him!* He grabbed the shovel and hit the man hard.

In 1981, he was arrested for indecent liberties toward a woman who was applying for a housekeeper job. That charge was dropped.

His temper got him into trouble again in May of 1984. He took his tractor to the bank of the Green River and starting scooping out dirt he wanted to use to fill up a hole in his field. He was undermining the carefully engineered bank. Confronted by a game warden, Hansen gunned his truck in anger. It slid and hit the game warden's truck. The warden called 911, and the message became garbled.

Marv Milosevich laughed as he recalled the chaos. "The operator heard 'Green River Road,' and the tact squad came in en masse, armed. They thought that the Green River Killer was hiding in the brush."

Most men would have been concerned to be a suspect in the Green River murders, an eighteen-year-long string of murders of more than fifty runaway girls or young prostitutes, many of whom were last seen on the Pacific Highway.

Captain Frank Adamson, who took over command of the Green River Task Force in late 1983, had a list of three prime suspects. And Bob Hansen was number one.

Adamson drove past Hansen's Spanish-style house on Green River Road occasionally, not really hoping to see anything but curious about the older man who lived there.

A young woman had reported Hansen as "a very peculiar person." She had answered an ad that he'd placed in local papers for a housekeeper.

The twenty-three-year-old woman agreed to have her possible employer meet her in front of a motel on the Pacific Highway on July 22, 1984. She sometimes worked as an escort and thought that his ad might have only been a front, especially when he mentioned the motel as a meeting place. She had been surprised that he was so much older than the "usual johns."

"He seemed nice enough at first," she told Green River Task Force investigators. "He took me to Valu-Village and gave me thirty dollars to buy some clothes. It's mostly a secondhand store, but they have some good things."

After she had chosen a few outfits, the old man drove her to his house. She saw that he owned several acres of property and a barn and thought he seemed to be wealthy.

"Once he got me there," she said, "he said he wouldn't take me back to the highway. I was there several days. He showed me a special police badge he had, but I didn't believe he really was a cop. He took me out to his barn—he was very proud of it, but I was afraid when I saw that one wall was covered with dozens of pictures of women. He even took pictures of me. I was afraid maybe it would be an awful kind of souvenir."

Afraid that she might also end up on the wall, she felt trapped. The man hadn't really hurt her, she said, but he kept her a prisoner and touched her inappropriately. She was afraid he'd never let her go. She was too far from the Strip to walk back—even if she could manage to get away from him.

At length, she had seen a chance to run, and she hitched a ride back to the Pacific Highway. She thought that the man who held her captive might be the Green River Killer.

There were hundreds of reports from citizens who were sure they knew who the river killer was, and, initially, the task force detectives thought that the young woman merely had an active imagination. But they changed their minds when she was able to lead them back to Bob Hansen's home and barn.

If there had indeed been females' pictures in the barn, they were gone by the time King County detective sergeant Jim Allen asked to look through the old barn.

He did find a camera with the pictures Hansen had taken of his most recent captive, along with a large cache of guns and knives. The barn had a round door high up in the ceiling, a trap door held in place with large spikes. Allen climbed up and searched inside—and found nothing.

At first, Bob Hansen was a little nervous about the King County sheriff's search—and he hired a private investigator to look into what the detectives had found. Nothing of import, his PI said, and Hansen bragged that the photos were there all along; he'd simply taken them off the wall and hidden them in a drawer.

The PI told Captain Frank Adamson where they were; they weren't salacious. They were, oddly, mug-shot-type photos. They weren't official booking photos, but Hansen had apparently taken them to look that way—snapping both front and profile views of about forty women. None of them were on the list of women—over fifty now—who were missing or whose remains had been found thus far.

Although Jim Allen found nothing definite that might tend to incriminate Bob Hansen in the string of serial murders, his home's location on Green River Road and his apparent taste for young prostitutes still made him a suspect.

For Frank Adamson and other investigators, Bob Hansen seemed to be a strong "person of interest." Then FBI profiler John Douglas and psychologist John Kelly from New Jersey—both of whom were often dead-on in their profiles of suspects—disagreed, and Hansen slipped toward the bottom of their "persons of interest" lists.

Dr. Kelly wrote of Hansen: "A wealthy and eccentric farmer . . . I believe him to have been a lonely, elderly man who wanted a woman to live with him and take care of him. He even advertised for such a woman. His house was important to him; he felt secure behind the heavy wooden door. I believe his house was much more important to him than the river or the woods. He was too conservative and concerned about his wealth and success, and would not endanger that by being in the river or woods with corpses or transporting them long distances. If he was the 'River Killer,' that girl would never have escaped from his house."

In some areas, Kelly was right about Bob Hansen. In others, he was very wrong. Bob knew the woods, rivers, lakes, and wilderness extremely well and had spent much of his life enjoying the outdoors as he fished, hunted, and camped out. He was not housebound in the least.

Had the psychologist known about the "elderly man's" long missing wife or the girl who never came back from a hike with Bob in Costa Rica, Kelly might have rethought his profile.

Bob Hansen wasn't charged with anything connected to the Green River cases, but he was charged with indecent liberties and unlawful imprisonment for his alleged sexual advances toward the young woman who had answered his ad for a housekeeper. He was booked into the King County jail on August 4, 1984, and his bail was initially set at $25,000. When a records check showed his 1981 arrest for indecent liberties, his bail was raised to $100,000.

There is, however, no record that he was convicted of his second sexual crime. Bob could handle his bail easily, and he could afford the best defense attorneys.

One thing about the search warrant of his barn concerned Bob Hansen. He'd had a wig and some kind of costume, Marv Milosevich recalled, and the investigators took that, along with his collection of knives. The disguise in the barn could have been a Halloween costume or it might have been used for something more sinister.

Bob told Marv that he had kept $5,000 in cash under the rim of a sink, and the sheriff's men hadn't taken that. "I don't think they knew it was there," he said to his old friend.

"Don't fool yourself," Marv said. "They knew it was there—they weren't looking for money."

A few days later, Bob came out to Marv's place in the country. He had $10,000 in a mason jar that was wrapped in rubber bands. He wanted Marv to keep it for him—just in case he needed emergency money. Marv wasn't sure where he should put it, and he really didn't want that much cash secreted on his property.

But Bob insisted, and he dug a hole on the edge of

LaVonne's flower garden and put the mason jar in it. He left, sure that his emergency money was secure.

"It wasn't a very safe hiding place," Marv said with a laugh. "My Labrador found it the first day and dug it up! I made Bob take it home and hide it at his place."

Bob Hansen's life had taken a downturn, and the older he got, the more paranoid he became. He begged Marv Milosevich to be the executor of his will. He wanted to be sure that none of his children or *their* children inherited any of his assets—money or property.

"They sent me pictures of their kids," he told the man he considered his best friend. "But I sent them back, unopened. I don't want to know anything about them."

That was hard for Marv to understand; his living room was full of photographs and mementoes of his children and grandchildren as well as friends who were as close as relatives.

Basically, Bob Hansen had always been something of a loner, and now he was isolating himself even more, building walls that grew higher and higher. He didn't need or want his two sons or their offspring. As far as he was concerned, his children had betrayed him. He would find friends in Costa Rica, he assured Marv.

It was true that Bob Hansen had often advertised for "housekeepers" when he was in between wives and/or girlfriends from Costa Rica. Living all alone, he was still seeking housekeepers as he passed eighty.

His son Ty had described Bob as "a terrible cook," and

he hadn't improved over the years. He kept a folder titled "Things to Do," and in April 2006 he wrote out a recipe for soup inside.

Garlic—1 whole clove
Onions—15 large yellow
Cabbage—2 heads
Carrots—4 packages
Celery—2 stalks
Chilis—5 (2 green and 3 red)
Culantro [*sic*]—2 bunches
Green onions—2
String beans—12 cans
Peas—1 large package frozen

Bob Hansen's recipe would have made an extremely large vat of soup. Life sustaining, perhaps, but hardly tasty. He did need a woman's touch in his kitchen, and for "companionship."

In 2009, Kathleen Huget found a copy of his most recent ad, along with a stack of mimeographed "applications" in his house.

His ad appeared on September 17, 2008, in the Domestic Care and Services sections of the *Seattle Post-Intelligencer*'s south county editions:

Auburn resident looking for live-in housekeeper. Female preferred. Light housekeeping, companionship, light cooking, shopping etc. Room and board + wages. Salary negotiable. Call 555-1234.

About half of Hansen's questions ignored equal rights edicts. He asked women who answered his ads to fill out his applications; they had to give their ages, their heights and weights, whether they had a husband or a boyfriend, if they smoked, used drugs, or drank. And he insisted that they respond to many more highly personal questions that were none of his business.

After he interviewed prospects for someone who would clean his house, cook for him, and be a companion, he scrawled his opinions in the margins of the applications. It was clear he wanted a housekeeper "with benefits."

Hansen's comments showed that. He was very picky and wrote "too fat," "too old," "too young, "has a boyfriend," and sometimes "too ugly."

Few women met his standards, and those whom he grudgingly hired didn't stay long.

For most of his life, Bob Hansen had exerted control, *power,* over almost everyone he came into contact with. He was essentially a heartless man who laughed at people who gave to charities or were concerned about others who could do nothing for them in return.

A psychiatrist probably would have diagnosed him as a person who, deep inside, had no sense of control, a man who had to micromanage everyone and everything to stave off panic.

Perhaps.

Flory, Hansen's third or fourth wife, was a devout Catholic who was often horrified by the way he treated other people. She asked him once: "Aren't you ever afraid of God's wrath?"

Bob was cruelly patronizing when he answered: "Flory, don't you understand? I *am* God . . ."

That had frightened her—for Bob's soul. He was asking to be struck down. She half-expected a bolt of lightning and a thunderclap from the sky. But nothing happened. He kept on living a hedonistic, controlling life.

Eventually, sometime early in the new century, Flory was able to find her way back to Costa Rica. She had paid dearly for her parents' house; she could no longer live like a butterfly in a cage, trying to deal with Bob Hansen's temper and blasphemy.

But there were so many more young women waiting in Costa Rica; when Bob started his new life there, he was sure he would have his pick.

His newly purchased condo in Costa Rica was lavish for that country, and he memorialized every room and all of its luxuriant details and features with his ever-present camera.

Located across the street from a park, the building was modern and Bob had selected comparatively expensive furnishings and paintings for every room. He could hardly wait to live there permanently.

The ironic thing about Bob's snapshots was that they were almost always a bit out of focus. He seemed to be trying to capture "things" and not people. Even Cecilia and Flory were universally posed against tourist attractions or something Bob wanted to brag about.

Chapter Fifteen
LOOKING FOR JOANN

In the early years of the new century, Cindy Tyler and Ty Hansen were still searching avidly for Joann Hansen, missing now for more than forty years. Beginning with Patricia Martin, they talked with everyone and anyone who might have some memory of Joann and what had happened to her. At one point, they hired an investigator to help them canvass possible witnesses to the lives of Bob and Joann back in the fifties and sixties.

"It seemed that each time we talked to someone new," Ty recalls, "they said the same thing. 'Wasn't she murdered and buried under a cement slab by Bob Hansen?'

"At first this response was shocking. But at some point, we were used to hearing the same thing. No one should become used to hearing about his mother being murdered and buried under a slab of cement."

Even when Cindy Tyler located one of Bob's attorneys who had retired to Chicago and asked him about his former client, she was shocked by his response.

"Oh—yeah," the attorney said. "He was the 'cement man,' wasn't he?"

Ty felt a sense of outrage that the mother he couldn't even remember had been accepted by people living in the south county area as a homicide victim and then quickly forgotten. Had everyone known but no one pursued the mystery of her disappearance when it had happened? Was it a matter of not wanting to be involved?

Well, Pat Martin had gotten involved, and so had Duncan Bonjorni. They were rays of hope and encouragement that someone still cared.

Ty and Cindy had never found a police file that might have existed shortly after Joann disappeared in August 1962. Patricia Martin had tried her best to file missing reports but no one would listen to her then.

They learned that there *had* been a case file more than forty years earlier, but it had been destroyed. That was a fairly common practice in the days before computers provided incredible amounts of storage space; very old files were shredded to make room for more recent cases.

At one point in 2004 or 2005 when Ty was in California, Cindy, hoping for clues—or even daring to hope Bob might confess to her—gathered her courage and knocked on Bob Hansen's door. No one answered, and she knocked again. She was just about to leave when the door swung open and she saw Bob towering over her.

"He let me in," she said, still surprised that he had.

"I stayed almost an hour. He showed me some clippings he had saved from the time Ty's 'Loan Arranger' car lot failed. He seemed happy that Ty had gotten into trouble.

"His whole conversation was about making everyone else look bad—even his own children."

At Ty's urging, the King County Sheriff's Office had updated his mother's case. She would remain officially listed as missing, and they periodically reviewed her case. They certainly had more recent files on Bob Hansen's temper tantrums, fights, and assaults. Of course, there was the case where he had held the young woman captive in his barn. Detective Jim Allen still did whatever he could to unravel the details of the long-vanished woman. If Joann was alive, she would be in her seventies.

If she was alive . . .

Some of the people Ty and Cindy had talked to thought that Joann was buried under Bob Hansen's barn (which no longer existed); some believed she was even closer to where she was killed; Bob had built the Willows Apartments next door to their house close to the same time she vanished. Pat Martin said, "I think she's in the foundation of those apartments on the Kent Des Moines Road."

That was an eerie thought; Bob had moved his children into those apartment units when they were in their mid- to late teens.

Under construction, the Willows Apartments had little vegetation around them and could be clearly seen from the heavy traffic that moved up and down the Kent Des Moines Road, and from the Chevron station across the street. It would have been extremely difficult for Bob to bury a body beneath the strip of half-built apartments without someone noticing.

But there were other apartments that Bob Hansen had constructed. The Valley Apartments were virtually identical to the Willows, and the one-story brick building stood a few feet from where the old white barn had once been.

Although Detective Sergeant Jim Allen and prosecutor Jeff Baird had turned Ty Hansen and Cindy Tyler away so many times, it didn't mean they didn't care or didn't believe that Joann Hansen had been murdered decades earlier. The biggest problem was the ever-shrinking budget the King County executive and the county commissioners specified for both their departments.

Ty and Cindy were convinced that the most likely place to dig on the grounds would be where the old barn had been; it had been reduced to rubble, and that area was now covered by an asphalt road with the Green River only steps away. Another likely spot was under the Valley Apartments.

Ty and Cindy were exploring the possibility that new forensic tools said to spot bodies hidden in the earth might help to find Joann's remains. It seemed such a long shot, and they knew it would be expensive.

In 2003, they contacted Bernard Housen, a geologist at Western Washington University in Bellingham, to see if it might be possible to use some kind of imaging—such as radar—to reveal a body buried in the ground. Cindy had read that an infrared process was being utilized in police investigations to spot disturbed earth and vegetation even though it wasn't obvious to the naked eye. Red splotches often meant that plants and trees were slowly dying because their roots had been disturbed when murder victims' graves were dug.

Housen explained that Ground Penetrating Radar (GPR) could reveal clandestine grave sites up to twenty feet below the surface. It wasn't foolproof, but with careful measurement of the areas to be searched, *and* by marking known objects already in the ground such as utility lines, buried storage tanks, or foundations long covered over with dirt, something unusual—an "anomaly"—might be seen and evaluated.

The old white barn where Ty and Nick used to play in the rafters, where Bob Hansen had temporarily imprisoned young women, was long gone now. An asphalt county road—S. 251st Street—had been built two to four feet over the barn's concrete floor.

And the Valley Apartments had been constructed some years after Joann had disappeared.

Joann had technically received this land and the barn that once stood there in the division of the Hansens' assets in 1962. But both had somehow ended up on Bob's side of the ledger soon after she disappeared.

One of the renters in the Valley Apartments told Ty Hansen that she had always felt there was something odd about the cement floor in the laundry room, which all the tenants could use.

The laundry room, too, was added to the proposed radar search.

There would be four "digs" that followed this first attempt on October 7, 2003.

Bernard Housen worked from a scale map drawn to the dimensions of the area to be searched. Fifty-three transect lines were run so that any finding could be triangulated and both suspicious anomalies and benign anomalies located could be marked on the map.

A GSSI SIR 2000 Ground Penetrating Radar unit with a 400 MHz antenna would be used to detect data. Working between four large steel nails that were placed in the ground to mark the corners of the site, Housen dragged the antenna along the surface of each transect line. He walked at a slow but steady pace.

Would he find an anomaly that proved to be Joann Hansen's bones? The conditions were perfect for the GPR search and both benign and unknown objects showed up.

Housen found three areas of "disturbed soil anomalies" from two to four feet below the cement barn floor pad.

"Areas A, B, and E are all consistent in depth and size to represent a clandestine grave site."

He warned, however, that there might be other causes for disturbed soil—such as the removal of stumps or rocks.

A GPR search of the Valley Apartments' laundry room showed some similar findings. The concrete slab floor was inordinately thick for a laundry area—two to three feet. It had no rebar to stabilize it.

The only way to be sure of what lay beneath the old barn floor or the laundry room was to dig, take core samples, and bring in cadaver dogs. Ty Hansen and Cindy Tyler were prepared to do that, even if they had to do the shoveling themselves.

Twice, Ty used an excavator to explore the area under S. 251st Street, digging six-foot chunks out of the dirt beneath the road.

He found nothing.

With fellow volunteers, Cindy Tyler and Ty began to cut through the cement slab in the Valley Apartments' laundry area and the lawn outside.

"When Ty and I started digging there," Cindy recalls, "both Detective Jim Allen and deputy prosecutor Jeff Baird grabbed shovels and joined us.

"There was a moment when I almost lost it," she says, "when someone found a large bone. I really thought we had found Joann and I started to cry. They had a sheriff's patrol car standing by and the bone was rushed downtown for the medical examiner's office to check it out.

"But it wasn't Joann; it was an animal bone. Eventually, we found so many animal bones, and every time we hoped we might have solved the mystery of where Ty's mother was.

"We didn't find her at the Valley Apartments, but we sure made a mess of the lawn," Cindy said. "My brother, Russ Tyler, went back there with grass seed to try to bring it back to the way it was."

From 2003 to 2005, the backbreaking work of exploring the earth for some sign of Joann Hansen continued. Luckily, there were many volunteers who joined Cindy and Ty in their sad project, ready to dig with shovels. They didn't have enough money to rent machines that would drill and then lift cores of dirt and "anomalies" out of the ground. Neither did the King County budget.

It was no wonder that both Ty and Cindy were burned out in their frustrating goal to find Joann and give her a proper burial where those who loved her could visit her and place flowers on her grave.

But, like phoenixes rising from the ashes, they always found new energy to continue.

Chapter Sixteen
A DIFFERENT APPROACH

Stymied by all the blocked pathways he had encountered, Ty Hansen had something else he needed to do. That was to confront his father with what he believed to be the truth. If he never found his lost mother, at least he could tell his father that he *knew* finally that she had never deliberately left him and his siblings. He wanted to get that message to the old man and accuse him of her murder.

He tried to do that in 2005 and 2006, but Bob turned a deaf ear and swore at him, threatening to call police if Ty didn't get off his property.

And then it was early in 2008.

Ty entered Bob Hansen's phone number into his cell phone and hit "talk." He heard an almost endless ringing before it went to voice mail. He wondered if his father had caller ID and was deliberately avoiding talking with him. He might be sitting there, listening. Maybe he had the kind of answering machine where he could hear his callers leave a message.

Ty was determined to have his say; if he had to leave

a message instead of confronting the old man, he would do that. He had missed the "beep" while debating what he should do, and he quickly redialed, and this time he began to speak when he heard the shrill tone.

"I know our mother never left us on purpose," Ty said. "I know you killed her—and I'm going to prove it.

"You hid her somewhere," Ty said evenly. "You murdered her way back in 1962. What did you do with her body?"

There was only silence on the other end of the line.

"I won't stop until I find her bones!" Ty shouted, before he hung up. "Not until I find her bones!"

That explained one of the yellow notes that Kathleen Huget found tacked to Bob's wall, the one that baffled her the most.

The frightened old man listening to that message wrote those words on a yellow note:

"Ty: 'I won't stop until I find her bones!'"

Bob Hansen was growing more paranoid, perhaps even having waking nightmares as many elderly people do. He had printed another note in late August:

"2 MEN IN BACKYARD. THEY RAN AND JUMPED BACK FENCE—ONE GUY DROPPED BACKPACK."

Chapter Seventeen
NOT QUITE CLOSURE

Ty Hansen had begun his quest full of resentment and rage. He was angry that he had lost his mother so early that he couldn't even remember her, angry at the physical and mental abuse he had suffered at his father's hands. He wanted some kind of justice, an ending to the lies about Joann that would avenge his mother—but he also wanted to punish his father. He may not have thought about this aspect of his crusade when he set out.

There came a point, however, when Ty realized that it wasn't all about him and his pain and loss. He was nearing fifty now. In a way, he had come to know the pretty dark-haired woman who had undoubtedly perished when she was much younger than he was. Through her friends who had never forgotten her, Ty's blurry picture of his mom began to fill in and take shape. He realized that she had lost far more than he had.

"And I also saw that my mother's disappearance had hurt so many people and changed their lives, and not for the better. I certainly didn't give up trying to find out the truth, but I wasn't just thinking about myself any longer.

"I guess, in that moment, I finally grew up."

Bob Hansen's eighty-fourth birthday was on October 13, 2008. Ty told Cindy that he wanted to go see his father.

Even though Bob hadn't threatened Cindy when she knocked on his door, she was worried about what he might do when he saw Ty. He'd had nothing to do with either Ty or Nicole for years, and she had seen his delight in criticizing both of his sons during the hour she'd spent with him.

Like everyone else who either knew Bob or knew of his reputation for violence, she was afraid for Ty.

But Ty was adamant. Bob Hansen's birthday fell on a Monday, and the two of them drove to Auburn. Alongside the road, the vine maples were scarlet and the big leaf maples golden as they neared the town where Bob lived.

They parked a few doors down the street from the neat yellow house that was now Bob's "pad" in America when he wasn't in Costa Rica. But when Ty knocked on the door, there was no answer—and there was no vehicle in the driveway.

Ty sensed that time was running out for his father. "I had gone through several of the first stages of grief by then," he recalls. "I was probably at a point of acceptance that my mother was dead, and I would still look for her, but I guess I wanted a final word with my father, some kind of peaceful conversation."

They waited for a long time; Ty was convinced his father was living there and determined to wait until he got home.

"I didn't realize then how frightened Cindy really was to be there."

More than an hour later, Bob Hansen's Toyota 4Runner came down the street and turned into his driveway, coasting into the garage.

After the old man crawled awkwardly out of the driver's seat, he went to the back of his SUV and was rummaging around, looking for something. Ty, followed by a nervous Cindy, walked up and they were standing behind him as he closed the rear hatch.

Bob Hansen was caught off guard as he turned around, shocked to see Ty.

"I want to talk to you," Ty said, and Bob turned away from him.

His father had grown very old, and he seemed afraid.

"Dad!" Ty called. "I forgive you. Do you hear me? I forgive you!"

The elderly man slowed down only slightly.

"I hope you can forgive me?" Ty shouted. He didn't regret his long hunt to find out what had happened to his mother, or feel guilty about contacting the sheriff. At the same time he realized that it must be hard on the old man.

Ty was torn, pulled in two directions. He and Nick had worked with their dad when they were younger, they'd learned things from him—if not ethics, then skills that they'd been able to use.

The vacations and trips had been fun once in a while— even though they never quite got over waiting for their father to get mad about something. Kandy Kay was gone, and Nicole had a completely different life. Ty's uncle Ken was gone.

"What I would have given to have a father like my uncle Ken," Ty lamented. "He was a really good man."

Ty still didn't trust his father; he still believed that his father had destroyed his mother—and he didn't want to spend time with him. He didn't want anything from him. But he hated the idea that one of them would die full of hate.

"Dad," Ty called again, "can you forgive me?"

Bob Hansen half-turned toward Ty, and his son could see hatred in his eyes. He brought his hand up and brusquely signaled with it in a dismissive gesture.

"Get the hell off my property!" Bob snarled. "You son of a bitch!"

Cindy tugged at Ty's arm and urged him to come back to their car. Bob had always had a lot of guns and ammunition in his houses, and there was no telling what he might do.

For an instant, the world stood still—and then Bob limped toward his house and disappeared. For Ty, there was a measure of satisfaction. His father had always forbidden them to mention their mother's name to him. And now the old man had had no choice but to hear Ty's angry accusations. Would it have any impact on him?

It was over so quickly. Ty hadn't said everything he wanted to, and he knew he might never know what his father's reaction was.

Marv Milosevich, however, heard about the confrontation between Ty and Bob.

"Bob told me that Ty scared him to death," Marv said when interviewed. "Bob said, 'I thought he was going to kill me.'"

Ty had no intention of killing his father, but he wanted some justice for his mother. He had frightened Bob, long after the years when he had been terrified by his father.

Later, Ty tried once more to speak to his father but was unsuccessful. "Whenever I'd come up to Washington State, I'd make it a point to drive by his house," Ty recalls. "I didn't feel there was any chance of talking to my dad, but I wanted him to see my car go by and know that I hadn't given up trying to find what had happened to our mother."

The encounter on his birthday only served to convince Bob Hansen that he needed to move to Costa Rica for good as soon as possible. He contacted an attorney in Washington and asked him to do research on how he could become a Costa Rican citizen.

He planned to take all his assets with him and hide them in Costa Rica.

Bob thought it would be far easier than it was. Bizarrely—since he didn't trust either of his living children—Bob had made friends with an American couple who had become Costa Rican citizens decades earlier. Herb Stuart* and his wife, Lily,* were about the age of Ty and Nicole, and they seemed to dote on the aging man. He had known them for twenty-five years.

But Costa Rican officials made immigration more and more difficult, and the Stuarts assured Bob that they could be his sponsors so he could achieve citizenship in Costa Rica.

But Herb Stuart said it would take money. Lots of money.

Although Bob usually kept his financial business close to his vest, Marv Milosevich believes Bob advanced as much as half a million dollars to the Stuarts. Either they told him or he had heard somewhere that it would take that much to prove his good faith to the proper government offices.

When Marv Milosevich heard that, he attempted to warn Bob that it sounded fishy to him. "I spent an hour and a half drinking coffee with Herb Stuart when he came up here," Marv said. "Apparently, he had told Bob that he had to prove to the Costa Rican government that he had enough funds to take care of himself so he wouldn't be a burden on his chosen country. Herb figured it had to be at least a million dollars. He told me that he and his wife were going to be Bob's 'personal advocates.'

"In my opinion, that guy was a con man, and Bob fell for it. I tried to warn him but he trusted Herb Stuart."

Bob Hansen wasn't the kind of immigrant that most countries would covet. There was still the mystery of the missing girl who'd gone hiking with him, and although he never served more than overnight jail time—including the sentence (then) Judge Duncan Bonjorni gave him—Bob had a record of numerous arrests in the Northwest. Most of them stemmed from fights where he'd physically hurt people or destroyed property.

He was required to present many documents to validate statements he'd given Costa Rican officials. He scrambled to get his birth certificate and proof of his place of birth in Junction City, Oregon, and he filled out a number of forms that he sent to the capital in Salem. He asked that his documentation be taken care of with all possible speed.

Hansen also contacted the Washington State Patrol offices to obtain a record of any rap sheet of arrests he might have. He seemed to luck out there; his record came back clean. It wasn't luck, however. Bob had cleverly changed his answers on the WSP form. He gave his birthday as October 16, 1924, instead of October 13, 1924. He also changed his name slightly—from Robert Milton Hansen to Robert Melvin Hansen.

The WSP report said that they had not found any felony offense under that *exact* birth date and *exact* name.

Whether Bob Hansen had any proof that Herb and Lily Stuart had actually *given* the half-million dollars he said he'd sent them to immigration authorities in Costa Rica—or not—nobody knows. Marv Milosevich doubts that they did.

Robert Milton Hansen had hurt people in one way or another all his life. Suddenly, *his* world was crumbling.

His efforts to get into Costa Rica as a citizen came to nothing. Officials there refused his application, and much of his fortune was gone. Nevertheless, he drew up a will leaving everything he owned—including his house—to Herb and Lily Stuart! It would be his final revenge on his sons.

But it wouldn't be a surprise. Ty had known for decades that he and Nick would get nothing in their father's will, just as the money set aside for them to collect on their eighteenth birthdays from their mother's estate had disappeared. They had both accepted that long ago.

"He really had no one else to leave his assets to," Ty says. "He had planned to leave them to Marv Milosevich, but he got mad at Marv over something."

At last, at eighty-three, Bob Hansen had begun to ponder his own mortality. He had a few of the ailments that came with old age—various aches and pains—but he was basically healthy and still quite strong, strong enough to walk along the Green River for miles every day, picking up trash. He had, however, stopped hunting and fishing.

He had no one to go with him to pursue the blood sports he had enjoyed for much of his life.

"When I get old," he once told Marv Milosevich, "I'm not gonna go to one of them rest homes. You sit in a chair, and they don't take care of you. I'm gonna go my own way—kill myself."

"That'd be hard to do, Bob," Marv said cautiously.

"I can manage it—I've made up my mind."

Since the midnineties, Bob had begun to doubt his own mind. He was forgetting things. To cover up for that, he kept a kind of journal, most pages riddled with misspellings, which Kathleen Huget found. There were also the yellow notes on the walls of his house. He jotted down miscellaneous bits of information—things he'd heard on *60 Minutes* or Fox News.

"Gold—Highest in 62 years"

"Ford Will Give Buyout to 75,000 employees—from $40,000 to $140,000"

"Venezuela's President called Bush a 'Diablo'—Devel"

"FEEMA is paying eleven million dollars per night for hotel rooms in Louisiana for flood victims"

"CATHOLIP BISHOP: No stem cell research, no abortions, no condoms or birth control devices"

There were scores of notations that seemed to have no pattern, although Hansen focused on countries that controlled oil, elderly celebrities who had died, war, disaster—and occasionally, sex transgender operations. He was either trying to keep his mind alert and current or he was writing down items because he had no one to talk to.

When Flory was still with him, he listed resorts and trip destinations, along with the names of high-priced hotels and motels.

He studied his notes constantly, trying to build muscles in his memory.

Hansen also wrote precise lists of things he had to accomplish, particularly when he was preparing for a visit to Costa Rica. One list had thirty-eight reminders for everything from "Put money in checking account to cover expenses while I'm gone," to "Unplug refrigerator and freezer—Put rocks in door."

What purpose rocks in the refrigerator doors served is obscure.

Bob Hansen was an intelligent man but a lousy speller. Some of his notes are laughable because of that. He wrote "VIAGRA—Pills for sex—Impudence [*sic*] Drug."

When he commented on President Bill Clinton's disastrous affair, he wrote "Monica Luinsky or Levinsky, Clinton's Lover."

Hansen also kept track in his journals of how many fish Marv Milosevich had caught. He did not list his own tally of fish.

From the time he was a young man, he'd kept precise listings of every penny he had spent on the women in his life. Bob Hansen had always considered that they "owed him" for the food they ate and the secondhand clothes he bought them.

The year 2008 was coming to an end. Marv and LaVonne Milosevich talked about asking Bob to come for Christmas dinner, but knowing that he would put a pall over the festivities, they kept putting the decision on that aside. Finally, they decided not to.

Bob Hansen had finally run out of friends—except for Lily and Herb Stuart in Costa Rica. His estate, estimated to be worth $5 million, would reward *them* for standing by him. Hansen's will specifically said that his wife, Joann Cooper Morrison Hansen, had left him, and it was worded in such a way that even if she should ever resurface, he wanted her to have *nothing*. His children were also disinherited in the will.

Later, Marv felt guilt about that last Christmas, but he had also become tremendously disappointed in his one-time mentor, the man he had tried valiantly to remain friends with. The meanness in Bob Hansen had only intensified as he had grown older, and there were few comfortable moments to be spent with him.

Bob was a racist, a miser, a misanthrope, the living image of Ebenezer Scrooge, a white supremacist, and a latter-day Nazi. He continued to blame everyone but himself for his misery. Maybe it had started when he was a little boy—when he had to go with his father to the dreaded Stump Farm, or for some other reason no one knew about.

It is said that in old age, we become who we were when we were young—only more so. Happy people are fun to be around even when they are long past social security age, and angry people are as sour as dill pickles when they are elderly.

In his almost eighty-four years, Bob Hansen had become only more paranoid and resentful of others.

Chapter Eighteen

THE SILENT HORN

On Tuesday morning, August 4, 2009, the neighborhood on 14th Avenue in Auburn was very quiet. Forty-seven years earlier plus six days, Joann Hansen had disappeared. Perhaps the date had some meaning for Bob Hansen. Possibly, he had chosen this day at random.

His next-door neighbor finished his breakfast and realized that he hadn't heard the familiar "ooga-ooga" of Bob's antique automobile horn.

He walked the ten or twelve feet next door and could see that the garage windows were fogged over. When he found a clear spot to look inside, he saw Bob Hansen sitting as still as death behind the steering wheel of his car. He knew instantly that Bob hadn't died of a stroke or heart attack; he had died the way he'd once told Marv Milosevich he'd chosen.

By his own hand. With the help of carbon monoxide. His skin was the characteristic bright cherry red that appears when carbon monoxide shuts off oxygen in the blood.

Some might say that Robert Milton Hansen's death was a prime example of "What goes around, comes around."

His life had ended in ashes. He was alone in an empty house and he had alienated everyone who might have been there for him when he was an old man.

Hansen would never achieve his dream of starting life over in Costa Rica with a new young woman. That country had barred him as a candidate for citizenship. The luxurious condo he had furnished lavishly wouldn't be his home—ever.

But he had avoided living in a nursing home.

He had told Marv Milosevich that he would go out of this world in his own way. He had accomplished that bleak ambition; his final act ensured that he was in control. Or was he? The chilling aspect of suicide by carbon monoxide is that, at a certain point, the brain is still active—but the subject cannot move. If Bob Hansen had changed his mind partway through his suicide plan, paralysis would have already overtaken his body.

There had been no going back.

There was little of any value in Bob Hansen's last house. Everything was secondhand, worn, and cheap. Hansen's yellow notes and his journals remained—on almost all of them he'd written about mundane things: reminders, his opinions, scraps and bits of disorganized news left behind for strangers to find.

Ty, Nicole Hansen, and Cindy Tyler removed only the stacks of photo albums that Bob had kept since he was twenty. There were faded pictures of their mother in some of them, and photos of themselves as babies and in their growing-up years. They could all see Joann's tenderness toward her babies; it was something to hold on to.

There were forty times as many photographs of Bob posing with dead animals, birds, and fish—his trophies from sixty or more years of hunting and fishing.

That was his legacy.

This was the house that Kathleen Huget had walked into a few weeks later, the rooms where she would "hear" both a silent cry for help and a sense of looming rage and danger.

"I'm not afraid of you," Kathleen had shouted into the empty rooms, and her voice didn't tremble at all. "I'm not afraid of you! You don't scare me, and you can't hurt me!"

Initially, she knew nothing about the man who had lived and died in this house, but the eerie presence of evil she sensed couldn't be denied.

The Realtor friend of Kathleen's had told her she could have anything she found in the house. A lot of it was usable if not new. She neither needed nor wanted it, but she didn't feel as if she could just take it to the dump.

"I had an estate sale," she said. "I figured if there was any profit, I could give it to charity."

Lots of people showed up on the day of the sale. Sophisticated bargain hunters soon moved on after they saw that there were no precious antiques or collectors' items in the yellow rambler in Auburn.

"But there were poor people who came," Kathleen recalls. "There were quite a few migrant workers in the area during harvest season in August and September. Most of them were barely making it. They were so happy to find six pairs of socks for a dollar, or a table for fifteen dollars. Before long, I cut the prices in half. An old bed meant so much to them, or some dishes that didn't match. Some of them called relatives and they came to the sale, too. In the end, I was giving things away, and it was a wonderful experience to see how grateful they were."

Having heard of Bob Hansen's stinginess and his scorn for anyone who gave to charitable causes, Kathleen admits that she took a certain satisfaction as she virtually donated all his possessions to people who basically had nothing.

"I knew he would have hated my doing that," she said with a smile. "He never believed in helping poor people, and now they were driving and walking away with the things he'd left behind, with their little kids jumping up and down with excitement."

Chapter Nineteen
A LANDMARK LAWSUIT

Ty had attempted to file a lawsuit against his father in 2006, believing that the only thing that might get the old man's attention would be to threaten his bank account.

"I didn't want his money," Ty says, "but I wanted to honor my mother, to somehow let her know that we were still fighting for her. We had run out of money to hire excavators and bulldozers in our search for her remains. If we could finally get the inheritance that our mother had left us, we could keep on looking for her. But I couldn't find a lawyer who would take my case."

The Christmas season was in full swing in late November 2009, and Bob Hansen had been dead for four months when Ty Hansen and Cindy Tyler finally located an attorney who would represent Ty and Nicole.

Dean Brett, a Bellingham lawyer, agreed to file a wrongful death suit on behalf of Joann Hansen's estate.

It seemed a unique legal situation. Their surviving children were suing on behalf of their mother, dead for almost five decades, against their father, also deceased.

*　　*　　*

A King County judge had ruled in 1969 that Joann Cooper Hansen was legally dead—even though her body had never been found. By 1975, thirteen years had passed with not one sign of her. Nor had her remains surfaced by 2009, despite the determined hunt kept alive by Ty Hansen and Cindy Tyler.

Sergeant John Urquhart, spokesman for the King County Sheriff's Office, said that as far as his department was concerned, Joann's case had remained open in 1975. "And it remains open today."

Urquhart said that Bob Hansen had, indeed, been a person of interest in Joann's disappearance, but that sheriff's detectives had never been able to find enough evidence to file murder charges against him.

"At the time Joann Hansen disappeared," Sergeant Urquhart added, "missing persons cases weren't pursued as vigorously as they are today."

So many people had been afraid of Bob Hansen, and Ty and Cindy hoped that frightened witnesses might feel safe enough to come forward now that he was dead. Someone, somewhere, had to have information—no matter how slight it might be—that could be tied with what *was* known to finally weave a net that would incriminate Bob. He couldn't be tried in regular court now, but he might be facing a higher judgment beyond life.

If her children could bury Joann's earthly remains in a cemetery with a headstone, it would mean the world to them.

No amount of money could ever compensate Joann's children for the loss of their mother when they were only toddlers, nor could it erase the pain and suffering she had endured in her brutal marriage and in her sad anticipation of her own death.

Local papers in Seattle and in adjoining counties carried the story of the bizarre lawsuit. Forty-seven years later, the *Seattle Post-Intelligencer* did cover the mystery of Joann Hansen's disappearance. KOMO-TV, the ABC affiliate in Seattle, heard from the network headquarters in New York after they did a comprehensive overview of Ty and Nicole Hansen's suit against their late father.

"Would Ty Hansen be willing to be interviewed by Chris Hansen (no relation) regarding the lawsuit he had filed?"

Of course Ty would! He had done his best to gain publicity that might reach someone who knew something about his mother. Her photographs and the history of the case were registered on the Doe Network, a successful clearinghouse for missing persons and unidentified bodies in America. Joann's face—as she had looked in 1962—was also on posters and fliers sent out by smaller organizations dedicated to locating the lost souls who had never come home.

Chris Hansen, famous as the NBC reporter who meets internet stalkers looking for underaged girls and boys on *To Catch a Predator*, conducted an interview with a man with the same last name. They were not related. Chris and Ty Hansen were almost the same age, in their early fifties.

Ty explained that he had always been told his mother deliberately left their family, and he had only become suspicious when he read his parents' divorce papers from 1962 and realized that his mother had claimed she suffered from violence and abuse.

"No matter who I've talked to, my father's friends, my mother's lawyer, and even my aunts—my mother's sisters whom I didn't even know existed—have told me the same story. They all say, 'Well, your dad killed your mom and he probably buried her down there at the barn site.'

"My father knew I was investigating, but he never reached out to say, 'Stop!' He just basically told me to go to hell," Ty Hansen continued. "I went to his house several times in 2005 and 2006, while I was traveling to do more legwork on the project. I'd visit him and confront him. I'd say to him, 'Dad, I think you killed Mom. I think you're a liar, a murderer, and a coward.' And he'd just cuss at me and tell me to get off his property."

Ty told Chris that he had also made it a practice to drive by his father's house in Auburn—not stopping, but letting his father know that he hadn't given up his crusade to find his mother.

And then their détente was over. The King County Medical Examiner's Office notified Ty Hansen in August 2009 that his father was dead. He had committed suicide by asphyxiation.

To say that Ty and Nicole grieved wouldn't be correct. Ty had attempted to forgive his father and to ask forgiveness for doing what *he* had to do. And Bob Hansen had wanted none of it.

"I think the prospects didn't seem very good to him," Ty told Chris Hansen. "So he decided he was done with it."

Ty said he'd discovered his father's tax records that indicated the eighty-four-year-old man's assets totaled almost $5 million. But he wasn't truly suing Bob Hansen's estate for monetary gain. Still, he'd already heard from people who accused him of greed and of dishonoring his father.

They had no idea of what the real story was.

"I was doing it for my mother," Ty explained. "Not for money. I don't care what people say about me. It doesn't bother me one single bit whether I get nothing or everything. It makes no difference. I'm still going to pursue this mystery."

Ty had far more supporters in his years-long hunt for his mother than he had detractors.

In the end, Ty and Nicole prevailed in the suit against their father's estate. It validated their knowledge that Joann Hansen had meant for them to have *her* estate when they reached eighteen. But they got very little money to help in the continuing exploration of the ground beneath where the old barn and the Valley Apartments had been. The amount of the settlement was just under $100,000, and it was divided three ways. Ty, Nicole, and Dean Brett, their attorney, each got one third.

Herb and Lily Stuart, Bob's friends in Costa Rica, got all the rest of his estate, including his condominium and the house in Auburn.

This is where things stood in 2010 when Ty Hansen, Cindy Tyler, and Kathleen Huget contacted me. None of them wanted money for the story of Joann Hansen; each of them begged me to write it only to keep her memory alive, and in the hope that this book might eventually help in their search for her.

Like Kathleen, I was quickly caught up in the mystery and tragedy of it all, and particularly in the injustice done to a young mother, close to my age, who lived a few blocks away from where I'd moved a year after she'd disappeared. If the timing had been just a little different, I probably would have known her. Maybe I could even have helped Joann escape safely from Bob.

If Joann had lived, Kandy Kay—the same age as my daughter, Leslie—would have probably been one of the girls in my Brownie troop, and she would likely be alive today. Ty, of course, did play baseball with my son, Andy.

But life is always a series of connections and near misses. Decades of "If only . . ." In the end, the one thing I could do for Joann and her abused children was to write her story.

And to try to find her earthly remains.

Chapter Twenty

COULD IT POSSIBLY BE?

Ty, Cindy, and Nicole had often been energized whenever news reports mentioned that an unidentified female body had been found—only to be disappointed when they learned that none of the remains were Joann's.

Beginning in 1974 with Ted Bundy's swath of terror in the Northwest, and continuing in 1982 with Gary Ridgway's Green River victims, there were scores of news flashes about young women whose bodies had been located. Bundy's victims were found in mountain foothills or in their own beds, Ridgway's in secluded wooded areas. Gary Ridgway buried some of the unfortunate young women he murdered in shallow graves.

Not all of the unidentified women could be traced to either of those infamous serial killers. And there were always women who, like Joann Hansen, had seemingly disappeared into the mists of time.

On September 7, 2010, a backhoe operator was working on the water system of a golf course in the new and expensive resort that had been built on formerly forested land. Suncadia is located between the towns of Cle Elum and Roslyn just beyond the eastern foothills of the Snoqualmie mountain range.

Ironically, one of the area's only tourist attractions before Suncadia was an acres-wide cemetery where Slavic coal miners and their families were buried early in the twentieth century. The gravestones bear photos of the deceased encased in celluloid. Although vandals have pried many of the photographs out, the graveyard is still a fascinating study in life, death, and tragedy of more than a century ago.

The other attraction is the town of Roslyn, where the wildly popular television series *Northern Exposure* was filmed. A giant moose is still painted on one of the downtown buildings.

Land for the Suncadia Resort was cleared in 2002. It now draws visitors, sometimes to the distress of old-timers who loved the old towns and the forests and lakes just beyond the hamlet's limits. They knew for years it was inevitable that wealthy investors would discover Kittitas County, and they dreaded it.

Now they had no choice but to accept it as progress.

The backhoe operator unearthed a shallow grave, not more than two feet below the surface.

A skeleton lay beneath. There was precious little evidence to identify him or her, only some blue clothing and a simple gold wedding ring in size five or six.

Kittitas County undersheriff Clayton Myers told reporters that it would take at least two days to remove the remains, as his department had contacted forensic anthropologists so that the skeleton could be very carefully lifted from the earth. They believed, however, that the body was that of a female between five feet four and five feet ten inches tall, and probably somewhere in the age range of nineteen to forty years old.

She had straight teeth and extensive dental work.

When I saw the forensic artist's drawing of what the woman probably looked like in life—using the dimensions of the skull—my heart stood still for a moment.

The sketch looked a great deal like Joann Hansen—the same long jaw, cheekbones, forehead.

Since Suncadia was only eight years old, the body had almost certainly been buried in the woods long before that. Hunters, fishermen, miners, and loggers were about the only humans who ventured deep into the wilderness.

Ty Hansen was doubtful; he had been through similar situations before, and he didn't let himself hope that this could be, at last, his mother.

Sadly, Ty was right. Kittitas investigators had checked out all the missing woman reports in the state of Washington, they had distributed photographs of the drawing and the gold ring, and they entered her dental records in the NCIC computer bank—all to no avail.

It was months later when one family came forward, hoping against hope that the body in the Suncadia Golf Course was *not* their daughter.

The mother of Kerry May-Hardy had allowed the Green River Task Force to take a sample of her own DNA in 2004, fearful that her daughter might be one of Gary Ridgway's victims. It hadn't matched any of the initially nameless dead girls.

It took months to compare that DNA with DNA taken from one of the bones of the still unidentified body found in September 2010.

But the FBI laboratory found an absolute match; the deceased was Kerry May-Hardy, who had disappeared from Seattle's Capitol Hill district in June 1972. She was twenty-two when she vanished. Kerry was married at that time. One of her relatives believed that Kerry had lived in an apartment on an upper floor of the building that housed the Crisis Clinic in 1972, but that wasn't true. There were no apartments in that towering old Victorian house, and the comings and goings of people who weren't authorized to be there were monitored very carefully.

As this is written, investigators are backtracking on Kerry May-Hardy's life, hoping to find information that will lead to *her* killer.

The search for Joann Hansen continues. This book may prove to be the one avenue that will lead Ty and Nicole Hansen and Cindy Tyler to the truth about what happened to a young woman who literally faced death so that she could be with her children and raise them in a loving home.

When I look back over the hundreds of disappearance and homicide cases I have been asked to explore over the last forty years, I realize that they all come down to human emotions that have somehow run off the tracks. Synchronicity and chance bring people together, and not all of these connections end happily. I still believe that Ty Hansen will find his mother, although I wouldn't wager on how long it may take.

One thing I do know: Ty, Cindy Tyler, and Nicole will never give up their search for Joann and the truth about the end of her life.

Anyone with information, no matter how slight, on Joann's life in August of 1962 should contact the King County Sheriff's Office in Seattle or myself at www.annrules.com. I will see that those messages reach Ty Hansen.

THE CASE OF
THE DEADLY
GIANT

One way to commit the "perfect murder" is for the potential killer to choose a victim who is a complete unknown to him—or her. Detectives cannot follow threads into the past histories of either the slayer or the victim because there *are* no connections. Serial killers invariably pick vulnerable targets that fit their perfect profile. But, beyond that, they search for someone they don't know at all. There are two reasons for that: (1) Their sadistic fantasies demand that there be no emotional ties to their victims and they look for potential "kills" that are mere objects to them, and (2) they don't want to get caught by pathways, however narrow, that wend their way back, giving investigators reasons to question them.

While assailants may stalk victims, those under observation are often as unaware of danger as a rabbit being watched by a coyote.

When two total strangers met on an Independence Day weekend—Saturday, July 3, and Sunday, July 4, 1971— one of them believed they were unobserved. The other had no inkling of the violence that lay ahead. It was a chance meeting that might never have been traced, except for the skillful and painstaking legwork by King County police detectives. They reconstructed in the most minute detail the movements of those two lives, movements leading inexorably to a fatal confrontation that would leave one dead and the other to face a jury of his peers.

The Fourth of July weekend in the Northwest promised three days off to most, but the weather was hardly appropriate for the celebration of a midsummer holiday. The air was as chilly as early April and rain drizzled on and off on Saturday, making the hopes for picnics, swimming, and fireworks dismal. Sunday, the Fourth itself, seemed a bit warmer but storm clouds still lowered, dropping rain on scattered areas of King County.

Ordinarily, Echo Lake, a small tree-lined body of water improbably set just west of Aurora Avenue's bustling traffic lanes, would be alive with celebrants on the Fourth of July. On this soggy holiday, only the homeowners whose property bordered the lake were there, and most of *them* were staying inside.

At 2:30 Sunday afternoon, a young woman who was renting a lakeside home took her dog for a walk close to the water's edge. She was idly gazing at the wavelets lapping against the dock when her attention was drawn to a patch of crimson bobbing up and down in the lake just below the surface.

It looked like clothing of some sort and she grabbed a stick and nudged it ashore.

She was surprised to see that it was a woman's red leather coat. It seemed to be in new condition, but it was ripped under one arm. When she looked closer, she saw stains of a much deeper red near the ripped area. There was something about the coat that gave her a chill of apprehension. She wondered what to do, and then gingerly carried the soaked coat up to a picnic table near her house. She left it draped on the table and dialed the King County Police Department.

Patrol Deputy Jess Hill responded to the call. He agreed that the sodden coat in almost new condition was, indeed, a peculiar discovery. It wouldn't have taken much mending of the torn lining to fix it, and it looked expensive.

While Hill was talking to the young woman, a teenage boy who lived with his parents in the Echo Lake Motel, which was several hundred yards from the lake's edge, made an even more ominous discovery. Attracted by the popping of firecrackers near the lake, he had wandered down the path that was an easement for motel visitors to reach the beach. He'd stopped for a few moments in a grassy clearing to watch a father and his three youngsters as they lit firecrackers. Then the boy headed toward the lake.

He was surprised to find some things on the ground directly ahead of him that didn't belong there. There was a woman's black purse—its contents scattered all over the grass. There was an address book, papers, cosmetics, and a checkbook in addition to the myriad items most women carry in their handbags. There was also a bra, a ring, and a broken necklace.

Near the purse, the grass itself appeared to be soaked in a wide pool of thickening blood that was at least three feet long and two feet wide.

The teenager backed away and ran to tell the man he had seen setting off firecrackers. Warning his own youngsters to stay back, the man walked to the bloodstained area. He, too, viewed the scattered possessions, noting there was a bloodstained card from Seattle Children's Hospital and a pack of Kool cigarettes, its label almost obliterated with drying blood.

He stepped to the shallows where he stared with apprehension into the weed-choked water. A pair of red hot pants and a single nylon stocking floated lazily near the shore.

"You stay here," he told the boy. "Don't let anyone down here. I'm calling the sheriff."

Detective Sergeant Bob Schmitz and Deputy Ben Colwell of the sheriff's north precinct sped to the Echo Lake address. They found Deputy Jess Hill already at the lake, and he had just learned from the radio dispatcher about the newest clothing discoveries that had been found just around an outjutting section of the shoreline.

The torn jacket and the hot pants and single stocking had probably been thrown in the lake at the same spot and then drifted apart with the tide.

Whatever had happened here at the now-serene lakeside didn't look good. Detectives Dan Nolan and James McGonagle soon arrived to join in figuring out the mystery at Echo Lake.

Viewing the blood-soaked patch of grass and the jumble of feminine paraphernalia on the ground, the detective crew had little doubt that someone had been grievously injured on the spot—if not killed.

They hoped that the woman—clearly it *was* a female—who had bled this much might have been rushed to a hospital by someone who had witnessed an accident or even a fight.

Already a group of curious bystanders had been drawn to the scene when they saw the ever-increasing number of squad cars parked on the road above. The investigators immediately cordoned off the lakeshore before anyone could edge too close and trample what could be vital physical evidence.

The sheriff's detectives stepped out on a dock adjoining the beach area. Despite the weeds, the water near shore was relatively clear and they could see not only the hot pants and stocking the teenager had discovered but several other items that did not belong in the lake: a multicolored change purse, a lipstick case, and a small plastic-bound case. There was, however, no sign of any victim of an attack that had surely taken place.

The woman who had shed so much blood had either managed to escape, naked, or she was in the lake floating silently just beyond the scope of their vision.

The detectives on the scene asked the police radio dispatcher to contact sheriff's divers George Zimmerman and Joseph Dollinger. The expert swimmers cut short their own Fourth of July celebrations with their families at once and drove to Echo Lake.

They arrived about 6:30 p.m., entered the water, and began to swim slowly side by side out into increasingly deeper water. The detectives waited tensely on shore as the silent search was carried out.

It only took ten minutes before Deputy Zimmerman suddenly dove toward the bottom and surfaced holding the body of a woman. He had spotted her lying facedown on the bottom in about twelve feet of water some twenty-five feet from shore. He and Dollinger brought the woman's body to shore. She was completely nude, save for the shredded remnants of a nylon stocking clinging to her right foot.

She wore a wedding band on her left ring finger.

The detectives who observed the petite form could only guess that she might have been attractive in life. Although the tiny woman's figure was voluptuous and well proportioned, her face—beneath wet strands of longish blond hair—was a ruin. Her forehead was split above her right eye, and there were open wounds over and under that eye as well as on the top and sides of her nose. Ugly bruises marked each side of her chin and two rows of round bruises—as if fingers had pressed deeply into her flesh— were apparent on the underside of her left arm.

The dead woman appeared to be in her late twenties or early thirties and was probably about five feet tall. She could not weigh more than 110 or 115 pounds.

"She hasn't been dead long," Nolan commented. "Her body is perfectly preserved. On a beach as popular as this one, her purse and clothes didn't go unobserved for long."

"I wonder what she could have done or said to make someone this angry," Ben Colwell muttered. "She's been hit again and again—and hit hard. She sure wouldn't make much of an opponent for anyone. She's just a little bit of a thing."

As they waited for deputy medical examiners from Dr. Gale Wilson's office, detectives carefully placed plastic bags around the victim's hands and secured them at the wrists to preserve possible evidence under her fingernails.

At 7:15 p.m. coroner's deputies removed the body to the King County Medical Examiner's Office to await a postmortem examination.

In early July, it doesn't get dark in the Northwest until almost ten p.m., and Sergeant Schmitz, Deputy Colwell, and detectives Nolan and McGonagle remained at the body site until it was fully dark, meticulously searching the shoreline and the shallows for every possible piece of evidence, anything that might somehow explain the incredible violence that had taken place and the motive behind it.

The two divers moved once again into the lake. This time they retrieved a wine-red jacket that obviously matched the short shorts found earlier. The jacket had been ripped to tatters. There was also a beige blouse—styled in leotard fashion—of sheer stretch fabric with panties attached. However, the blouse had been ripped into two pieces and the panty half floated separately. The divers swam in widening circles one hundred feet from shore searching the bottom of the lake for a possible murder weapon.

They found no weapon. Seventy-five feet from shore, Deputy Zimmerman located a woman's white crisscross sandal in new condition. Could someone have thrown it that far? Or had the wind stirring up the waves carried it there?

Dan Nolan photographed the scene and all the evidence and then assisted McGonagle as they took triangulation measurements of the area and bagged the evidence in plastic containers. The triangulations would allow them to pinpoint exactly where the woman's body and the evidence had been—if they had to return to the site or needed to re-create it.

As they went over the scattered contents of the black purse, they consistently found one name: Mrs. Bethany Stokesberry.* Credit cards, doctor's appointment cards, and letters alike bore that name and gave an address, some six or seven blocks south of Echo Lake.

"I don't think there's much question that the dead woman is Bethany Stokesberry," Nolan remarked. "If she has a family at this address, we can probably get positive identification tonight."

McGonagle nodded grimly. No amount of experience in homicide investigation can inure an officer to the dreaded task of informing a family that someone they loved is dead.

As the investigative crew finished gathering evidence and darkness settled over the peaceful setting, it fell to Dan Nolan to contact possible family members at the residence whose address appeared in the victim's belongings. Nolan, a veteran of the King County Police Department, is a native of Ireland, a congenial soft-spoken man whose voice still carries a trace of brogue in relaxed moments.

Now he approached a pleasant dwelling where he was greeted by a man in his thirties who said he was Beth Stokesberry's husband, Martin.

The worried husband fought for composure as he said he and Beth had been married for ten years. Responding to Nolan's gentle questions, Martin answered that his wife was missing.

"She didn't come home last night," he said anxiously. "And I haven't heard any word from her today either. That isn't at all like her—she always calls."

Bethany, whom Stokesberry said he had met and married in Scotland while he was stationed there in the air force, had occasionally stayed away all night with friends. "I didn't want to file a missing persons report on her—and embarrass her," he said. "But I'm really worried now. It isn't like her to be gone for more than twenty-four hours."

Stokesberry agreed to accompany Dan Nolan to the King County Medical Examiner's Office in downtown Seattle to view the body of the woman taken from the lake.

As the long drawer slid out from a wall of body containers, Martin Stokesberry turned pale.

"It's her," he said, barely breathing. "It's my wife, Bethany."

"Are you sure?"

"Yes—there's no doubt at all."

When the shocked man was able to talk more, he told Nolan that he, his wife—who was thirty-one—and their two sons, seven and nine, had lived in Seattle for about four years, and that he had been employed by the same company as an electronics technician for five years.

She was a good mother, he said, but Bethany was at home with the boys all day and Stokesberry worked a lot of overtime. His wife missed the camaraderie of pubs that were neighborhood meeting spots in Scotland where everyone knew one another and drank a few pints with their friends or played darts.

"I was tired after working twelve-hour days," Martin said, "and was usually glad to stay home with our boys while she went out for a few hours. She drove herself or she'd go with couples who were friends of ours."

"Were you ever jealous—I mean, was it possible that she might have been seeing someone?" Nolan asked quietly.

"No. Never. We trusted each other."

As Stokesberry described the night of July 3 to the detectives, he said he had driven his wife to the Frontier Tavern, a neighborhood meeting spot where she often went on weekend nights to drink a few beers and chat with friends. It had been between ten and ten thirty when they had arrived and Bethany had spotted a car that looked like one belonging to Brian and Susan, a couple who were friends of theirs.

Stokesberry warned his wife to be sure to come home with the couple. Then he wouldn't have to worry about her. Bethany was wearing her new pantsuit and a red leatherette coat that evening, and carried about $60 in cash with her.

In response to further questions, Stokesberry confirmed that his wife smoked Kool cigarettes. He also emphasized that she could not swim. In fact, she was almost obsessively afraid of the water.

Stokesberry then explained that he himself had driven home because he had promised a friend—who was making his debut as a radio disc jockey—that he would tape his show that evening. He had turned on the recording device, alternately checking the transcription and watching a late movie. He couldn't recall the name of the movie; he remembered only that it was some kind of war movie. He hadn't watched it continuously.

At a little after 1 a.m., Stokesberry said he'd gone to bed for the night, confident that their mutual friends would give Bethany a ride home.

"When I left her off at the Frontier, that was the last time I saw her, and I didn't hear anything from her until you [Detective Nolan] came to tell me that she was probably dead."

Many husbands would have been jealous to have their wives go to taverns alone, but Martin Stokesberry again assured the investigators that he didn't mind. He understood that she needed to have adult conversation and a few glasses of ale occasionally. He didn't believe she was interested in any other men.

Even minutes count in homicide investigations, and, for the crew of King County homicide detectives, the combination of the holiday and the late-night hour when Bethany's body was identified could not have been worse. Although the sheriff's detectives were prepared to work all night on July Fourth, they had no luck in finding witnesses. Not only were many lakeside residents away from their homes on vacation, but when the investigators visited the Frontier Tavern, they found it was closed. Their phone calls to the number listed for the owner went unanswered.

Long after midnight, the weary detectives were forced to temporarily halt their search for Bethany Stokesberry's killer.

However, a few hours of sleep were all they could get. They were up with the first filtered morning light.

Dan Nolan and Sergeant Don Actor were back in the north King County area early Monday morning. The tedious but vital door-to-door search began. They talked to many residents living in the houses surrounding Echo Lake.

In addition to the scores of homes in the area, there were two sprawling apartment complexes with almost a hundred expensive units facing the lake. Again and again, the two detectives received the same disappointing answers; either the occupants had been away from home the night before—or they had heard nothing unusual because of the boom of fireworks.

At length, Nolan and Actor struck pay dirt that at least gave them some estimate of the time of the attack on Bethany Stokesberry. A homeowner, who lived almost directly across the narrow lake from the spot where her belongings were found, told them that he had arrived home shortly after midnight. While he was fixing himself a late snack in the kitchen, he had been alarmed by what he termed a "penetrating, serious female scream."

"I thought it might be just some hijinks because it was the Fourth of July, but it was frightening enough that I went outside on my dock to hear better. I carried my flashlight, but I couldn't make out anything across the lake. It was absolutely still for moments and then I heard it again. It was definitely a woman, but all I could make out was the word 'help!' I kept listening but there was nothing else. It was all quiet by about a quarter after twelve."

The man explained that he hadn't called the police or checked further because shouts and screams on the lake were common during the summer months.

Nolan and Actor canvassed the taverns and motels along Aurora Avenue North on Monday, July 5, with negative results. Most of the taverns were closed for the holiday—at least until evening—and the motel managers had no information at all about a woman screaming for help.

Their repeated calls to the owner of the Frontier Tavern continued to be unanswered.

"If Bethany Stokesberry went into the Frontier Tavern after her husband let her off around ten thirty," Nolan surmised, "and she was screaming for help at midnight, the chances are pretty good that she met her killer inside. And if the bartender is as observant as most of them are, we may get lucky."

"Right," Actor agreed. "But until we find him, we haven't any way of knowing who else was in the Frontier Saturday night—unless we get a call from someone who hears about the murder on radio or television."

Luck, however, was not with the detectives. If anyone had seen Bethany Stokesberry on Saturday night and recalled who she had left the tavern with, he or she obviously did not want to become involved. A second night passed with no real clues to the victim's movements on the last night of her life.

At 6 a.m. on Tuesday morning, Dr. Gale Wilson, King County medical examiner, performed the autopsy on the five-foot-tall, 120-pound blonde. Although she had been beaten savagely, the worst violence had been done to her head. There were nine wounds concentrated on her face and skull—some up to nine centimeters in length. Her nose was broken at the bridge, and she had severely bitten her lower lip when she was struck forcefully in the jaw. The tooth marks in her lip were her own.

The wounds were what Dr. Wilson termed "upper force" injuries with crushed edges, as if the hapless woman had been struck with some manner of blunt instrument. She had suffered severe brain damage called contrecoup injuries, which macerate the brain as it slams against the opposite side of the skull from where the force of the blow struck. That damage was severe enough to have rendered her unconscious almost immediately—causing her death within hours if she didn't get emergency medical help.

Even with that, Dr. Wilson doubted that the woman could have survived.

Bethany Stokesberry had been the victim of a savage attack. The medical examiner noted more human tooth marks—not her own—encircling one of the victim's nipples. Both breasts were bruised extensively along their outer walls.

Had a sexual attack sparked the violence that ended in death? The victim's nudity and her breast injuries strongly suggested it, but she had been in the water for too long before she was discovered for Dr. Wilson to determine if she had been raped or molested.

The postmortem made one thing patently clear: something the victim had said or done had enraged her killer to the point of maniacal fury. Ironically, despite her grievous wounds, Bethany Stokesberry had not succumbed to the multiple head injuries. Her cause of death was drowning.

Her lungs were completely filled with water and death would have come quickly, as it always does with freshwater drowning, as the human bloodstream, with a higher salt content than lake water, actually sucks water into the blood.

Dr. Wilson determined that the victim had died at about 2 a.m. on the morning of July 4—with an hour's leeway in either direction. A test of her blood showed no alcohol or drug content at all.

Bethany Stokesberry had fought her attacker, as nail scrapings taken from beneath her broken fingernails revealed.

Detectives observing the autopsy preserved and labeled strands of her hair. If they found her killer, he might have some of her hair on his clothing or person. DNA as a forensic tool was unknown at the time.

The burning question for the detectives was, Why? What had transpired in an hour and a half on July 3–4 that had ended in the death struggle on the shore of Echo Lake?

Shortly after the autopsy on Bethany Stokesberry was completed, Nolan and Detective DuWayne Harrison checked the Frontier Tavern and found the owner had finally returned.

"Sure, Bethany was in here Saturday night," the owner-bartender replied, after explaining that he had been out of town since closing his bar that night. "She sat right there," he added, pointing to a stool at the bar.

"She was alone?"

The bartender nodded. "Bethany used to come in often—usually on a Friday or Saturday night. Used to talk with whoever was here. Sometimes she left with a gentleman—could have been her husband—sometimes with another couple."

"And Saturday night?"

"Well, we're usually pretty busy on Saturday nights. I can give you the names of several people who sat at the bar. Bethany talked to all of them—but she left with Long-tall-Paul* and another couple."

"Long-tall-Paul? Do you know his last name?" Harrison asked.

"Nope. He's been in maybe eight or ten times. All I know him by is 'Long-tall-Paul.' He's a really tall fellow with a beard. He comes in to play pool. About the only other thing I could tell you is that I hear he works part-time at Melby's Tavern down the road."

"Did Mrs. Stokesberry seem to have known this Long-tall-Paul from before?" Nolan questioned.

The bartender shrugged. "Maybe—but I don't think so. He was trying to get her to go to another tavern with him and I guess she must have agreed because, as I say, they left a little before midnight with this other couple who were sitting there."

Asked about Bethany Stokesberry's clothes, the tavern keeper mentioned that she had been wearing some kind of hot-pants outfit. "She got up once and twirled around beside the bar and asked everyone how they liked her new outfit. She was very outgoing and cheerful."

The detective duo next went to Melby's Tavern, where Long-tall-Paul was supposed to have a part-time job. Entering this tavern, which was only a block or so down the street from the Frontier Tavern, Detectives Nolan and Harrison nodded to its lone occupant. The man identified himself as the part-time bar manager and explained that he was principally occupied with his duties as owner of the Echo Lake Motel.

"Do you know a guy called Long-tall-Paul?" Harrison asked.

"Sure do," the man responded amiably. "He's not here now. He's probably over at the motel."

The investigators exchanged glances.

"Long-tall-Paul lives at my motel—upstairs with Al and Cindy. He works here some of the time, but I'm not expecting him in this morning."

After days of frustration in attempting to find anything that might lead back to Bethany Stokesberry's death, the officers were now being handed the name and address of the last person seen with her. They headed back to the motel building whose main entrance is a few scant feet from Aurora Avenue. The unit number given by the owner was on the second level at the far end of a narrow hallway.

Detective Nolan knocked at the door. When it opened slowly, he found himself looking at a giant of a man who stood before him with a blanket wrapped around his shoulders.

As Dan Nolan told me later, "There was a step up into the apartment as it was, adding to the illusion of height, but the man who came to the door appeared to be about eight feet tall."

The man identified himself as Paul Anthony "Long-tall-Paul" Vinetti* and said he would be willing to talk with the detectives if they didn't mind being exposed to the flu, as he was sick.

When they walked into the motel unit, the two detectives saw that Long-tall-Paul Vinetti was almost as tall as he had first appeared in the doorway. He stood well over seven feet!

Questioned about Bethany Stokesberry, Vinetti said that he had talked with her briefly in the Frontier Tavern on July 3, but he hadn't left with her.

"Did you know her?" Nolan asked.

Vinetti shook his head. "Not before Saturday night—I made some conversation with her while we were sitting at the bar."

Before pressing him further on his statement, detectives Nolan and Harrison made arrangements to talk privately with the couple he lived with: Al Rigglestatt* and Cindy Mateska.*

That way they might have a clearer idea if Paul was telling them the truth about Saturday night when they questioned him in depth.

Dan Nolan talked with Rigglestatt just outside the motel unit, while DuWayne Harrison talked with Cindy. The revelations gleaned from these interviews cast serious doubts on Vinetti's statement that he hadn't left the tavern with the murder victim.

Rigglestatt told Detective Nolan that he had met Long-tall-Paul, twenty-three, at Smokey Joe's Tavern in downtown Seattle about six months earlier.

"When I found out that he didn't have any place to live and no job and hardly any money, I felt sorry for him and invited him to live with me and Cindy. We didn't have any beds or couches in our unit that he could fit into—he's about seven foot two or three—but he was happy to sleep on this kind of makeshift pallet on the floor."

Paul had chipped in on their household expenses whenever he made a few dollars, and Al and Cindy found him a docile, easygoing houseguest who was always willing to help clean or walk the couple's pet dogs.

"What happened on Saturday night?" Dan Nolan asked.

"Well, Cindy and I were both home when Paul came in between twelve thirty and one. He was breathing heavy and he seemed pretty upset. He had blood all over his shirt and Levi's and on his arms. I asked him what happened. He said he was in a fight at the Frontier Tavern.

"He told me the name of the other guy in the fight, and I believed him because he's a fellow we've had trouble with. Paul said, 'I really beat the guy—I took my boots to him.'

"When he took his boots off, I noticed blood up on the instep and long hair caught in the cleats. I told him he'd better just go to bed and he did. Cindy took his clothes and threw them in the closet, and I took and washed his boots off and pulled the hair out of them. Cindy washed the blood off his arms. Then Cindy and I went downtown for a while, but I got to worrying about the guy Paul beat up, so I drove back to the Frontier Tavern, but I couldn't find anyone in the alley.

"Paul had told me, 'Every time the guy moved or moaned, I kicked him,' and I was afraid he might really have been hurt bad.

"The next day, Cindy went down by the lake and came back and said, 'They're taking some young girl's body out of the lake. She's been raped and murdered.' When I told this to Paul, he seemed nervous and sick."

In the meantime, Cindy Mateska was telling Detective Harrison an identical version of Paul Vinetti's homecoming on Saturday night. "Paul came in with his sleeves rolled up and blood all over his hands and arms. He knows I disapprove of drinking and I scolded him and told him to go to bed. He gave me a twenty-dollar bill and two or three ones to hold for him and he gave Al a five-dollar bill. He said it was the five that this fellow he beat up owed us for a guitar we'd sold him.

"The next day," Cindy continued, "when I told Paul about them bringing a girl's body up out of the lake, he seemed completely surprised."

Although the couple who had "adopted" Paul Vinetti were only a dozen years older than he was, they seemed to the detectives to have assumed a parental role with him. Rigglestatt recalled that the hair he'd cleaned from the metal cleats of Vinetti's boots had been blond or light brown and about four and a half inches long.

Informed by detectives Nolan and Harrison that they intended to take Vinetti downtown for further questioning, Rigglestatt said that he had some loaded guns in the unit and that he would be willing to go up first and unload them before any attempt was made to take Vinetti into custody.

He didn't think Paul would be dangerous when they arrested him, but he wanted to be sure.

Weighing Vinetti's mild demeanor during previous questioning against the maniacal rage that had exploded on the lakeshore, and knowing that Al and Cindy's motel unit was at the dead end of a hall—with Paul waiting inside—the detectives agreed that loaded guns might well turn the apartment into an armed fortress. They waited until Rigglestatt returned to tell them that the guns were secured.

Joined by Sergeant Don Actor, Nolan and Harrison knocked once more on the door of the second-floor unit and informed Vinetti that he was under arrest. He was handcuffed and advised of his rights.

"I know my rights," the hulking suspect responded, but finally he agreed to read the card that outlined his constitutional rights.

The King County investigators obtained a search warrant—although Al and Cindy were completely cooperative—and Sergeant Actor and Detective Howard Reynolds removed several items of clothing that Paul Vinetti had worn on the night of July 3: jockey shorts, a black short-sleeved turtlenecked sweater, a white T-shirt, and a pair of heavy black boots with horseshoe-shaped cleats on the heels.

At the sheriff's office, Paul Anthony Vinetti gave two statements to Harrison—statements that would lead to second-degree murder charges being filed against the lanky suspect. However, these statements would not become known to the public until Vinetti's trial in Judge Nancy Ann Holman's courtroom during the first weeks of November.

In extensive preparation for that trial, Dan Nolan and DuWayne Harrison contacted many witnesses. Among them were people who had sat at the bar of the Frontier Tavern with Vinetti and Bethany Stokesberry. One of these witnesses was Tom Fogarty,* whose name was given to the detectives by the bartender.

"We were there, all right," Fogarty said. "My girl, my sister, and her husband stopped in at about eleven or eleven thirty, after we'd been out to dinner. We sat at the bar and had one or two schooners of beer. Long-tall-Paul—who I'd seen before maybe once or twice—was there and a woman we met as 'Bethany' sat beside him."

"To your knowledge, was either of them intoxicated?" Nolan asked.

"No, sir. As far as I could tell, they hadn't had any more to drink than we had. This guy—Paul—asked me if I wanted to play a game of pool for four-fifty, and I said no. At one time, he called me over to the side of the bar and asked me, 'What's Bethany's problem?' I didn't know what he was talking about so I just shrugged."

"But Bethany and Paul left with you and your girlfriend. Is that right?" Nolan asked.

"I guess you could say that. But it was just because

Long-tall-Paul asked if I'd drive them down to Melby's. I don't know if Bethany wanted to go there or not. At first I hesitated because my car's a sport model that only holds four people—but then my sister and her husband said they'd wait for us in the parking lot, so we drove the two of them down toward Melby's. When we got to the car wash place, Paul said, 'This is close enough,' and he pulled her hand, and they got out on Aurora."

"You didn't see them after that?"

"No, sir. We let them off about midnight and drove on home after we picked up my sister."

The Bethany Stokesberry–Paul Anthony Vinetti case took a backseat to other news in Seattle papers as summer eased into fall. And then, as "Long-tall-Paul" Vinetti faced a jury of five men and seven women in Judge Holman's court, it once again made headlines.

The huge defendant himself sat placidly in the courtroom, dressed in slacks, a long-sleeved shirt, and sandals. His brown hair was long and he wore a mustache and a Vandyke beard. He was extremely thin.

Occasionally, as he wrote continuously on the yellow legal pad in front of him, the tattoo described by those who had sat with him in the Frontier Tavern was exposed to our view—an ironic combination that drew murmurs from the press bench. It was the image of a devil, under which the words "Love Forever" were inscribed.

Prosecuting the case from King County prosecutor Chris Bayley's office were deputy prosecutors Roy Howson and Douglas Dunham. Because Vinetti could not afford to employ counsel for his own defense, two extremely capable lawyers on the permanent staff of the King County Public Defender's Office were retained for him; they were Frank Sullivan and Rich Brothers. They would not deny that the beating had taken place but they would deny vigorously that Vinetti had thrown Mrs. Stokesberry into the lake, causing her death by drowning. Further, they would attempt to establish proof of "diminished responsibility" on the part of the defendant—the result of a long-standing mental disorder triggered by a daylong drinking marathon and marijuana binge on July 3.

I attended every day of Paul Vinetti's trial. I remember that I wanted to take a picture of him to include with the article I wrote about the case. He agreed right away—but he said he would pose only if I would stand beside him afterward so he could get a photograph of the two of us together.

It seemed only fair. I recall that the top of my head came just above his elbow. I don't have the picture I took of him any longer; I don't know if he still has the image of the two of us smiling for the camera that the court deputy held.

The rail in front of Judge Holman's bench became cluttered with piece after piece of physical evidence—macabre physical evidence, the tattered and bloodstained remnants of the new outfit Bethany Stokesberry had proudly shown off only hours before her death and Paul Vinetti's heavy black boots with metal cleats on the heels.

A score of witnesses appeared for the prosecution to recall again the holiday atmosphere in the Frontier Tavern on the Fourth of July weekend. All of them confirmed that Long-tall-Paul Vinetti had appeared sober at that time.

Sheriff's investigators testified to the bloody scene beside Echo Lake and to the recovery of the victim's beaten body from deep water not far from shore.

Attorney Rich Brothers made the opening statement for the defense. Brothers, under thirty at the time, was already an accomplished criminal defense attorney. It was obvious that he had spent as many hours preparing for the defense of an indigent client as he would were he in private practice. He would now detail to the jury the events on that day of death and the horrendous life the huge defendant had endured in his twenty-three years.

"We don't deny that an assault took place," Brothers told the jury. "But we are going to show you that there was no design to effect the death of Bethany Stokesberry. There was no intent to defraud or to take money." (Vinetti had also been charged with grand larceny in the alleged theft of the victim's money.)

Brothers gave the time line of Vinetti's day on Saturday, July 3. He had begun by drinking several pitchers of beer in Melby's Tavern well before noon. And he had progressed through more beer in seven other taverns.

Brothers described Vinetti as a man who was "a loner, moody, depressed," who had been deserted by his own mother at the age of six months. The defendant's father told him once: "Your mother had a choice between you and a pair of roller skates, and she took the roller skates."

His attorney explained Vinetti's extreme sensitivity to remarks about his height. He said that Bethany Stokesberry had taunted Paul about the two things that distressed him most: his mother and his height.

In many murder trials, the defendant does not take the stand in his own defense, but Long-tall-Paul Vinetti chose to do so. There, before a courtroom hushed so that spectators could hear his muted voice, he answered his attorney's questions about the events on July 3.

"I went to Melby's Tavern at ten thirty Saturday morning. I had about four beers before the others came in."

(The "others" were an Edmonds, Washington, couple and their nephew who had joined Vinetti in the long day of drinking.)

"Then we went to the Forum Tavern and they waited while I went to my friends to look for some stuff."

"Stuff?"

"Pills. Acid. Mescaline. Speed. But I didn't find any."

The defendant told of going next to Smokey Joe's, Tiger Al's, The Hideout, Blue Moon—and then back to Melby's. And finally, to the Frontier. He said he'd smoked almost an entire lid of marijuana—sharing it with a man whose name he couldn't recall—as the day wore on.

"I staggered—the way I see it—up to the Frontier Tavern. I don't remember if Bethany Stokesberry was there or not when I got there. I had never seen her before. I don't remember talking to her although I might have."

"Do you remember leaving with her?"

"Yes. I remember going in a car and getting out at the Elephant Car Wash. She wanted to go for a walk so we ran across Aurora Avenue. I remember that she had some kind of accent. We went down toward the water and along the gravel path to the dirt path."

"Did she say anything to you then?"

"When I put my arm around her, she was foul-mouthed. She said my dad was a bastard and my mother must have been a terrible person to have a son like me. She made fun of my height. She asked if my brothers were tall, too, and I said we were all over six foot six. Then she said when I was born I must have been dropped on my head and then pulled out and stretched like a string to get to be so tall.

"She kept on and on when I told her to shut up. I felt angry inside. I started swinging on her with my fists. Everything went blank. I felt like I was fighting to stay alive. I didn't see her while I was hitting her—it was dark out. She fell and got up. I hit her again. Then I threw her against the tree headfirst. Then I kicked her—with the heel of my right boot. I ripped off her clothes with my hands. I just grabbed them at the throat and tore."

Vinetti vehemently denied throwing Bethany Stokes-berry into Echo Lake. "I remember seeing something white on the ground. I picked it up and split. She was lying right by the tree when I left. My foot was next to her when I was reaching for the money. She wasn't in the lake."

Vinetti explained that his reaching for the money had been involuntary—a reflex action from the times as a child when he had had to survive any way he could.

Perhaps the most damaging testimony Vinetti gave was his reply to prosecutor Roy Howson's question about how he could be so sure he had not thrown the victim into the lake.

"I hit her. I threw her against the tree. I used my boots. That's three different ways—and that's all I did."

As in all murder trials, there is one side of the story that is never heard: the victim's side. Was Bethany Stokesberry a malicious termagant who consciously or unconsciously sought out a man's weakest side and finally went too far with the wrong man with her caustic comments?

Or were the remarks attributed to her by the defendant the product of his own imagination, which was fueled with beer, marijuana, and possibly other illegal substances?

Whatever the provocation had been, the jury didn't believe that anything the petite woman might have said excused Vinetti's brutal attack.

We will never know why she went with him, or if she willingly got out of her acquaintances' car and walked to a deserted lake at midnight. She may have simply wanted to go home, or Paul Vinetti may have physically pulled her from the car before she could protest.

Nor will we know what she said to her killer at the lakeshore. Why would she have courted disaster by taunting a man twice her size? The words Paul Vinetti recalled might have been from someone else he'd met that day, and, very much under the influence of alcohol and drugs, he could have confabulated the day's events in his mind.

Bethany Stokesberry never had an opportunity to tell her side of the story. So we have to give her credit for what she could not say. She was a bored housewife who probably dressed too provocatively when she went to the

Frontier Tavern that night in July. But I tend to believe her silent voice rather than Vinetti's drunken recall of what really happened.

We do know that *she* was not intoxicated at all. She had no alcohol in her blood.

The jurors in Paul Vinetti's trial seemed to hear her silent plea for justice, too. Paul Anthony Vinetti was found guilty of second-degree murder and grand larceny.

Perhaps he had no choice in life either. When his mother picked a pair of roller skates over her baby son and abandoned him, she may have sealed his fate.

And the fate of Bethany Stokesberry.

THE MOST
FRIGHTENING
CRIME OF ALL

PART ONE

THE DAYLIGHT RAPIST

In many ways, the crime of rape is always the same—the forcing of one individual's sexual desires upon a helpless victim.

In other ways, it is always different.

When I worked in the Sex Crimes Unit of the Seattle Police Department, I came to realize that there were no rules or parameters in sexual assaults. Since then, as a true-crime writer, I have covered a dozen or so rape cases that defy imagination.

There was the case of a rapist who insisted that his victim fix him a pork chop dinner—after he had assaulted her! He gobbled it down and left without hurting her further. And one sex criminal was so violent that he "raped" his victim with a .32 caliber pistol, actually firing it into her vagina. Miraculously, she survived and was even able to bear children after this happened to her. Another dangerous felon arrived at the apartment of three young women with a note of recommendation from one of their friends—which he had forged. A still more bizarre case involved a fastidious offender who demanded that his victim take a long bath before he raped her.

I remember a paroled felon who had his college tuition paid by the state—to help him succeed once he was out in society. Sex crimes detectives discovered he was skipping class at least two times a week so he could commit rapes in the university neighborhood. One of his victims was the daughter of a police officer.

I suppose we shouldn't be surprised by the peculiar obsessions and actions of sexual criminals. Although most look like ordinary people, they are very different from law-abiding citizens.

It is virtually impossible to teach women how to avoid and/or survive the crime of rape; what works for some puts others in terrible danger. We all know the basics, although we don't always adhere to them:

- Lock your doors securely.
- Lock your car even when you run into a store "just for a minute or two."
- Don't pick up hitchhikers.
- Don't meet an absolute stranger in your home—or his.
- Arrange to meet in a public place and let someone know where you are.
- Don't walk alone in bad neighborhoods after the sun goes down. Or *any* neighborhood!
- Don't believe everything prospective dates list about themselves on internet dating sites.
- Check out someone you don't know as carefully as you can.

• Don't open your car door or your home's door to someone you don't know. If it's an emergency, tell them you will call the police for them.

Most of this is simple common sense. Rapists don't all look daunting. Nor do most serial killers. Often, they are quite handsome, charming, and persuasive—until they manage to get a woman in a lonely place far from anyone who might help her.

Experts advise women to do anything they can to alert others that they are in trouble. Scream, shout, kick, and fight. Sadly, more bystanders react to "Fire!" than they do to "Help!"

Anyone over sixty remembers Kitty Genovese of Queens, New York, who screamed "Help!" on the frigid, pitch-black night of March 13, 1964. Kitty, a petite, dark-haired twenty-eight-year-old bar manager, encountered a sex killer at 3 a.m. as she got out of her car and headed for her apartment. Thirty-eight people heard her cries and ignored them, not wanting to get involved, believing someone else would save her.

Winston Moseley, twenty-nine, had set out to kill a woman that night—any woman—when Kitty saw him approaching in her Kew Gardens neighborhood. Without saying a word, he stabbed her twice. She called out, "Oh, God! He stabbed me. Please help me!"

Windows lit up and a few people looked out. One man even called out, "Leave that girl alone!" Still, no one called police or rushed downstairs to help her. Moseley was alarmed by the lights going on, and was preparing to drive off when the windows darkened again. Like a cat stalking an injured mouse, he followed Kitty to the doorway of her apartment house. Once more, she cried out, "I'm dying! I'm dying!" He stabbed her again—and raped her.

Finally, a neighboring apartment dweller called for police and paramedics, and then bravely ran downstairs to rock Kitty in her arms. But Kitty was dead.

Arrested, Moseley admitted to detectives that he had killed another woman. He escaped custody for a short time and raped a pregnant woman. Kitty Genovese has become a tragic poster girl for the apathy of people who look the other way when they see someone in danger.

If Kitty had yelled, "Fire!" would she still be alive? Psychological studies have shown that when a number of people witness an accident or a crime in progress, it's easy for them to believe someone else will help.

A few years ago, I spoke at a rape prevention seminar in Nashville, Tennessee. One of the other presenters was a detective who told of a case he'd worked on—a story I've never forgotten. A young woman was kidnapped in broad daylight, and her abductor told her to sit quietly in the passenger seat of his car. To make sure she did, he held a hunting knife against her ribs, and he promised her he wouldn't hurt her if she just did what he said.

They stopped at a red light. The kidnapper's car was in the left turn lane, and a marked patrol car pulled up beside it to the right. It was a hot day, and both vehicles' windows were down. The kidnap victim was barely a foot from the uniformed officer in the patrol unit.

"If you say anything," the abductor warned, "I'll stab you right here."

She said nothing. The police car went straight ahead when the light turned green, and the car she was in turned left. A few miles down the road, the man with the knife pulled off into an orchard. There, he raped her, and then cut her throat.

If she had screamed or cried out for help, she might have lived—but she trusted the promise of a psychopathic killer.

Legal definitions of rape state that it is *any* penetration of an unwilling victim's body—from intercourse to sodomy. And yet rape is difficult to categorize; each sexual assault is different from others. Some rapists are cautious, seizing their victims in dark and deserted places where there is only a slight chance that any cries for help will be heard. Others, like the crimes of a man who prowled two counties in Washington State for almost a year, are blatant; he took such incredible risks that it seemed he was crying out to be caught. Perhaps it was the extreme danger of possibly being discovered that enhanced the sexual excitation he felt.

One factor is invariably true, however. Rapists—like almost all criminals—have clearly defined MOs. They repeat their crimes with little variation.

During the time I was a Seattle police officer, I worked for months in the Sex Crimes Unit—then called, oddly, the Morals Division. The rapists seemed to be considered to have "bad morals." Some people believed that that meant the victims were immoral, too. I took many statements from victims of sexual assault. Later, as a true crime author, I have written a few dozen articles about more recent cases. I don't think laymen realize how terrifying sexual attacks can be—most of them involve far more than "missionary position" intercourse.

Some of these cases stand out in my memory. This story of a serial rapist is one I won't forget. His series of sexual assaults shared a plotline so consistent that they must have been carefully planned and scripted. As always, I have changed the names of victims to spare them any more invasion of their privacy.

It was the fourth day of August, 1976, an uncommonly steamy day in Edmonds, Washington. Edmonds is a picturesque town a half hour's drive north of Seattle, and it hugs the shore of Puget Sound.

Ashley Varner,* twenty-three, was typing some quarterly reports in the office of a church in Edmonds. It was shortly after two in the afternoon. Surely, there could be few safer places than a house of God on a sunny summer afternoon.

The pretty young woman heard the main church door open and then footsteps approaching the office where she worked. She looked up to see a tall man in workman's clothes. There were some repairs under way at the church, so it wasn't at all unusual to have workers come into the office. Ashley thought that he probably needed to use the phone.

That wasn't it at all. She was startled when the man pulled a knife from his pocket and began to extract the blade. She was horrified by his rough command: "Take your clothes off!"

"What?" she asked, still unable to believe her own ears.

"I said to take your clothes off!"

There was nothing for her to do but comply, and pray that someone would enter the church to help her before it was too late. She removed all her clothing except her bra, and the man barked, "That, too."

He remained fully clothed, but he unzipped his trousers and ordered the terrified girl to perform oral sex on him.

She bent to obey, still incredulous that this could be happening. She was afraid of the sharp knife he held, and realized that he was at least sixty pounds heavier than she was. She was trying to survive, hoping someone would see what was going on. After a few minutes, the intruder, still fully dressed except for his open fly, attempted to rape her. Although he had achieved a full erection, actual intercourse proved impossible; Ashley was a virgin and that, combined with her utter terror, made penetration impossible. Disgusted, the man ordered her to perform oral sex on him again. He ejaculated in her mouth as she choked and vomited with revulsion.

"That's all there is to it," the man said airily. "If you report this to the cops, though—I'll come back and kill you."

He walked from the church and she heard a car start, and tires squeal. Quickly, she threw on her clothes and locked the church. Once safely home, she didn't know what to do. Like many sexual assault victims, she was ashamed. And she also believed that the man would come back and kill her if she called the police.

Ashley took a bath, desperately scrubbing away the scent of the rapist, but also unintentionally washing away semen that might have been matched to any suspect's bodily fluids. After spending a sleepless night, she felt she had to tell someone. Ashley confided in a friend who urged her to tell the minister of their church. "You can't just let it go—he'll hurt somebody else."

The reverend counseled her to call the police.

Detective Marian McCann, a longtime veteran of the Edmonds Police Department, gently elicited the details of the attack and assured Ashley Varner that she had done the right thing in reporting it. Ashley described her attacker as a white male about twenty-five, quite tall, with dark curly hair and a two-day growth of beard. She said the man wasn't bad-looking; in other circumstances, she would have said he was handsome.

Forensic artist Robin Hickok drew a composite picture based on Ashley's description and copies of the composite were distributed to all of the area police departments.

There was little more McCann and Hickok could do at that point. The victim hadn't seen her attacker's vehicle— if he even had one. She was positive that she'd never seen him before. The detectives knew from long experience that the man was likely to attack again, but where or when was impossible to guess. They checked with nearby jurisdictions, but none of them reported similar sexual assaults. No one recognized the composite picture.

Two months later, on October 7, an eighteen-year-old bride who lived in rural Snohomish County, was mowing her lawn at two in the afternoon. As it was in the case of the first attack, it was a weekday afternoon, a Thursday. Dressed in jean cutoffs and a beige top, she concentrated only on the task before her, mowing both the front and side yard. Then she went into her house through the side door to check on clothes she had in the dryer. Finding them dry, she carried the load into the kitchen to fold. She turned the stereo on, not terribly loud, but loud enough to drown out quiet noises—stealthy noises.

The young housewife, Jill Whaley,* was sitting at the kitchen table with her back to the door, going over her grocery list, when suddenly, muscular arms encircled her neck. She felt the blade of a knife against her flesh. Rigid with shock, she stared straight ahead, and heard the deep voice saying, "This is a rape!"

"What?" she cried. Later she would tell Snohomish County detectives, "Then I just went crazy and kept begging him not to do that to me."

She realized that the knife was not actually cutting into her neck. By dropping her eyes and using peripheral vision, she could see it was a small pocketknife with the blade open. The man's hands were more frightening: he seemed very strong.

"Go into the bedroom," he ordered, and she obeyed. Once in the room, he said, "Take your clothes off."

For the first time, Jill turned to face him. He was very tall, inches over six feet, Caucasian, between twenty-two and thirty, and he had medium brown hair that grew almost to his shoulders. He wore blue jeans and a heavy, service-type jacket.

He closed the knife with his left hand and put it in his pocket, saying, "If you behave, I won't have to use this."

Jill was sobbing now and begging the stranger not to hurt her. She pulled off her knit top and unfastened her bra. The man bent over and began to kiss her breasts, asking her if she would touch him on his genitals.

"No! Please, I can't," Jill murmured. The man stepped back for a few moments and watched her as she removed her cutoff jeans and panties. Then he pushed her onto the bed. "Spread your legs!" he commanded.

While she closed her eyes and bit her lips, her attacker attempted penetration. It wasn't working, and he commented that she was "sure tight for being married."

As before, with Ashley Varner, the would-be rapist had lost his erection. After a matter of a few seconds, the man jumped up and said, "Forget this. Where's your money?"

"I'll check and see if I have any," she said, stalling. She threw on her clothes and produced her wallet, showing him it was empty. He walked toward her again and she cried, "Please don't hurt me—I'm pregnant. Please don't hurt my baby."

The big man studied her for a long moment and then walked toward the door. He turned to look at her and said, "I'm sick."

"Just go," Jill cried. "Just go and I won't tell anybody."

She didn't mean that. She watched him walk past her neighbor's home and then break into a run. When she was sure he was gone, she ran to the neighbor's house, where she called the Snohomish County Sheriff's Office.

Jill's report to Snohomish County detective Ken Sedy was quite similar to the statement Ashley Varner had given after she was attacked in the Edmonds church two months earlier. In this assault, too, the rapist had not removed his own clothing, had only unzipped his fly. Both women were assaulted on a weekday in the afternoon. Their descriptions of the stranger were close. And each of the terrified young women mentioned the size of the man's penis, so large that he had been unable to have intercourse with either of them.

Similar attacks, yes, but there was really no sure pattern yet. The attacks were some distance apart, and the rapist's MO matched several other unsolved cases just as closely as it did the Edmonds and the rural Snohomish County cases.

Jill Whaley's shorts, panties, and bedspread were sent to the lab for analysis, but, since no ejaculation had taken place—no semen or pre-ejaculatory fluid was detected—nothing of evidentiary value was found.

Almost exactly two months later, on December 6—a Monday—a twenty-seven-year-old King County housewife, Dorian Bliss,* and her five-year-old daughter drove home after a trip to the grocery store. It was just before noon and the little girl was hungry, so Dorian hurried as she made several trips from her car into the house, carrying bags of groceries. She had left the front door open because her arms were full. Later, she couldn't be sure if she had closed the front door on the last trip.

She heard someone coming in the front door, assumed it was her husband, and looked up expectantly. Instead, she saw a perfect stranger. Alarmed, she said, "Who are you, and what are you doing here?"

The man responded by clapping his hands together and ordered, "Get rid of the kid!"

That, of course, was her first thought: if there was danger—and there certainly appeared to be—she wanted her child safe. She led the little girl into the child's bedroom and turned on her record player, warning the youngster to lock her door and not to come out—no matter what.

The intruder, a very tall, husky young man, pushed Dorian into the family room. "Take your clothes off," he snapped. She tried to dissuade him, protesting that she couldn't do that, that what he was suggesting was crazy. Finally, she slowly started to take off her sweater.

"No," he said. "I want you to take *all* your clothes off."

The man knelt before her and lifted her skirt, rubbing her pubic area through her underclothing with his hand. "Damn, that's beautiful," he breathed, and then he bit her.

She knew she couldn't scream; her daughter might run out and be hurt. Instead Dorian pushed him away from her by kicking him. It didn't seem to faze him. He stood up and methodically began to undress her.

He kissed her mouth and breasts and he was furious because she would not respond. "Damn it . . . kiss me!" he ordered the trembling woman.

She wouldn't. She couldn't.

The huge man pulled her panties and panty hose over her shoes, and began to kiss her all over her now naked body. Finally, he mounted her. The rape itself lasted for a short time—only five or six thrusts—and she was quite sure he hadn't climaxed when he suddenly withdrew and stood up.

The man walked toward the kitchen, saying, "I didn't plan for this to happen—I'm sick, you know."

She called him back, afraid he was going to her child's room. "Why don't you go for help?" she cajoled. "There are people who could help you."

The big man now turned toward the front door. "No one can help me. Go ahead and shoot me, lady. I wouldn't blame you at all."

And then he was gone. She ran to bolt the door behind him, threw on her clothes, and calmed her little girl. Then she called the King County police and her neighbor.

King County detective sergeant Ben Colwell took Dorian's statement. She was then taken to a hospital for treatment. She was asked to remove her clothing while standing on a sheet. This would prevent any minute evidence from being lost—hairs, pubic hairs, fibers—anything that might be matched to a suspect, if they ever found one.

Once again, there had been no ejaculation, so there was no semen to check for blood type or DNA. There was really nothing more than Dorian's description of the man: tall, collar-length brown hair, mustache, fairly good-looking, wearing a jeans outfit and only one glove. She had never seen him before, and if he had followed her home from the supermarket, she wasn't aware of it. She didn't even know if he'd had a car; he'd just suddenly been there inside her house.

Ben Colwell contacted all police agencies in the north end of King County. He made sure that Detective Marian McCann in Edmonds knew about this attack. Dorian Bliss's house wasn't far from the Edmonds church where Ashley Varner had been assaulted. McCann did have the unsolved church rape in August, but that rapist hadn't made any comments about "being sick," and he had been more interested in oral sex than rape.

At that point, the MOs appeared to be different.

On December 10, Jill Whaley was driving toward her home when she observed a car parked in her driveway— an unfamiliar car. As she approached, the car backed out and left at a high rate of speed. The spunky woman followed it until it pulled into another driveway. She pulled her car across the sidewalk there, virtually blocking the driver. She saw that he was a young male who looked a great deal like the man who'd raped her.

Irritated, he rolled down his window and said sarcastically, "Can I get out of here?"

She backed up just enough to allow the car to leave but she continued to pursue it. She lost the man's car in traffic—but not before she wrote down his license number.

Colwell ran the number through the Department of Motor Vehicles on his computer. He found it registered to an Edmonds area man. When he confronted the possible rapist, Colwell saw that the man certainly matched the description given by Jill Whaley. He was irate and indignant and insisted he'd merely been looking for an address. On December 17, he agreed to take a polygraph test. Surprisingly, the results of the lie detector showed he was telling the truth.

The weekday, daylight rapist was still at large. However, if he struck again during the first months of the new year, his victims did not report it.

And then on March 14, a twenty-one-year-old Edmonds housewife, Leann Cross,* underwent a horrifying experience. She and her husband had advertised an antique car for sale. Shortly after noon, Leann answered the door to find a tall, handsome young man standing there. He smiled and asked, "How much do you want for the antique car?"

"We'd have to have something over a thousand dollars," she replied.

Instantly, the man's demeanor changed. "That's too much—how much do you want for a fuck?"

Before the shocked woman could react to the obscene question, the stranger was inside her house. She started crying but her tears had only a stimulating effect on him. He pushed her toward her bedroom and he was so strong that there was no question of resisting. "I'm a hired killer," he told her. "Don't fight me."

As the stranger took her clothes off, Leann heard her eight-month-old baby crying in the kitchen. She was afraid he would hurt the baby, and she vowed to do whatever she had to in order to protect her child.

And then, oddly, he placed a pillowcase from the bed over her head. Rape was clearly what he had in mind—but he was unsuccessful at that. "I can't even do this right," he moaned, moving off her. The man explained that he was an ex-marine as well as a "hired killer," yet he was not proving to be a very efficient rapist.

"Get me a rope to tie you up with," he ordered.

She found a thick sash cord and her husband's bathrobe belt. The intruder tied her hands behind her and bound her ankles loosely with the bathrobe sash. Leann held her breath and prayed he would not harm her still-screaming infant. Then she heard the front door close. Hobbling over to the phone, she managed to get one hand free to dial her sister-in-law who lived next door. She rushed over to untie Leann.

The two frightened women called the Edmonds police and patrol officers responded, followed in minutes by Detective Marian McCann.

Leann's description of her assailant had a most familiar ring: white, male, thirty, six feet two, 210 pounds, medium brown curly hair, brown eyes, mustache, jeans and jean jacket. Possible witnesses on the street where Leann lived reported that they had noticed an orange van parked in front of the victim's house. It was possibly a ten-year-old Dodge.

Detective McCann immediately put out a teletype on the van and description of the rapist. Almost at once, she was deluged with reports of orange vans and/or unsolved rapes. She was appreciative of the response, but it meant checking out over a dozen orange vans and their drivers. Some were easy to eliminate; one spotted by a victim's relative in a grocery store parking lot was driven by a skinny man with shoulder-length red hair who in no way matched the description of the rapist.

Others weren't so easy. McCann visited a rural farm in Snohomish County where three brothers were supposed to own an orange van. She spent hours staking out the place, even talking to some young women who were also waiting for their "suspects." None of the brothers turned out to match the description of the man.

Detective McCann conferred with departments as far away as Spokane County at the eastern end of the state, and Mason County many miles south of Edmonds, but nothing matched up. In the meantime, she dreaded the repeat that must surely come if the rapist was not found—and soon.

McCann combed her files and surrounding departments' files for mug shots of men with previous sex offenses. A fellow detective, Wally Tribuzio, recalled an incident in December 1976 when he had assisted the Lynnwood Police Department in the arrest of a suspect in an alleged burglary-rape at the Bali Hai Sauna.

"This guy supposedly went in there and shot up the place, and then stole a desk because he couldn't get the drawers open to get the money out," Tribuzio recalled. "He was driving a panel truck, only it was white then. We traced the license number they got to a Tom Barrington.* I went out to his residence to help out the Lynnwood officers. Anyway, just as I turned down the street, I saw the panel truck parked—the license was right—and I parked out of sight and waited. There was somebody in the van, and he seemed to be fooling around with what looked like a huge box. I called Snohomish County Dispatch and they told me that the man they were looking for had stolen a desk. Apparently, he was stashing the drawers in the bushes while I watched."

Tribuzio had moved in and arrested the man.

"He fits the description to a T," Tribuzio recalled to Marian McCann. "Big guy, two-day growth of beard, brown hair. We found a bunch of Bali Hai business cards in his glove box. He claimed to have thrown his gun away and we never found it."

Possible—although a rape in a massage parlor is a good deal harder to prove than a sexual attack on a housewife in her own home. McCann learned that Tom Barrington was awaiting trial on the Bali Hai case, and she obtained a mug shot of him from the Lynnwood police to include in the ten-mug laydown of pictures to show to Leann Cross.

Unfortunately, she could not identify any of the mugs in the laydown as the man who had assaulted her and tied her up that harrowing day.

Worse, the attacks continued. On April 26, a South Everett housewife was in her own home at two in the afternoon when a man suddenly appeared. A big man, white, around thirty, with stubble on his face, dark hair, a good-looking man. He wore jeans and a blue plaid shirt.

The intruder forced Mrs. Lillian Mercer* into her bedroom, placed a pillowcase over her head, and raped her. He also told her he was "scared," which was mild compared to the way the attractive housewife felt. When he left, he took her wallet containing $119 in cash, eight credit cards, and three bank savings books.

Snohomish County detective Sedy listened to the description and felt it sounded much like the man who was now being sought by practically every department from North King County on.

All the attacks had taken place on weekdays, all had occurred around late morning or early afternoon. "We're either dealing with a man who works nights or a guy who takes advantage of a long lunch hour," one detective remarked. It was only a matter of time before someone was going to get hurt. The rapist was not only described as huge and husky, he was hostile and aggressive and often carried a knife. So far, his victims had been terrified into submission. What if one of them attempted to fight back? Would that send the big man into a rage that might end in a crime far more final than rape?

But how do you catch a phantom? He was here, there, then miles away in his attacks. McCann suspected he was staking out his future victims. He always seemed to know when they were home alone, possibly having checked their husbands' working hours. Perhaps he followed many of them home from grocery stores, knew that they would leave their doors open while they carried in armloads of groceries.

On June 7, it happened again in Snohomish County, near Lynnwood. It was 1:30 on a weekday afternoon when Tula French* was in the bathroom washing her face while her small daughter brushed her teeth. She'd left the front door open because it was an exceptionally warm, sunny day. She wore only a bathing suit because she'd been sunbathing.

Suddenly, unbelievably, a man walked into her bathroom! He had a peculiar expression on his face and held his hands near the zipper of his jeans.

To gain time, Tula faked a smile and said, "Hi, how are you?"

"I've come to rape you," he answered.

"You're kidding! What do you really want—can I help you with something?"

"I'm not kidding," he snarled. "I'm going to rape you." He pushed Tula's four-year-old daughter into the bathroom and locked the door, dragging the mother out into the hallway.

"What is the matter with you?" she asked incredulously.

"Don't you know I'm crazy?" he said as he began to tear her bathing suit top off.

Inside the bathroom, Tula French's daughter cried, "You leave my mommy alone!"

"You shut her up, lady, and cooperate with me or I'll rape her, too. Now you get in that bedroom or I'll hurt you bad . . ."

Tula was a fighter and clung to the door frame in the hallway while she screamed to her neighbor for help.

It only served to further enrage the huge man who was struggling with her. "Shut up, bitch, or I'll really hurt you!" he threatened.

The man threw her to the floor, and she came up fighting, grabbing his leg and butting him in the stomach as hard as she could with her head. It knocked a bit of the wind out of him, and he loosened his grasp for a moment. Tula ran for the front door, then realized she couldn't leave the house—her little girl was hiding in the bathroom and the man was still inside. She saw her German shepherd in the yard and ordered, "Get him . . . get him!" But the dog had been raised as a pet, not as an attack animal; he merely stared quizzically at his mistress.

However, with the front door open, Tula opened her mouth and screamed as loudly as she could again and again. This was too much for the would-be rapist. He ran by her, and she slammed the door behind him. She called the Snohomish County Sheriff's Office at once, and four deputies arrived within three minutes. They checked the heavily wooded area around the Frenches' home where the man had fled on foot—but he was gone, swallowed up in the thickets of fir and alder.

Tula had been very lucky. She had saved both herself and her little girl, and suffered only bruises and a bad scrape on her leg.

But the siege was not over yet. The rapist's desires had not been slaked, and this time he struck again in a much shorter time.

Three weeks later, another pretty young housewife, Linda Miller,* had just returned from the grocery store shortly after noon and was busy carrying armloads of groceries into her kitchen in Edmonds. Her three-year-old daughter was sitting at the kitchen table eating a hamburger while Mrs. Miller went to the bathroom. As she stepped out, a huge man approached her down the hallway with a knife in one hand and a black case of some kind in the other.

Before she could even scream, the man grabbed her around the neck with one powerful forearm and pushed her into the bedroom. He snatched a pillowcase from the bed, and she started to run. He caught up with her within a few feet and led her back to the bedroom. "Try that again and you'll both get hurt," he growled.

She watched in amazement as he removed a Polaroid camera from the black case. Then he placed the pillowcase over her head; she could see only vague outlines. The man removed her slacks, blouse, and bra and ordered her to stand, wearing only her panties, next to the dresser. She could hear the click and whirr of the camera. He was taking pictures of her!

Then he rustled through the drawers of the dresser until he found some panties he liked better. "Change into these," he ordered, handing them to her.

If she had any hope that he was merely a picture freak, a man with some kind of weird fetish, that hope was dashed. He closed the drapes tightly, and she could see through the thin weave of the pillow case that he was unzipping his jeans.

"Spread your legs more," he demanded. Then he raped her.

When he was finished with her, Linda pleaded, "Leave—just leave!"

"No, I have to tie you up."

That frightened her. Her little girl was still in the kitchen. If the man tied her up, she wouldn't be able to protect her child. She pleaded with him not to tie her.

"Okay, I won't—but you have to give me all the time I need—an hour."

She promised. With rapists, a good rule is to promise them anything; ethics don't enter into it—survival does.

The big man walked down the hall, then suddenly returned to check on her. He found her still sitting on the edge of the bed as he'd left her and appeared satisfied. This time, he left and she heard the front door slam.

Linda threw on some clothes and ran to check on her daughter, relieved to find the child still munching on her hamburger, unaware of the struggle in the bedroom. The child couldn't understand why her mother was sobbing and holding her so close.

Then Linda ran to the phone and called 911. Almost immediately, the streets around her house were alive with patrol cars.

By this time, however, the audacious rapist's luck had just about run out. While Marian McCann talked to the distraught victim, every detective and patrol car in the Edmonds Police Department was searching the area around Linda's home. They were looking for a tall man with semi-long dark curly hair, a mustache, jeans, a white T-shirt with a flowered design, and ankle-high boots. They didn't know if he was on foot or in a car, but if ever they were determined to catch someone, it was this man.

Captain L. L. Neuert was proceeding south on Olympic View Drive at 12:43 p.m. when he received radio information that a rape had just taken place eight blocks away. The description was a good one, and the man should be easy to spot if he was on the street.

Neuert turned around and headed northbound on Olympic View Drive. At that moment, he heard a Lynnwood car advise that he was in the area of Meadowdale High School and would block off that area. Neuert decided to go down the Meadowdale Beach Road in an attempt to intercept anybody coming eastbound. Just as he turned onto the Meadowdale Road, he spotted a white

Chevrolet at a stop sign. The driver was a dead ringer for the suspect being sought.

Captain Neuert made a U-turn and headed back in pursuit of the Chevrolet. He found he had to hit 70 miles per hour even to get close to the white car. He turned on his blue flashing lights and the car ahead finally pulled over to the side of the road.

Neuert hopped out of his car as a very tall man exited the Chevrolet and began to walk back toward him. Neuert ordered the man to return to his own vehicle, put his hands on the trunk, and spread his legs. Neuert's pat-down search netted only an empty black knife case at the rear of the big man's belt.

Captain Neuert handcuffed the suspect and radioed to ask if the suspect had been wearing a floral-patterned T-shirt. The answer was yes. Dennis Kelly, of the Lynnwood Police Department, arrived at that moment and the subject was placed in the back of Kelly's patrol car. He was advised of his rights.

"Do you want to talk to us?" Neuert asked.

"Talk about what?" the suspect countered.

"About a young woman who was raped near here a few minutes ago," Neuert answered.

"I don't know anything about anything like that."

"Well, you match the description—right down to your T-shirt."

"I don't know what you're talking about."

The man said that he was living in Edmonds and had become lost on his way home from Everett; he was only coming up the hill in an effort to find the road home.

There was no further conversation. Captain Neuert then received information from the officers at Linda's residence that the suspect had had a Polaroid camera, and Neuert located the case for a Polaroid in the back of the white Chevrolet behind the driver's seat and the camera itself under the right front seat.

Neuert and Detective Wally Tribuzio transported the suspect to the Edmonds Police Department for further questioning.

The man was twenty-five-year-old Thomas G. Barrington—the same man Tribuzio had arrested the previous December in the Bali Hai Sauna robbery! Looking at the mug shot taken in that case—sans mustache—Detective Marian McCann could see why it might be difficult for a victim to identify it as a likeness of the man before her.

Barrington signed a rights waiver and talked to Detective McCann. He said that he was unmarried, had lived with his parents since the previous October. He explained that he was in an alcohol treatment program and was also addicted to heroin, and "would be hurting soon."

Barrington told Detective McCann that he had started seeing a psychiatrist and had had one appointment. He readily admitted the charges against him in the Bali Hai Sauna case and said he had been convicted of robbery only—not the rape charge—a few weeks before. But he didn't remember it—his mind had "blacked out," he said. He was employed at a Seattle newspaper and worked nights. He repeated the phrase that so many of his suspected victims had heard: "I need help."

At that point, Barrington requested permission to call

his attorney, and it was granted. There, the interview stopped.

Detective McCann called Detective Sedy of Snohomish County and told him of the arrest of Barrington. Since Sedy had been investigating so many similar assaults in his county, he was elated to hear the news.

Detectives Robin Hickok and Marian McCann transported Barrington, and he was booked into the Snohomish County Jail.

With the help of Snohomish County deputy prosecuting attorney Tom Wynne, a search warrant was obtained for Barrington's parents' home. The parents were extremely cooperative, although understandably stricken at the charges against their son. They had tried repeatedly to obtain psychiatric help for him, and he was presently being seen at a VA hospital. Everything had seemed to be better for the man who had come home from service in Vietnam a changed man. Beyond his psychiatric problems—drinking and drugs—Barrington had had surgery for a cancerous testicle; it had been removed. Whether this particular kind of surgery might have been enough to have any influence at all in turning a man into a compulsive sexual criminal is a question that only a top team of psychiatrists could determine—if, indeed, even they could.

Asked if Barrington owned a Polaroid camera, his parents said he didn't—but they did. However, when they looked for it, they found it was missing.

The physical evidence against Thomas Barrington mounted steadily. When Detective Tribuzio searched him, he found a pair of turquoise panties trimmed with lace in the suspect's pants pocket—a "souvenir" from the attack on Linda Miller.

Officer Terry Minnihan, searching the probable escape route from Linda's home to Barrington's vehicle, found three Polaroid photos showing a woman with a pillowcase over her head, a woman wearing different panties in each shot.

When Barrington's car was processed, a large buck knife was found under the cardboard flooring of the white Chevrolet. The Chevrolet was registered to Barrington's father, but McCann learned that his brother-in-law owned an orange van.

A canvass of the neighborhood where Linda lived turned up two fourteen-year-old girls who had been frightened by a man answering Barrington's description just before the attack on Linda Miller. He had parked and stared at them so intently that they had run for home as fast as they could.

The long hunt by detectives from three jurisdictions seemed to be over: Ben Colwell from King County, Ken Sedy from Snohomish County, and the Edmonds police detectives. Still ahead lay a lineup before the women who had been attacked. This was set for July 6, 1977. The handsome suspect shaved off his Fu Manchu mustache before his lineup; it did little good.

When Tom Barrington stepped forward from the group of men who were similar to him in height, weight, coloring, and age, he was asked to repeat phrases—phrases the victims would never forget: "I am sorry, lady, I'm sick. I need help." "I've come to rape you." "This is a rape—"

Linda Miller, Tula French, Jill Whaley, and Dorian Bliss positively identified Thomas Barrington as the man who had attacked them. "There simply isn't any doubt," Jill said.

Later, although Ashley Varner, the young woman who had been attacked in the Edmonds church, was unable to pick Barrington in the lineup, Barrington himself admitted to Detective McCann that that, too, was his crime.

Thomas Barrington subsequently pleaded guilty to first-degree rape in the case of Linda Miller, first-degree burglary in the attack on Tula French, and armed robbery in the Bali Hai Sauna case. He received a twenty-year sentence in each case with a ten-year minimum—to run consecutively. That meant that he had at least thirty years to serve on Snohomish County charges.

On September 30, he pleaded guilty to first-degree rape in the Jill Whaley attack in King County and received a life maximum sentence, fifteen-year minimum sentence. If this sentence ran consecutively to the Snohomish County sentences, it would be at least forty-five long years before Thomas Barrington saw the world outside prison walls.

One thing will continue to puzzle Detective Marian McCann: She could never get Barrington to tell her how he picked his victims—how he knew they would be alone, why he almost always chose pretty young housewives with small children. Did he stalk them, or were they only spurof-the-moment choices? He took incredible chances at being discovered—or did he? Did he think his only adversaries were helpless women and children? Did he forget that some of the best detectives in three departments were after him and would surely catch up with him? It is now only conjecture; Barrington's yearlong reign of terror is over.

PART TWO

THE HANDSOME RAPIST

Despite the current proliferation of books, articles, and television shows about rapists, there are still many laymen who believe that most sex offenders attack women because they are losers in the dating game, men too unattractive to obtain sex through socially acceptable means. Not true. Many rapists are good-looking enough to pick and choose among the female population. But they don't get sexual satisfaction through intercourse with a willing female. Rather, they are turned on by the terror they evoke by grabbing a woman by force in the dark, making her submit, and, for some, the thrill they get when they hear the satisfying crunch of their fists against a soft cheek.

These are the men who most alarm sex assault detectives. The psychic scars left by a "gentle" rapist are bad enough; the injuries helpless women suffer at the hands of a punitive rapist tend to increase with each attack and very often result in the death of a victim.

The man who terrorized Seattle women for four months through the winter and spring of 1980 was a good-looking ex-con who liked to brag that he looked like actor Peter Fonda. He expected compliments on his sexual prowess and technique, although he left his pretty victims bruised and battered. There was a definite pattern to his attacks, but, unfortunately, several women had to suffer utter terror before that pattern began to emerge.

Ordinarily, Kitty Amela,* nineteen, would not have been out so late on a Sunday night, but on February 16, 1975, the young nurse had a visit to make after finishing her late shift in the emergency room of a north end hospital. Her fiancé was in the hospital, about to undergo emergency surgery, and she stayed with him until after one a.m., when he was wheeled away to the operating room. Then she left to go home for a few hours of sleep before she came back to sit beside him when he awakened from the anesthetics.

Kitty lived with her family in a quiet residential neighborhood, but her relatives were away for the weekend. She had carefully left the lights and radio on at home so that it wouldn't seem quite so much like coming back alone to an empty house in the wee hours of the morning.

The porch light was on, and she felt safe as she drove into her own driveway. She set the emergency brake and jumped out of the car to lock the doors. It was very still, but only for a few moments. As she headed for the front door, she heard footsteps behind her. She turned around, but before she could say anything, she felt a fist crash into her forehead. The blow made her knees sag, but she stayed conscious.

Kitty screamed as loud as she could, hoping the next-door neighbors would hear her. She knew they were probably all asleep, but she held on to the slight hope that someone might hear.

Before her scream had faded in the quiet night air, however, strong hands grabbed her coat and pulled it over her head. She heard a male voice ordering her to be quiet or she would be killed.

Kitty screamed again—but her cries for help were muffled now. No one heard. No one had heard her first scream either. The neighbors' windows were all closed, and the drumming of a heavy rainstorm had dulled sound even further.

She could tell that the man who gripped her tightly was tall and very strong. He pinned her arms to her sides and walked her northbound away from her yard. The first house they passed was vacant; the second had lights on, but she didn't dare scream again.

Evidently not satisfied with the location, the man walked her back past her own house and into the backyard of the next house.

Suddenly, he threw Kitty on the ground, and ripped off her slacks and panties. Still holding her coat over her forehead, he kissed her. And then he raped her.

After he climaxed, he asked her for money.

"It's in my purse," she sobbed.

Displeased with the mere two dollars he found there, the rapist began to beat Kitty with his closed fists. A dozen times or more, she felt pain as his blows thudded against her face.

"That's too bad about the money," he grunted. "I need more than that."

He ripped two rings off her fingers. Her diamond engagement ring was worth at least a thousand dollars, and her other ring was a rare opal valued at almost four hundred dollars.

As if to justify his brutality, he told Kitty, "Don't think I'm sick or a junkie, but I have a four-hundred-dollar-a-day habit." And then he laughed, adding, "I'm sorry you have to be a victim of this sick society."

And so, indeed, was Kitty Amela. "Take what you want, but don't hurt me," she begged.

"I won't hurt you, sweetheart," he said, his voice soft now. "Don't get up for a couple of minutes and you'll be okay."

After the man left, Kitty lay still, afraid that he might come back. But a few minutes later, she heard a car start and drive away.

She estimated that the attack had lasted almost twenty minutes. Painfully, she made her way back to her car and drove to the emergency room where she'd gone off shift earlier in the evening. Nearly hysterical, she fell into the arms of a nurse friend, whimpering. "Oh, Mary—I've been raped."

Kitty Amela's clothes were almost torn off and she was covered with dirt. She had a contusion and abrasions all over her face. A vaginal exam confirmed that she had, indeed, been raped.

But the coat blindfold hadn't worked. Kitty had seen her attacker's face in the porch light that shone that Sunday night.

When she was calmer, she told Seattle police officers J. A. Nicholson and D. Hilliard that her attacker was a man in his early twenties, Caucasian, tall and slender, with shoulder-length dark hair cut in a shag. He had a scraggly goatee and a pointed chin. She hadn't seen his car, but she believed he had left in one.

After she had been treated for her injuries, the officers accompanied the young nurse to the yard where she had been attacked so they could help her recover anything she might have dropped there. They found her coat, one shoe, her purse, and its contents—which had been scattered over the ground.

In a city the size of Seattle there are, unfortunately, a number of rapes reported almost every day. Sex Crimes detectives Joyce Johnson and William Fenkner had learned to evaluate the MOs used in sex attacks. They know that rapists rarely stop with one attack and that they tend to follow an almost fetishist pattern.

A few days before Kitty Amela was attacked, another young woman had reported that she had been raped by a tall, thin man with shoulder-length hair.

"He followed me after I got off my bus in the north end," she told the detectives. "I didn't think there was anything dangerous about him, but then he walked past me, turned around suddenly and grabbed me around my neck and my head. He forced me into a garage off an alley."

After she was raped, the young woman said that the stranger had stolen two dollars from her, chagrined at how little money she had in her purse.

"He told me to count to fifty before I left the garage."

Fenkner and Johnson realized that the two rapes had followed an almost identical scenario.

"Except that the first victim wasn't brutalized like the second," Joyce Johnson mused. "They are so alike."

There would be more that seemed similar.

On March 10, Cory Bixler* left her apartment in the near north end of Seattle a half hour after midnight, intending to walk a few short blocks to a friend's house. At the corner of North 39th Street and Linden Avenue North, a dark figure stepped from the shadows and grabbed her from behind, putting his hand tightly over her mouth. Although Cory fought hard, her assailant was much stronger. He began to drag her into the bushes, and her screams didn't deter him in the least. Cory's purse fell on the sidewalk as the man threw her roughly beneath a thick stand of laurel bushes.

"He ripped off my clothes," she recalled later. "And he wrapped my coat around my head. Then he raped me, and he kept hitting me in the face and stomach with his fists when I tried to crawl away."

Cory recalled that the rapist's voice was quiet and soft—an odd contrast to the violence of his fists and the fact that he said he would kill her if she didn't cooperate.

Once he had ejaculated, he turned his thoughts to money and asked Cory where her purse was. She pointed to the sidewalk where it had fallen in the struggle, and he left her for a moment as he moved to retrieve it.

As soon as he let go of her, the plucky young woman got up and ran across the street, darting between dark houses, until she reached Aurora Avenue, which was always full of traffic—day and night. There, Cory found a motel office still open and begged the manager to call the police.

444

Patrol officers from the Wallingford Precinct, along with K-9 patrolmen and their dogs, responded at once.

But the rapist was gone, gone so completely that the highly trained German shepherds could not track his scent much beyond the spot of the attack. That meant that the assailant had probably gotten into a nearby vehicle.

When Cory Bixler talked to detectives Johnson and Fenkner, she revealed a decidedly weird facet of the rapist's personality: "After he had raped me, he made me lie there and he kept telling me, 'You're dead. Just act like you're dead'—and then he started throwing dirt on me. Almost like he was trying to bury me."

Her attacker had taken Cory's purse with him. On March 18, some of her papers turned up coincidentally. A friend of Seattle police robbery detective John Boatman called to tell him that his (the friend's) Volkswagen had been stolen. It was recovered, but by then it was in very poor mechanical condition.

On March 18, a garage mechanic working on the "Beetle" found some identification documents belonging to a Cory Bixler under the seats. The car's owner had never heard of anyone by that name and commented on it to Boatman.

John Boatman worked in the Crimes Against Persons Unit a few feet from Bill Fenkner's and Joyce Johnson's desks. Boatman had heard of Cory Bixler, and he knew she was the young woman who had been the victim of the vicious rape and assault—with robbery—the week before. Evidently, the rapist had stolen the Volkswagen for his getaway and inadvertently left Cory's ID on the floorboards after he rifled her purse.

It was a good—though frustrating—lead. At this point the Volkswagen was of no use for fingerprint evidence. Most of its surfaces had been touched by half a dozen people in the garage and any latent prints were destroyed.

And the car thief—was it the rapist?—had been punctilious about removing his own possessions.

The sadistic sex attacker was out there, and, so far, he had been clever at avoiding detection. His victims all described him as young, slender, tall, and strong as an ox. He had a mustache and dark shag-cut hair to his shoulders.

Detectives knew he would probably not stop his attacks unless he was caught. They waited tensely for the next time he surfaced.

For almost two months things were quiet; none of the rape reports coming in sounded like the man who'd tried to bury his last victim—either actually or symbolically. It was quite possible that he was still active and his latest victims were afraid to report him. Many rape victims don't report what happened to them because they are embarrassed and fearful. This benefits no one but the sex criminal.

It was near closing time—nine p.m.—at the huge Northgate Mall on May 13 when the rapist came out of hiding again.

Lynn Rutledge* walked toward her new car, which she had parked near the Bon Marché store. She had just put her purse on the backseat when she sensed that someone had walked up behind her. It was a man who was muttering some words she didn't understand. Then she realized that he was telling her to hand over her purse.

"I've only got two dollars left," she answered, and tossed her keys out onto the parking lot to divert attention. She kicked the stranger as he pushed her toward her car. Angry, he called her, "Bitch!" as he retrieved the keys.

"Get in the car," the man ordered. When Lynn didn't react quickly enough, he struck her in the face twice. He pushed her into the passenger seat and got into the driver's seat. Brutally, he forced her head toward the floor. "Keep it down," he barked.

It was full dark as the man drove away from the lot, and he seemed satisfied that no one had noticed them. He drove to the corner of North 95th Street and Fremont Avenue North and ordered Lynn out of the car, pointing toward a thick cluster of bushes.

After he put his own shirt over her eyes, Lynn's abductor ripped her blouse down the front, tearing the buttons off. Then he stripped off the rest of her clothes. He spread them on the ground and directed her to lie down on them.

And then he raped her.

When he had finished, he allowed Lynn to get dressed, and he made her walk in front of him back to her car. As he drove back to the Northgate Mall, her attacker said he had friends waiting for him there.

He apologized to her, and he told her he had a wife and child.

"I'm sorry I had to hit you," he said, almost pleading for forgiveness. "I've been good to you, haven't I? I didn't hurt you, did I?"

"Not really," she murmured, praying that he would see his friends and let her go. But when they got back to the mall, he couldn't find his friends.

"I guess they left without him," Lynn Rutledge told Joyce Johnson later. "That made him really upset."

Now Lynn's nightmare began a replay.

"Get your head down, bitch," the tall man snarled, calling her "bitch" again and again. He drove around aimlessly, perhaps looking for his friends—if they ever really existed. Lynn could see him well now. He looked to be about twenty-five, was tall and slender, and had a medium-length, sloppy, grown-out shag haircut and a small mustache. She studied him covertly, memorizing every detail of his clothes. He wore a white pull-on shirt with short sleeves and a three-quarter zipper and light-colored brushed denim jeans. And well-worn cowboy boots.

The nervous rapist talked continually. "Would you believe I have a college education?" he asked, and Lynn nodded, figuring that flattery might save her. He told her he had majored in sociology and then served in Vietnam, where he'd become hooked on heroin.

"The army didn't help me, so now I have a three-hundred-dollar-a-day habit. I was a parole officer before I was drafted."

"Don't you think I look like Peter Fonda?" he asked. "You know, Henry Fonda's son?"

"Yes, you do," Lynn said, adding, "but you're better looking. You shouldn't have to kidnap a girl—you could easily find lots of them that wanted to go out with you."

Trying to be sympathetic to his drug addiction, she suggested that he might try the methadone program.

"I tried it, but they couldn't help me even though I want to quit."

Lynn Rutledge's mind raced as she tried to keep her kidnapper talking and, at the same time, agree with him. It was a delicate balance. She was afraid of what he might do next. But none of her talking was doing any good.

She realized that the handsome rapist was heading her car right back to the same corner where he'd attacked her before. She balked at walking into the berry patch again because she'd lost her shoes. That made him mad, and he started calling her "bitch" again as he pushed her into the bushes. His emotions were mercurial and he was instantly violent again. He punched Lynn twice in the face, and then he picked her up and threw her bodily farther into the brush.

Even through her fear, Lynn was reminded of a child who was having a tantrum. She had tried everything to placate him, but all of her amateur psychology had only landed her back in the dark corner.

"Oh, no! You don't want to do this again?" she asked him in horror.

In answer, he hit her in the left cheek and she staggered as he hit her again. She began to cry, and that made him madder. He thumped her hard on the back, virtually knocking the wind out of her. She stopped crying and submitted.

Oddly, until now, she hadn't been afraid he would kill her. But as he raped her for the second time and threatened to inflict various perversions on her, she realized he might very well murder her. She moaned in terror—and that seemed to please him. He asked if she was enjoying the sex and she finally lied and said, "Yes."

She meant to stay alive if she could.

Nothing seemed to satisfy him. He threatened anal sodomy and she cringed. She knew she would scream and that he'd wring her neck if she did.

Finally, her attacker seemed to finish this second sexual attack. Was he going to force her back into the car again? No, he was gathering up her clothes and preparing to leave. She begged him to let her have her clothes and he finally relented, tossing them back at her.

"It's my first rape," he crowed. "Wow! I just raped somebody!"

She cowered in the bushes, wondering if he was so enthused about his conquest that he'd turn back to her, but it looked as though, this time, he was leaving.

"I'll leave your car at Northgate," he called back.

Lynn Rutledge had hidden her diamond ring under the seat. If he found that, he might be furious and come back to hit her again or kill her. As soon as she heard the car drive off, she put on her ruined clothes and ran to a nearby house, where she begged the owner to call 911.

Patrol Officer G. Meyers responded to the call and, on the way, received a "possible" sighting report of the stolen car. It turned out to be an identical car—not Lynn's. Officer Meyers drove the injured kidnap victim to a hospital for treatment of her many cuts and bruises. Then the brave young woman volunteered to go with the officer in a search for her car—and the man who had abducted her.

They toured the parking lot at Northgate and did not find her car. Lynn, however, spotted it parked along the street near the Wallingford Police Precinct. It was impounded for processing and fingerprint expert Jeanne Bynum was able to lift one good partial latent print.

The shaggy-haired rapist was long gone once again. It was certainly possible that he lived in the neighborhood where the car was found; several of the other attacks had occurred in the same general vicinity. The latent would do no good alone: AFIS (Automated Fingerprint Identification System) was not yet in place at the time, but it would be vital if a suspect was found so they could compare his prints with the latent in evidence.

On June 2, Detective Fenkner got an anonymous call saying that the Northgate kidnapper was Grant Wilson,* twenty-three, who had been released from the Monroe Reformatory within the last year. Fenkner pulled Wilson's file and found that the parolee had a rap sheet going back eight years, but none of the charges against him had involved sex offenses.

Wilson's bookings had resulted from auto theft, grand larceny, burglary, and assault. He had served thirteen months at the penal facility at Shelton and fourteen months at the Monroe Reformatory for parole revocation. He had been released from Monroe two days before Christmas a year earlier, and in February, he'd been arrested as a burglary suspect. Since then, he hadn't been arrested.

Wilson's current location was unknown, but a look at his mug shots revealed he fit the general description of the man who had been terrorizing women in the north end of Seattle. He was six feet tall, weighed 165 pounds, and had brown hair and blue eyes. He occasionally had worked as a carpenter.

While Bill Fenkner and Joyce Johnson attempted to track down the elusive ex-con, the rapist was still busy. It was two days later, at 11 p.m. on June 4, when twenty-six-year-old Carol Brasser* drove up in front of her home in the near north end. She parked and got out, idly noting that a man was walking eastbound along the sidewalk.

Carol had just reached her front steps when the man called out, asking her for the time. As she turned to answer she grabbed her, covering her eyes with her coat. She screamed several times while he dragged her to the yard of the house next door. Her first thought was that he was trying to force her into a car, and she told him she would do anything he wanted.

The man was evidently confident that she had no choice in the matter anyway, and he continued to drag her behind a fence where they would be hidden from the street. Once there, he tore off her slacks and panties. He forced his fingers roughly into her vagina, bit her breasts cruelly, and then he raped her.

Not satiated, the man forced her to endure both oral and anal sodomy. During the attack, he tried to keep her eyes covered. The coat over her mouth and nose was smothering her and she told him she couldn't breathe. Hearing that, he'd let up the pressure on her face a little.

Carol suddenly heard the sound of other voices—young

voices. They were asking her attacker what was going on. Her assailant answered, "We're just making love."

She was so afraid. The man hit her in the chest and she feared he would beat her to death if she called for help now. The children wouldn't be capable of stopping him and might be hurt themselves. She managed to tell them she was all right, hoping that they would realize that she wasn't and go for help.

Carol heard their feet running away. The rapist seemed nervous now, even ashamed. He asked if she was okay, and allowed her to put her clothes back on.

Then he fled.

The youngsters had run to their mother and cried, "Mommy, there was a man and he grabbed a girl and she screamed and he dragged her into the bushes and put his hand over her mouth!"

The woman called police and Wallingford Precinct patrolmen arrived almost at once. But, just as before, the rapist had disappeared into the night, leaving behind only drops of blood from his feet, which had been cut by nails on the fence.

Carol Brasser was taken to a hospital, where doctors confirmed she had been sexually assaulted, had received deep scratches on her neck, sternum, and back.

Carol gave Sex Crimes detectives a now-familiar description: tall, thin, ragged shag haircut, mustache, in his twenties.

Her attacker's MO matched that of the earlier attacks almost exactly. The man stalked lone women late at night, kept their eyes covered, and not only subjected to sexual indignities but also seemed to enjoy beating them. And when he was finished with his victims, he apologized, and seemed to be asking for forgiveness.

What was most alarming was the increasing frequency of these copycat assaults. It was quite possible that the rapist assumed his victims had not seen him, that he felt perfectly free to continue his pattern. He had gotten away clean every time. If he felt safe, even overconfident, he might slip, and thereby betray himself.

Or he might kill his next victim. The number of rape victims who have ended up dead through strangulation or beatings is overwhelming. Sometimes the rapist goes further and uses more force than he intended. In cases of serial murder, the "thrill" of a "simple" rape is no longer satisfying for the sex criminal and he progresses to murder.

It is a very thin line.

On June 10, eighteen-year-old Moira Drew* attended a party at a friend's house in the north end. There were several people she knew there—and a few she didn't. One stranger was a tall, good-looking man with a mustache. As she left the party between 1:30 and 2:00 a.m., the handsome man approached her and asked if he could have a ride to Aurora Avenue.

"Sure." She nodded, and pointed out her car.

She felt no apprehension. After all, she had met the man at her friend's house.

Once on their way, the man, who had told her his name was Neil O'Leary, changed his mind about his destination. He asked her if she would mind taking him to North 91st

Street and Linden Avenue North. It was only a few more blocks out of her way and she agreed.

"Hey, move over closer to me," he said softly, as she pulled over at his corner.

It seemed like a simple pass. She shook her head and said, "No, I don't know you."

As quickly as a cobra strikes, the man's hand reached out and seized her by the throat, powerful fingers cutting off her air entirely. A black curtain dropped over her eyes and she saw pinwheels of light as she fought to breathe. With her last strength, she leaned on the horn.

"If you don't shut up," Neil O'Leary hissed, "I'm going to kill you . . ."

But Moira Drew kept her hand on the horn, its bleating staccato shrieks blasting through the early morning air. A car pulled up, paused, and the driver looked curiously over at Moira's car.

It was enough to spook "Neil O'Leary," and he leapt from her car and took off running.

Moira Drew was not a fragile little girl. She was perfectly proportioned, and she was five feet eight inches tall and weighed 135 pounds. She had fought her would-be strangler with such ferocity that she had literally forced the brake pedal of her car to the floor, making the brakes inoperable. She didn't realize that until she pulled into a nearby 7-Eleven parking lot, and found she had to pull on the hand brake to keep from crashing into the store's front window.

There was a police car parked there with Officer G. J. Fiedler inside. The distraught teenager approached the police unit and Fiedler could see the angry red marks on her neck—perfect imprints of someone's fingers.

At last, the handsome rapist had run out of luck. He had attacked a woman who knew people he knew. Moira called her host at the party and asked who the "tall, good-looking man with the mustache" was.

"Oh, him—that's Grant Wilson," the man responded.

Grant John Wilson was already a suspect, but unaware that Sex Crimes detectives were closing in on him, Wilson continued his penchant for brutal attacks on women.

Seattle police burglary detective Bill Berg had been investigating Grant Wilson, too—on burglary cases. Berg had information that tied in with his fellow detectives' case. Even better, he had a line on where Wilson could be found: He was living on Northwest 56th Street, not far from the cluster of violent sexual attacks.

Bill Berg arrested Wilson on suspicion of rape in the case of Lynn Rutledge, and the other victims' cases would follow. Grant Wilson would now have to face his accusers in a lineup arranged by Sex Crimes sergeant Romero Yumul.

On June 11, the ex-con moved across the lineup stage with several other men who looked a great deal like him. He had always been very careful to cover the eyes of his victims, nearly smothering some of them, but they had seen him, and they had remembered his face well.

Kitty Amela, the young nurse, recognized the man who had beaten her nearly unconscious. Carol Brasser, raped, beaten, and tormented, had his face emblazoned on her brain. Moira Drew, his last victim, picked him out of the lineup instantly. Lynn Rutledge, kidnapped from Northgate and raped twice, would never forget him. The children who were witnesses to the attack on Carol Brasser also identified Grant Wilson.

Cory Bixler, whose attacker had thrown dirt on her after the rape and tried to bury her, was not positive; she had only seen him briefly in the blackness of night. The other young women who had been attacked where there was little light couldn't be sure either—but they all recognized his voice.

It didn't matter. There were enough victims who were absolutely sure that Grant Wilson was the man who had raped and beaten them. In Lynn Rutledge's case, King County deputy prosecutors Paul Bernstein and Lee Yates filed charges of rape, robbery, and kidnapping. In three other cases where victims had picked Grant Wilson from the lineup, rape and/or sexual assault charges were filed.

With the arrest and confinement of Grant Wilson, who was held under $100,000 bail, there were no more attacks that fit the parameters of the rapist who had stalked women in the north end.

Direct physical evidence was piling up on the man who raped Carol Brasser. He had cut his feet on the picket fence as he ran from the sound of approaching police sirens; Grant John Wilson's feet showed healing nail punctures.

Bill Berg knew where the bloody male clothing Wilson had discarded was. Semen samples taken from the rape victims matched Wilson's blood type.

Grant Wilson had no alibis for the dates and times the attacks had occurred. In addition, the burglary charge Bill

Berg had arrested Grant Wilson for in February had many aspects that made it look much more like a rape attempt than a burglary.

Pry marks were visible around the windows of the home where Wilson was caught. Inside that house, a particularly beautiful woman lived alone. Wilson claimed that he had only been siphoning gas at that address. His trial on that charge had ended in a hung jury.

Detective Bill Berg wanted Wilson, and he had long believed the handsome suspect was potentially very dangerous. Now, Berg worked countless off-duty hours to help prosecutors Bernstein and Yates build their case. The investigative trio revisited each attack site and took photographs. They interviewed and reinterviewed the victims— all young women who were not only intelligent but had fantastic memories for detail as well. The case file grew as the prosecuting attorneys and the burglary detective gave their own free time to compile a loophole-free dossier against the brutal rape suspect.

As they learned more about Wilson's relationships with women, an interesting psychological profile emerged. There had been no dearth of women in the ex-con's life, but Grant Wilson had fought with most of them, beaten one severely, and had never taken even a hint of rejection without seeking revenge.

Strangely, he didn't fight any rejection by the women in his life by hurting *them*. Instead, he had taken his rage out on the victims of his sexual attacks, on hapless women who were complete strangers.

After each fight or breakup, Grant Wilson had gone

prowling, looking for a pretty woman on whom he would vent his wrath.

Interesting, too, was the fact that most of the attacks had taken place in the same neighborhood where Grant Wilson had grown up—one directly across the street from his boyhood home. Since his release from prison, he had been on the move, living with one friend or another in the north end of Seattle.

Grant Wilson was slated to go on trial for attacking the four young women in August. But when Wilson was faced with the voluminous evidence that detectives Joyce Johnson, Bill Fenkner, and Bill Berg, along with prosecutors Bernstein and Yates, had gathered against him, he changed his mind about going to trial.

He was allowed to plea bargain, to plead guilty to a charge of first-degree kidnapping and robbery in the case of Lynn Rutledge. The other charges were dropped. The kidnapping charge meant a mandatory life sentence.

Grant Wilson is safely behind bars for a long, long time. But the scars on his victims will not soon fade. One young woman is afraid to walk on the street by herself—even in the daytime. She no longer feels safe to live alone. Another suffers from painful recurring migraine headaches. Rape is a crime that often leaves lifetime nightmares for its victims.

And yet Grant Wilson's victims were lucky. They escaped with their lives. If he hadn't been captured when he was, forensic psychologists believe it was only a matter of time before his sexual attacks escalated to murder.

As girls grow up, at least a quarter of us have had some kind of encounter with sexually deviant offenders. Most often, we are not in physical danger, but it is shocking to be approached by a flasher—who seems to get satisfaction by exposing his genitals. Police call them "Lily Wavers," and they come from every level of society.

There are also the voyeurs—the window peepers—who stare into windows, hoping to see a female in some state of undress. Those who do not know better say that exposers and voyeurs are not dangerous, but they are wrong. Almost every sex killer I have written about began with these seemingly "safe" intrusions into victims' lives.

I was accosted by a flasher in a movie theater when I was twelve, and it scared me half to death—scared me so much that I didn't even tell my mother for three years!

Perverts like Jerome Brudos (the Lust Killer) began as a voyeur and an exposer. Then he progressed to stealing hundreds of pieces of women's undergarments from their bedrooms as they slept unaware.

Rape was his next step, and finally, a series of gruesome homicides.

I don't want to frighten women—but I certainly want them to be aware and alert, especially when they are having a bad day. Ted Bundy, like many serial killers, had the ability to perceive vulnerability in his prospective targets. The hapless young women he killed all encountered him when they were temporarily distracted. They had the flu, they were suffering from premenstrual tension, they had just flunked tests or had been up all night studying for a final, their hearts were broken because they had just severed romantic ties with a boyfriend, or they were running away from home. Some weren't wearing their glasses—and vanity cost them their lives.

The list is endless. We all make mistakes in judgment—especially when our lives have gone off the tracks for a time. We must be extra cautious during those times in our lives.

The sex killers I have written about for the last three decades are coyotes, watching for the crippled lambs that they can easily cut out of the flock even though they wear charming masks.

The title of this book is *Don't Look Behind You*. My message to you is *do* be aware of what is happening around you. Look back, to the side, and straight ahead with your head held high and walk with purpose. *Do* look behind you, and have your subconscious programmed so that you will react automatically should danger suddenly confront you.

You are the very first line of your own defense, and you can save your own life.

Acknowledgments

So many people opened their hearts and searched their memories to help me reconstruct mysteries of long ago in this book. For many, this meant opening old wounds and bringing up heartbreaks of the past, recollections that were, perhaps, best left alone. And yet the victims and the families they left behind need to be remembered.

My deep gratitude to: Gypsy Tarricone, Gina Tarricone, Claire Evans, Dean Tarricone, Rosemary Tarricone, Ben Benson, Denny Wood, Dawn Farina, Mark Lindquist, Marjean Denison, Rhonda Miller, Diane Benson, Curtis Wright, Jan Rhodes, Bill Haglund, Jerry Burger, Travis Haney, and Matt Haney.

And to: Ty Hansen, Nicole Hansen, Kathleen and Jeff Huget, Cindy Tyler Wilkinson, Patricia Martin, Duncan Bonjorni, King County detective sergeant Jim Allen, deputy prosecutor Jeff Baird, LaVonne and Marvin Milosevich, Barbara Kuehne Snyder, Chris Hansen, King County captain Frank Adamson, and profilers John Douglas and John Kelly.

I learned the ins and outs of included cases from King County sheriff's detectives DuWayne Harrison, Dan Nolan, Ben Colwell, Bob Schmitz, and James McGonagle, and sheriff's divers George Zimmerman and Joseph Dollinger. Seattle police detective Joyce Johnson, an expert on sexually motivated crimes, taught me the ropes when I was a young rookie. She and Bill Fenkner, along with Edmonds Police detective Marian McCann, caught a serial rapist who believed he was invincible.

Thanks once again to Gerry Brittingham Hay, my designated first reader, and tender critic.

And blessings to Andy, Lindsay, Laura, Rebecca, Matt, Miya Dawn, and Amari Violet, Leslie, Mike, Marie, Holland Rae, and Bruce, Machell, Olivia, Tyra, and Logan. I love you all very much.

Keep a-goin' to Donna Anders, Kate Jewell, Shirley Hickman, Sue Harms, and Barb Thompson, who have all proved that starting over and succeeding is possible if you believe in yourself. I'm proud to have you as friends! To the Boeing Ladies Who Lunch, and the forever young Jolly Matrons.

For Pat Kelly, Matt Parker, and Mike Morrow. Just Because.

To my ARFs (self-declared Ann Rule Fans): I love and appreciate all of you!

I always thank my lifetime literary agents, Joan and Joe Foley—who have been with me for many decades—because they deserve my sincere appreciation, as does my theatrical agent, Ron Bernstein of International Creative Management!

ACKNOWLEDGMENTS

To the gang at Waters and Wood who demolished my kitchen and living room and then remodeled them to rooms more beautiful than I could have imagined. The remodel and this book ended on the same day! Thanks to Bryan Christensen, Bryce Salzman, Eric Hamilton, Mark Rice and his second-in-command, Dan, Mark Kerkof, Francisco Diaz, Dave Myers, John Edwards, Bobbi Fritcher, Tara Foster, and Joy Mitchell!

And when I say, "I couldn't have done this without them," I mean my treasured team at Pocket Books: my publisher, Louise Burke; my editor, Mitchell Ivers, and his able assistant, Natasha Simons. The production crew keeps me on time and accurate, even when I keep thinking I need a vacation! They are production manager Liangela Cabrera, production editor Stephen Llano, managing editor Sally Franklin, copyeditor Ela Schwartz, proofreaders Adrian C. James, Wendy Warren Keebler, and Laura Cherkas, and book designer Meghan Day Healey.